From Postgraduate to Social Scientist

A Guide to Key Skills

From Postgraduate to Social Scientist

A Guide to Key Skills

edited by
Nigel Gilbert

 SAGE Publications

London ● Thousand Oaks ● New Delhi

Editorial arrangement and Chapter 1 © Nigel Gilbert 2006
Chapter 2 © Annette Boaz, Adrienne Sidford 2006
Chapter 3 © Nina Wakeford, Kate Orton-Johnson, Katrina Jungnickel 2006
Chapter 4 © Mark Israel, Deborah Hersh 2006
Chapter 5 © Keith Punch, Wayne McGowan 2006
Chapter 6 © Linda McKie, Jonathan Tritter, Nancy Lombard 2006
Chapter 7 © Alison Firth 2006
Chapter 8 © Nigel Fielding, Jonathan Allen 2006
Chapter 9 © Rowena Murray 2006
Chapter 10 © David Mills, Lucy Atkinson 2006
Chapter 11 © Jeanette Holt 2006

First published 2006

SAGE Publications Ltd
1 Oliver's Yard
55 City Road
London EC1Y 1SP

SAGE Publications Inc.
2455 Teller Road
Thousand Oaks, California 91320

SAGE Publications India Pvt Ltd
B-42, Panchsheel Enclave
Post Box 4109
New Delhi 110 017

British Library Cataloguing in Publication data

A catalogue record for this book is available
from the British Library

ISBN10 0 7619 4459 1   ISBN13 978 0 7619 4459 1
ISBN10 1 7619 4460 5   ISBN13 978 0 7619 4460 7 (pbk)

Library of Congress Control Number: 2005928386

Typeset by C&M Digitals (P) Ltd., Chennai, India
Printed on paper from sustainable resources
Printed in Great Britain by The Cromwell Press Ltd, Trowbridge, Wiltshire

Contents

Notes on Contributors

Jonathan Allen completed his MSc in 2001, during which time he tutored undergraduates in the Sociology of Contemporary Societies. Upon completion of that course he took up a post as a Research Officer in the Home Office's Research Development and Statistics Directorate, working on the British Crime Survey (BCS). He is currently a Senior Research Officer on the survey, where responsibilities include research into violent crime and the fear of crime.

Lucy Atkinson is researching for a PhD in Anthropology at Edinburgh University on the lives of refugee children from the Democratic Republic of Congo in camps in rural Zambia.

Annette Boaz is a research fellow in the ESRC UK Centre for Evidence-based Policy and Practice, Queen Mary, University of London. She is currently involved in a programme of training, development and methodological work relating to evidence-based policy and practice. Annette has previously worked at the Department of Health and at the Universities of Oxford and Warwick, carrying out research in a wide variety of policy areas. She has completed evaluations for the UK Cabinet Office and Home Office and worked in the Policy Research Programme at the UK Department of Health, learning about research commissioning, management and utilisation. Her recent publications include articles on evidence-based policy in health, education and social policy.

Nigel Fielding is professor of sociology at the University of Surrey, co-director of the Institute of Social Research, and co-director of the ESRC-supported CAQDAS Networking Project, which provides training and support in the use of computers in qualitative data analysis. He was editor of the *Howard Journal of Criminal Justice* from 1985 to 1998 and is co-editor of the *New Technologies for Social Research* series (Sage). His main research interests are in qualitative research methods, new technologies for social research, and criminal justice. In research methodology his books include a study of methodological integration/triangulation (*Linking Data*, with Jane Fielding, Sage, 1986), an influential book on qualitative software (*Using Computers in Qualitative Research*, with Ray Lee, (eds) Sage, 1991), a study of the role of computer technology in qualitative research (*Computer Analysis and Qualitative Research*, with Ray Lee, Sage, 1998) and a four-volume set, *Interviewing* (ed., Sage, 2002). He is presently researching the application of Grid/high-performance computing applications to qualitative methods, and the impact of community policing on public reassurance.

Alison Firth qualified as a barrister, practising in intellectual property chambers from 1983, following a first degree in physics and teaching in London and Lima. Since 1987, she has held full-time university teaching posts, first at Queen Mary, University of London, and now at the University of Newcastle, where she is professor of commercial law. Her research centres on the law of intellectual property and its interaction with other areas of the law. She is honorary legal adviser to the British Copyright Council. She has written a number of articles and books on intellectual property law and was editor, with E. Barendt, of the *Yearbook of Copyright and Media Law*, Volumes IV, V and VI (Oxford University Press, 1999–2002).

Nigel Gilbert is professor of sociology and Pro Vice-Chancellor at the University of Surrey, Guildford, UK. He is editor of *Researching Social Life* (Sage, 2001) and co-author (with Jane Fielding) of *Understanding Social Statistics* (Sage, 2005). He has also written or edited 15 other books, including *Simulation for the Social Scientist* (with Klaus G. Troitzsch, Open University Press, 2005), and many scholarly articles. He started one of the first full-time Masters courses in Social Research Methods in the early 1980s at the University of Surrey and more recently a Masters course in Digital Technologies and Society. His main research interests are in new social science methods, especially social simulation, and in innovation.

Deborah Hersh completed her PhD in 2002. She is a Senior Speech Pathologist at Julia Farr Services, Adelaide, Australia, and a member of the Ethics Board of Speech Pathology Australia.

Jeanette Holt studied for a BA in English Literature and Ancient History (University of Wales), followed by a Diploma in Careers Guidance. She has 18 years' experience as a careers adviser. She began by working in schools and then in Colleges of Further and Higher Education and joined the University of Surrey's careers team in March 2001. She currently advises undergraduates and postgraduates in psychology, sociology, biological sciences, physics and electronics. She has written and contributed to various publications for the Association of Graduate Careers Advisory Services, including an occupational profile of a Social Researcher.

Mark Israel is professor of criminology and convenor of postgraduate studies in the School of Law at Flinders University in Australia. He has a degree in law and post-graduate qualifications in sociology, criminology and education from the United Kingdom and Australia. He has published over 50 books and articles, including *South African Political Exile in the United Kingdom* (Macmillan, 1999) and *Ethics and the Governance of Criminological Research in Australia* (NSW Government, 2004) and is co-author of *Research Ethics in the Social Sciences* (Sage, forthcoming). In 2004, Mark won the prestigious Prime Minister's Award for Australian University Teacher of the Year.

Katrina Jungnickel is a researcher interested in new technology, urban sociality and visual methodologies. She has worked on various commercial and interdisciplinary research projects within the fields of visual culture, art, technology and sociology, and is currently a postgraduate student at INCITE (Incubator for Critical Enquiry into Technology and Ethnography) at the University of Surrey.

Nancy Lombard has worked as a research assistant for the Scottish Executive and a caseworker at a Women's Aid refuge. She has just completed the first year of her PhD looking at the attitudes and understandings of 10 and 11-year-olds to violence against women.

Wayne McGowan completed his doctorate at the University of Western Australia in 2004. During this time, he was made an inaugural Whitfield Fellow, which enabled him to prepare his thesis for publication. He has extensive experience in teachers' professional development, educational leadership and policy development. His research interests include political philosophy, especially in education, and the changing sub-jectivities, technologies and rationalities of power within the administration of educa-tion. Forthcoming publications are based on his PhD thesis and include: *Thinking About the Responsible Parent: Freedom and Educating the Child* (Edwin Mellen Press) and 'Flexibility, Community and Making the Responsible Parent' in the *Journal of Education, Philosophy and Theory*.

Linda McKie is research professor in sociology at Glasgow Caledonian University and associate director at the Centre for Research on Families and Relationships. Her cur-rent research work includes the topics of gender, policy and violence, and concepts of care in combining life and work. In addition to recent journal articles on gender and care, gender and violence, and aspects of health in *Sociology, Sociology of Health and Illness* and *Social Science and Medicine*, book publications include *Families, Violence and Social*

Change (Open University Press, 2005) and *Families in Society*: *Boundaries and Relationships* (edited with Sarah Cunningham-Burley, Policy Press, 2005).

David Mills is lecturer at the University of Birmingham and Anthropology Co-ordinator at Sociology, Anthropology, Politics (C-SAP), part of the Higher Education Academy. The post involves promoting research and debate into the teaching of anthropology. He has published on the post-war history of British social sciences and on the forms of knowledge created within universities. He is co-editor of *Teaching Rites and Wrongs: Universities and the making of Anthropologists* (C-SAP, Birmingham, 2004) and is currently completing a book on the political history of British social anthropology.

Rowena Murray is reader in the Educational and Professional Studies department of the Faculty of Education at the University of Strathclyde (in Glasgow). Her area of research is academic writing. She has produced video packs on thesis writing, research supervision, the viva and writing for publication. In addition to many research papers in various scholarly journals, she is the author of *How to Write a Thesis* (2002) and *Writing for Academic Journals* (2005), both published by the Open University Press/McGraw-Hill, Maidenhead.

Kate Orton-Johnson completed her PhD as a member of INCITE (Incubator for Critical Enquiry into Technology and Ethnography) at the University of Surrey, where her doctoral thesis examined student use of new technologies and innovations in teaching and learning in higher education. Her research interests are centred around the sociology of new technologies, the implications of technological innovation in higher education, 'virtual' and 'online' research methodologies, the practical and ethical issues surrounding ICTs as both research tools and field sites, and representations of identity and the self online. Kate joined the Department of Sociology at Surrey as a lecturer in September 2004 and teaches courses on the Sociology of Technology and Youth Cultures.

Keith Punch is professor in the Graduate School of Education at the University of Western Australia. His teaching interests now concentrate on empirical research methodology, and on training researchers for quantitative studies, qualitative studies and mixed-method studies. His research interests cover the sociology of education, educational administration and policy, and different aspects of international education. Recent books include *Introduction to Social Research: Quantitative and Qualitative Approaches* (2nd edition, Sage, 2005); *Survey Research: The Basics* (Sage, 2003) and *Developing Effective Research Proposals* (Sage, 2000).

Adrienne Sidford is in the second year of a PhD evaluating a countywide physical activity referral scheme at the University of Gloucestershire. She is investigating the effect of the referral processes and the demographic characteristics of the participants upon their involvement in the scheme.

Jonathan Tritter is research director, Health Strategy and Management in the Institute of Governance and Public Management, Warwick Business School and Senior Lecturer in the Department of Sociology at the University of Warwick. His main research interests relate to public participation and lay experience in health and policy making, particularly in relation to cancer, mental health and environmental policy. He teaches on a broad range of methodology courses and is interested in the challenges of multidisciplinary, multi-method and international research. His recent publications include *Improving Cancer Services Through Patient Involvement* (with N. Daykin, S. Evans and M. Sanidas, Radcliffe Medical Press, 2003).

Nina Wakeford is director of the Incubator for Critical Inquiry into Technology and Ethnography. (INCITE) research centre in the Department of Sociology, University of Surrey. Her previous research projects include studies of internet cafés, women's discussions lists and the use of ethnography by new technology designers. Along with colleagues at INCITE she is interested in the ways in which collaborations can be forged between ethnographers and those from other disciplines, such as engineering and computer science. As part of the Intel-funded project studying the 73 bus route in London, she has begun to research blogs as a data collection tool.

Acknowledgements

I thank Patrick Brindle, Senior Commissioning Editor at Sage, for his advice and encouragement. The original idea for the book was Michael Carmichael's, but Patrick made it into a practical proposition and has guided its development throughout. The book is dedicated to the memory of my father, for whom all these skills came naturally.

Nigel Gilbert
Guildford

Becoming a Social Scientist

1

Nigel Gilbert

This book is for you if you have already obtained a first degree in one of the social sciences and are now on track to becoming a social scientist. There is a considerable difference between getting a degree in social science and being a social scientist: for the latter you need a range of professional skills as well as a deep knowledge of social science. One almost essential qualification to become a social scientist is a further degree: a Masters or a PhD. To obtain these, you are likely to have to undertake courses to advance your knowledge and expertise in social science. But often, these courses give too little attention to the skills needed to be a proficient social scientist.

This book, in contrast to most books on research methods and similar topics, is focused on the skills that do not form part of the standard academic social science curriculum. These include how to conduct a systematic literature review, how to use the internet to maximum effect as part of your research, how to write research project proposals, how to manage research projects, how to give a presentation, how to give tutorials and classes to undergraduates, and what you can do to get a job once you have finished your degree.

These and other skills are needed if you are to survive as a professional social scientist. In the past, they were skills that one generally picked up 'on the job', but it is much quicker and easier to learn from the experts who have taken time to systematise their knowledge than it is to learn from listening and watching what colleagues do.

This has also been the view of some of those who fund graduate programmes. In the United Kingdom, for instance, over the last ten years the Economic and Social Research Council has developed its *Training Guidelines* (ESRC, 2005), and is becoming increasingly firm about requiring courses on professional skills in the programmes that it recognises. More recently, some of the other UK Research Councils have begun to demand the inclusion of similar topics as part of the education of research students.

This introductory chapter begins with a consideration of what it might mean to be a professional social scientist and then summarises the content of the following chapters.

How to become a professional social scientist

The idea of a 'professional' social scientist is rather a new one. Most learned societies for the social sciences were founded during the middle of the last century (exceptions are the Royal Geographical Society, founded in 1830, and the British Psychological Society, 1901), and these foundations marked the start of the idea that there were distinct social science disciplines, although not yet professions. It was not until the 1960s and the widespread employment of social scientists in central and local government, and later in business, that one could begin to consider social science as a profession as well as an academic vocation.

For this reason, what it means to be a professional social scientist is much less well defined than is the case, for example, for a lawyer, architect or doctor. Clearly, there is much professional knowledge involved, such as one might learn in a first degree or Masters. But just possessing a degree would not seem to be sufficient. In addition, one needs to gain entry to a community of practice (Brown and Duguid, 1991), in which one can call upon and be respected by one's fellow professionals. This is often explicitly recognised in training for a PhD where, as well as an 'original contribution to knowledge', it is expected that candidates will have begun to make links with other researchers in their particular field of social science, perhaps by attending conferences and giving presentations about their work.

Professional social scientists, then, are people who use their social science knowledge in their everyday work and who are also linked into a network with other social scientists. Many social scientists also try to contribute to social science in some way: through formulating new knowledge, perhaps, but also by passing on the ideas of social science to others through teaching or writing. If being a professional social scientist is seen as a set of linked activities, rather than as describing the qualities of a person, it becomes clearer why there are some specific skills involved in becoming one. These skills can be learned in much the same way as one can learn about social science concepts or methods. It is the various skills that are needed to be a professional social scientist that are described in the following chapters.

Each of the chapters follows a similar pattern: a general overview of the topic, some detailed advice, a short retrospective section from a graduate student reflecting on his or her own personal experience, and a selection of readings for pursuing the topic in more depth.

An essential preliminary to doing any social scientific research is to conduct a review of the literature. This has two primary functions: to ensure that your research question has not already been answered in a previous study, and to relate your research to what has gone before, so that it contributes effectively to a growing body of knowledge. The literature review is an essential chapter in any dissertation or PhD thesis and will inform the writing of project research reports. However, while anyone can gather together a few relevant articles and review them, there is considerable skill in doing the job properly. In Chapter 2, Annette Boaz shows how one should set about a review in a systematic manner, first defining the topic, locating sources, evaluating the quality of the sources, synthesising what they say and finally reporting the results. If you carry out a review in this way, there is some chance that you will identify all the significant prior work and, importantly, be able to explain and justify the method you used to do so.

One new type of source for previous literature is the internet, which provides an immensely rich, but also tricky resource for researchers. The internet also offers a wholly new site for data collection. In Chapter 3, Nina Wakeford shows how the world wide web can be used to search for existing literature, both of the conventional published kind, but also in the form of databases of citations and surveys. She also describes how the internet can be the basis for primary data collection through observation of the traces of internet users revealed in email, chat rooms, blogs and websites. Many of the traditional techniques of the social scientist, such as standardised surveys, interviews and even focus groups, can be adapted for use over the internet, as this chapter explains.

Internet research introduces some ethical issues additional to those encountered in more conventional research sites. In Chapter 4, Mark Israel examines the range of ethical questions likely to be raised in all types of social science research and describes the increasingly tightly regulated processes of obtaining ethical approval. He begins by considering the main areas where ethical dilemmas occur: consent, confidentiality and privacy, harm, and relationships with subjects, organisations and institutions. He then reviews the current structures of ethics governance in the United Kingdom and compares them with the structures to be found in the USA and the Commonwealth. Finally, he shows how to prepare a submission to a research ethics committee in preparation for developing a funded research proposal.

Researchers always grumble about the amount of time they spend writing proposals for projects, rather than doing research, but as Keith Punch shows in Chapter 5 on developing and writing proposals, so long as one knows the basic rules about what to include, writing good proposals can be a creative and satisfying task – especially if you then get the money. As he points out, the secret of a good proposal is to present a logical argument that meets the reader's expectations about what should be requested and why that is necessary in order carry out the research. The question to be addressed in the research must be clearly specified and the methods to be used must be laid out in a way that convinces the reader, that is, those in control of the funding, that the research will yield valid, reliable and significant results.

Once you have gained project funding, you will need skills in project management. These skills can also be very helpful if you are a lone researcher, for example, doing research for a higher degree. Linda McKee and Jonathon Tritter offer a wealth of advice in Chapter 6. They observe that managing a project is likely to call on skills in negotiation with participants, supervisors and funders, as well as time management and estimating and managing the use of resources. One of the critical factors is ensuring that there is adequate communication between all those involved. Another is being clear about what outputs are expected from the project and how these will be created. And since sometimes, even with the best managed projects, things go wrong, it is a good idea to lay out some contingency plans.

It is increasingly recognised that the results of research count as 'intellectual property' and consequently have a legal status. Researchers may need to protect their work against others' attempts to purloin it, for example by copying reports wholesale, or may need to counter the refusal of sponsors to allow results to be published. In many universities, some intellectual property belongs not to the researcher, but to the institution. For these reasons, it is essential to understand the laws that protect and assign intellectual property. In Chapter 7, Alison Firth outlines the meaning of intellectual property rights and explains what you can and cannot do, not only with conventional reports, but also with databases and collections. She also explains how you can register your rights and how employment and research sponsorship contracts can affect them.

While most projects will need to disseminate their results to a wider range of audiences than just the research community, it is still the case that every project, no matter how large or small, is required to publish its findings in the academic literature before the results are treated as having any scientific validity. In Chapter 8, Nigel Fielding outlines the structure of a typical dissertation or thesis and what should go into each section or chapter. He describes how academic reports get written and identifies some of the problems that new authors are likely to have to overcome. Writing policy-relevant reports can have unexpected perils, as well as the gratifying feeling that you are contributing to the policy process. He includes a case study that examines some examples of the problems and rewards that he experienced when reporting his own controversial research.

Nowadays, in addition to contributing to the academic literature, the results from social science research are often distributed through press releases, lectures at workshops, presentations at conferences and on websites. In Chapter 9, Rowena Murray describes the audiences that these different modes of reporting can reach, and how the work you present needs to be tailored for each medium and each audience. She begins by describing how to select a journal and how to target your writing to the journal's requirements. She explains how to construct a proposal to a book publisher and emphasises that a book is very different from a thesis. Writing for the media (newspapers, magazines and the 'trade press') demands not only a distillation of your message but also a quite different style of writing from the usual academic repertoire. She concludes with some advice about making effective verbal presentations. Throughout, the message is that it is necessary to 'translate' your findings into forms appropriate for the audience you are trying to reach.

It is very common for postgraduates to contribute to undergraduate tutorials. In many departments, postgraduates are an essential part of the teaching mix and one that is welcomed by undergraduate students. But all too often, postgraduates are thrown in at the deep end without much in the way of training or mentoring. In Chapter 10, David Mills redresses the balance by offering some good advice about how to make your first steps as a teacher. He also addresses the important question of whether you should accept the task when it is offered, or reject it as a distraction from your studies.

Finally, in Chapter 11, Jeanette Holt considers the career paths that will open up for you as a social scientist with a postgraduate qualification. A job as an academic in a university is the dream of some postgraduates, but it can be a tough and poorly paid career. This chapter outlines the many alternatives, from social research in government and private sector organisations, to jobs where social science is a useful but not essential background, such as social work. Even when you have selected the kind of job you want, there are still the hurdles of finding a vacancy and getting a job offer. The chapter therefore also takes you through the processes of locating jobs, preparing a persuasive CV and making an application.

Social science is becoming more and more indispensable to the functioning of society. Social policy has nowadays to be 'evidence-based', and that evidence is the product of social science research. Media commentators rely on social science for many of their critiques. Advertising and market research techniques rely on the results of social science research. Social science informs the work of charities and non-governmental organisations about their policies. In all these areas, the contributions of professional social scientists are needed. We, the authors of the chapters in this book, hope that it will help to make your path to becoming a social scientist easier and more certain.

Reviewing Existing Research

2

Annette Boaz with Adrienne Sidford

- Literature reviews can be approached systematically to locate as much relevant literature as possible. This chapter shows you how.

- Reviews are needed to identify what is already known, to bring together results from different studies, and to provide a starting point for new research.

- Reviewing involves defining the topic, identifying sources, evaluating the sources, synthesising and reporting.

Whereas single studies are often based on small samples and offer different results, a review can go beyond individual studies to identify trends and patterns in research findings. A literature review can be defined as follows:

> A systematic, explicit and reproducible method for identifying, evaluating and interpreting the existing body of recorded work produced by researchers, scholars and practitioners. (Fink, 1998: 3)

Of course, there is a huge volume of research out there on almost any given topic, so any attempt to review the literature needs to be guided by a clear plan of action. There are different ways of going about doing a review, and this chapter will help you to decide on an approach and put together a plan.

Why you might do a review

There are a number of circumstances in which you might choose to conduct a review of the literature. Researchers (including PhD students) may need to summarise existing research to provide a platform for further work. For students, the literature review often takes the form of a discrete chapter in a thesis which seeks to summarise the 'body of knowledge' relevant to the chosen topic. Other academic studies take a similar approach, devoting a section of the final research report to a summary of the relevant literature. This 'foundation laying' literature review is perhaps the most common application of research review techniques.

In addition, research commissioners, such as funding councils and government departments, sometimes require literature reviews as ground-clearing exercises at the start of programmes of research. Reviews can also be used to survey a field in order to identify research gaps or directions and to help develop an agenda for future funding programmes.

These functions, though important, have in the past relegated research reviewing to the methodological wilderness, with limited debate about its role, conduct and quality. Increasingly, however, reviews have been commissioned in their own right for quite different purposes. Researchers and research commissioners are promoting reviews as an opportunity to go beyond the individual study (with all its weaknesses) and to seek out and synthesise the huge body of research that already exists on almost any topic. Reviews have become a crucial part of the 'what works?' agenda in the UK, with its focus on finding out which public policy interventions are the most effective in bringing about change (Davies et al., 2000). As a result, literature reviews are finding their place as a mainstream research methodology. They offer new analytical insights and fresh ideas, and skills in reviewing will soon be an indispensable part of the researcher's methodological portfolio.

Why might you do a review?

- To understand what you know already about a given topic
- To identify gaps in the evidence base or generate a research agenda
- To build a platform for future work
- To complement primary research
- To 'go beyond' individual studies on a given topic
- To use the individual studies as data to explore a topic or question

The need for more 'recycling' of existing research is now widely accepted. At the very least it makes sense to check whether a research study has, in effect, been done already.

It is sometimes surprising just how much research there is, even in relation to quite specific topics. For example, a team at Glasgow University in Scotland conducted a literature review on the topic of gentrification – the rejuvenation and renovation of run-down urban areas by the middle class (usually resulting in the displacement of resident lower-income communities). This might be assumed to be a relatively small and specialised field of study. However, the search identified research from all over the world, including Australia, Europe and North America. The research team identified 17 existing literature reviews on the topic, in addition to the mass of primary research (Atkinson, 2002).

Literature reviews should be undertaken to the same high standards as primary research. Reviewers need to demonstrate clarity of purpose, use appropriate methods and demonstrate objectivity and rigour in their work. Review findings and methods should also be clearly reported.

By taking each step of the review process in turn we shall consider how to conduct a good-quality review that is something more than a dry summary of the state of knowledge on a given topic. The key steps of the review process are:

1. Defining the review topic or question

2. Locating sources

3. Judging the quality of studies identified

4. Synthesising the studies identified

5. Reporting the findings of the review

It is worth noting that, while the stages are presented as a linear process, most 'real world' reviews do not follow a simple progression through stages 1 to 5. For example, searching often continues (or should continue) throughout much of the review process as the reviewer develops a closer understanding of the topic.

Review methods

At first glance there seems to be a suite of literature review methods from which to choose. Common terms you might have come across include literature review, scoping review, systematic review, narrative review, meta-analysis and rapid review. However, on close inspection, the terminology is confusing and unhelpful. The list does not constitute a menu of methods.

There is a growing interest in conducting reviews more systematically and transparently (Boaz et al., 2002). There are a number of organisations, such as the international Cochrane and Campbell Collaborations, which support the conduct of systematic reviews in health, social welfare, criminal justice and education (see the Further Reading section at the end of this chapter for more details), and various organisations have produced 'how to' guides and training for individuals interested in using this approach. These include the CRD report 4 (NHS Centre for Reviews and Dissemination, 2001) and the EPPI-centre review companion (eppi.ioe.ac.uk/EPPI WebContent/downloads/ReviewGroupCompanion.doc).

This chapter does not seek to replicate these comprehensive resources. Instead it discusses some general principles that might apply to anyone conducting a good-quality literature review. Illustrations are drawn from two reviews of the literature on mentoring (Table 2.1). Mentoring is used as an intervention in a wide range of settings, including education, youth justice and the workplace (Boaz and Pawson, forthcoming). Mentors act as role models, counsellors or teachers, providing support to mentees with less experience. The mentoring reviews discussed here describe themselves differently (as a literature review and a meta-analysis), but they have common features, as we shall see below.

Defining the topic

Focus

When embarking on a review of the literature it is important to think carefully about its focus. Reviewers too often try to cover everything there is to know about a given topic, an over-ambitious goal that usually results in a review with little space to reflect on the literature identified. While the first of the mentoring reviews addresses a relatively tightly defined topic, the second sets out to answer a whole set of questions, including: what is mentoring, does it work, what makes it work and how is it viewed by different stakeholders? The sheer volume of literature identified presents a daunting task to the reader.

As with good primary research, systematic review guides promote the development of a precisely defined review question in the hope that this will lead to a more focused

Table 2.1   Two reviews of the mentoring literature

Bibliographical details	Type of review (author description)	Main findings
Dubois, D., Holloway, B., Valentine, J. and Cooper, H. (2002) Effectiveness of mentoring programs for youth: a meta-analytic review *American Journal of Community Psychology* 30(2): 157–197	A 'meta-analysis'	There is evidence that mentoring programmes are effective interventions (although the effect is relatively small). For mentoring programmes to be as successful as possible, programmes need to follow guidelines for effective practice. Programme characteristics that appear to make a difference in promoting effective practice include ongoing training for mentors, structured activities, frequent contact between mentors and mentees and parental involvement.
Hall, J.C. (2003) *Mentoring and Young People: A Literature Review* The SCRE Centre: University of Glasgow, 51pp	A 'literature review'	Mentoring is an ill-defined and contested concept. The US evidence suggests that mentoring is an effective intervention, although the impact may be small. Successful mentoring schemes are likely to include: programme monitoring, screening of mentors, matching, training, supervision, structured activities, parental support and involvement, frequent contact and ongoing relationships. The UK literature concludes that mentoring needs to be integrated with other activities, interventions and organisational contexts. Most mentors are female, white and middle-class, and report positive personal outcomes, including increased self-esteem.

review. In its original form in medicine, reviewers have been encouraged to formulate their review question in the way shown in Figure 2.1.

For example, are young offenders (the population) who undergo a mentoring programme (the intervention) less likely to re-offend (the outcome)? How do they fare compared to other young people who have not been involved in the mentoring programme (comparison, control and/or context)? While many of the questions reviewers address in social policy areas are more complex than this, it is sometimes useful to apply this simple formula (called PICO – Population, Intervention, Control, Comparison and/or Context and Outcomes) when thinking about a review question.

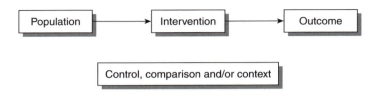

Figure 2.1 Population, intervention, control, comparison and/or context, and outcomes

Scope

It is also useful to consider a number of other dimensions that will have an impact on a review's scope, and thus on its findings. For example, will the review contain literature from one country or from a range of countries? This can be an issue of real significance. Consider, for example, what the implications might be for a UK review of gun crime that relied only on literature from the USA, where policies towards gun ownership are very different from those in other countries.

It is also important to think carefully about the time period covered by the review. The coverage needs to be congruent with the review question. For example, a review of the impact of mobile phones on communication skills might only consider looking at the literature from the last ten years (although it has been argued that the first mobile phone was invented in 1924! – see www.galaxyphones.co.uk/mobile_phones_ history04.asp). If the time period has not been dictated by the review question, there has to be some explicit reason why this is the case (e.g. lack of time, resources etc.). The Dubois mentoring review examines literature from 1970 to 1998 and the Hall review focuses on research published after 1995. Neither reviewer is explicit about their reasons for choosing a particular time period.

Most reviews only include research (as opposed to evidence contained in policy documents and articles in newspapers and magazines). Non-research evidence is often sidelined on grounds of quality. Reviewers are concerned that the evidence in newspapers and policy documents cannot be trusted. However, there have been some attempts to open up a debate about the quality and contribution of different types of evidence (Grayson et al., 2004). In particular, non-research evidence can often provide useful information about context and can help to fill gaps in the research evidence base.

Sometimes reviews even focus on specific sorts of research, usually reflecting the terms of the review question. For example the first review in Table 2.1 includes only studies that evaluate interventions because the review question focuses on the impact of mentoring. However, the second review looks at a wide range of review questions and pulls together lots of different types of research to address them.

Defining the topic: the mentoring review

The Hall review sought to address the following list of questions: What is a mentor/mentoring? What works/doesn't work? What is the evidence of positive outcomes for young people? Is there a case for regulating mentors? What are the views and experiences of mentors and mentees? What are the views and experiences of commissioning bodies and/or employers? The review included research from the UK and 'other relevant countries' from 1995 onwards.

The Dubois review focused on the impact of mentoring programmes on youth. The review included evaluation studies that used either before and after comparisons or control groups. The review focused on research published between 1970 and 1998. All the studies seem to be from the USA.

It is important that all these details about the scope of the review are written down in a protocol or project plan. This has the advantage of recording the reviewer's decisions for all to see, thus promoting transparency. For example, the scope of a review is often progressively narrowed for practical reasons, such as lack of time and resources (translation costs for large numbers of papers can be high, for example). It is important to articulate these issues to allow readers to place the review findings in context. It also allows the reviewer to revisit his or her decisions later on in the review process.

Locating sources

Searching

Searching for the raw material of a review is about much more than pulling down a set of books off the shelf. In order to find as much literature as possible that is relevant to the topic or question, a research reviewer needs to employ a range of tools and techniques. The search might typically include: a key word search of relevant databases, internet searches (discussed in more detail in Chapter 3), hand searches of key journals and a search through the bibliographies of papers, reports and conference proceedings. These more formal approaches are often complemented by informal contact with key individuals working in the field under review. This strategy is particularly useful for picking up unpublished research and work in progress.

Database searching is the most common approach to identifying the literature. Electronic bibliographic databases are particularly strong in the peer-reviewed academic literature, but can also cover the grey literature (unpublished research and/or research from non-academic sources) and PhD theses.

Some well-known social science databases

- ASSIA (Applied Social Science Index and Abstracts)
- ERIC (Educational Resources Information Centre)
- IBSS (International Bibliography of the Social Sciences)
- Sociological Abstracts
- Criminal Justice Abstracts
- Worldwide Political Science Abstracts
- INSIDE (British Library database)

Searching for mentoring studies

The Hall review searched the following databases: ERIC (Educational Resources Information Centre), BEI (British Education Index) and ERSDAT (the Educational Research in Scotland Database), looking for the key word 'mentor'. The reviewer also searched relevant websites, checked lists of references in other literature and contacted key individuals in the field, requesting copies of any relevant documents.

The Dubois review searched the following databases: PsycINFO, ERIC, Medline and Dissertation Abstracts, using both subject (index) terms (e.g. mentor) and free text words (e.g. the names of popular mentoring schemes). The reviewers also searched the internet using several search engines, and checked the reference sections of the studies identified for inclusion to check that nothing had been missed.

Reviewers in the social sciences can face significant problems as a result of the multiplicity of electronic databases (small and large, general and specialist, free and priced), their variable coverage of the different kinds of publication media in which useful social science evidence appears, and the need for skills and experience to carry out thorough searches (Grayson and Gomersall, 2003). These difficulties make the support of information specialists of particular importance, and reviewers often draw on the support of information scientists and librarians in designing and carrying out searches. However, courses are also available for researchers and reviewers interested in developing their own search skills. For example, the NHS Centre for Reviews and Dissemination at York University in the UK provides sessions on literature searching as part of its three-day course on systematic review and critical appraisal, and the ESRC Evidence Network also runs day courses on search skills. There are also some developments designed to improve access to social policy research, including the launch of a new database entitled 'Social Policy and Practice.'

It is unwise in any review to rely solely on the results of database searches. Careful reviewers will hand search key journals and other bibliographic sources, and scan the bibliographies of all retrieved papers, reports and books to pick up related material. They will often complement searches of bibliographic databases by looking at research databases (e.g. the ESRC's REGARD database) or at conference proceedings (e.g. via the British Library's INSIDE database) to identify relevant ongoing and unpublished work. Contacting professional networks and experts in the field to check for gaps and to identify any very recent or unpublished research can also be very productive.

To facilitate the search for relevant material a search strategy is recommended, making it clear to readers of the review how the studies included were identified. The search strategy is likely to outline the key words used to search databases. For example, the search strategy for the Hall review on mentoring and young people looked for papers that included the search term 'MENTORS', but excluded a long list of terms alluding to other types of mentoring, such as 'NURSING EDUCATION', 'TEACHER IMPROVEMENT' and 'GRADUATE STUDY'. It might also include a list of databases, contacts to be followed up, websites to be checked, etc. The strategy is likely to be an evolutionary process, probably beginning with fairly broad searches to establish the main outline of the topic, followed by a series of more detailed searches as the reviewer develops a closer understanding of the issues. Searching may continue throughout much of the review process and should be carefully documented, with details of the sources and search terms used.

Sifting

Using a broad set of search terms on a number of databases is likely to identify a very large number of papers. Many will be irrelevant to the review and an initial sift can often be done on titles. For example, a literature search for a systematic review on new roads (including bypasses) identified 23,000 studies, many of which were concerned with coronary artery bypass operations rather than road bypasses (Egan et al., 2003)! Papers that look promising based on their titles can be checked for relevance through abstracts or summaries, although it is important to remember that the quality of abstracts in social science databases is often inadequate and the choice of 'promising' papers should be liberal. The roads reviewers ordered 700 papers, of which 100 were relevant to the review. Of these, 32 met the inclusion criteria (the reviewers were only interested in the impact of roads on human health so environmental studies, for example, were excluded). In a review such as this, which has a tightly defined question and quality criteria, the reviewer will often only need to read a small subset of the papers identified through the initial searches. A PhD student doing a review for thesis purposes, or a researcher doing a scoping review with a broader question (and no quality threshold) may well have to read a great deal.

In order to manage the task of sifting and sorting, many reviewers use a data extraction tool to record basic information about the individual studies identified, such as title, author and key findings. The advantage of completing a sheet about each study is that it acts as a record for the reviewer and can be a useful resource for anyone aiming to update the review. At the very least, a reviewer should make a note of the full reference for each study, either in a word-processing package or in a reference organising programme such as Reference Manager or EndNote.

Judging quality

A reviewer may decide to include all the literature relevant to his or her review topic. Here 'fitness for purpose' (or fit with the review topic or question) is the primary concern when deciding which studies to include in the review. This is the approach used in the Hall review on mentoring.

In particular, some reviews aim to include in scope all the relevant literature identified through searching in order to understand what is known about a given topic. Similarly, a review aiming to identify gaps in the evidence base or to generate a research agenda is often less concerned with the quality and more concerned with the coverage of existing research. While occasionally a reviewer might focus on the studies that offer the most explanatory power or the clearest conclusions, they have rarely explicitly excluded studies on methodological grounds.

In contrast, systematic reviewing has brought with it a renewed interest in the methodological quality of the studies identified as potentially relevant for review. This approach involves the use of quality criteria, frameworks and checklists to sift out poorer quality studies (e.g. studies with inadequate sample sizes). Where possible, review teams try to employ more than one person in the appraisal process.

However, choosing to exclude studies on the basis of methodological quality is not without its challenges. Perhaps the biggest problem is the lack of transparency in the reporting of primary studies. Often crucial methodological details are missing from research papers and reports, whether as a result of oversight, the pressure of word limits or the perceived low importance of methodological details.

A further difficulty can arise if the majority of the evidence relevant to the review question is deemed to be of poor quality. Here reviewers get caught in a trade off between the quality of the research, the relevance of the research to the review question and the current availability of evidence. One review team, considering the evidence on water fluoridation, got around this problem by reporting a wide range of evidence of different quality, but presenting it with a quality mark of either A, B or C to allow the reader to decide whether to consider the poorer quality results (NHS Centre for Reviews and Dissemination, 2000). Many review groups seek to address the issue of poor-quality evidence on their chosen topic by setting out a clear agenda for future research at the end of the review. Even if they cannot come to firm conclusions on the topic, reviews offer a valuable opportunity to reflect on the quality of, and learn from, the conduct of other research.

For some research methodologies (such as randomised controlled trials), quality criteria, tools and checklists abound, while for others it is difficult to find a critical appraisal tool to use (NHS Centre for Reviews and Dissemination, 2001). Within the social sciences there is a lack of consensus on what counts as good-quality research in some areas, such as qualitative research, while some researchers argue that the appraisal of quality is inappropriate and unhelpful (Pawson, 2004).

Whether or not reviewers use formal criteria or checklists, their own judgement of quality is a crucial element in any review. This is informed by their private understanding of what should count as a useful and reliable piece of work. However, seeking to articulate this process of judgement (for the benefit of the reader) is a challenge for the reviewer.

The two mentoring reviews discussed here took different approaches to appraising the quality of the literature.

Appraising the quality of mentoring studies

The Hall review sifted the papers on their relevance to the review.

The Dubois review team first sifted papers on their relevance to the review question. Second, as the review was concerned with effectiveness, they excluded studies that did not evaluate the effectiveness of mentoring programmes using specific research methods: either studies with a comparison group (controlled studies) or studies that compared participants before and after participation in the programme (pre and post-test studies). No details are given of any quality checklists or criteria applied to these studies.

Synthesising results

Perhaps one of the biggest challenges facing the reviewer is how to make sense of the mass of literature identified, retrieved and neatly piled ready for analysis. Most reviewers hope to pull together the research into a chapter or report that says something additive, that is, the plan is to produce a review that is greater than the sum of its individual parts (or studies).

The extent to which the studies are integrated in a synthesis depends in part on the purpose of the review (for example, a review might aim to give an overview of the current literature, and thus just order and assess coverage rather than integrate) and in part on the methods used (for example, a meta-analysis combines data from individual studies).

Perhaps the most straightforward approach to bringing the literature together is to describe each study briefly and draw some conclusions. This is less of a synthesis, more a description of the literature. Sometimes, it might take the form of an annotated bibliography, or it may consist of paragraphs of text describing the different studies in turn. The moment of synthesis then rests in a section that draws conclusions from this descriptive text.

However, some reviewers have tried to achieve a greater degree of integration. For example, the most common methodology for synthesis in medical research reviews is meta-analysis (Egger et al., 2001), a way of numerically combining the results of existing studies in order to calculate the size of the overall effect for an intervention. However, meta-analysis is only possible where there are appropriate and comparable quantitative data from more than one study. This is rarely the case in social policy research, where multiple outcomes lead to diverse measures, and where quantitative data may be entirely lacking.

Synthesising mentoring studies

The Hall review organised and synthesised the literature around a set of questions provided by the review commissioners. All the literature relevant to each question was described under question headings. For example, in addressing the question 'Does mentoring work?', the review draws on a similar evidence base to the Dubois review (and the Dubois review itself), whereas in addressing the question 'How is mentoring viewed by different stakeholders?', the review draws together a very different literature.

The Dubois mentoring review synthesises the literature in a meta-analysis of the 55 relevant studies identified. The review team had to find a way of pooling together very different outcome measures (such as school achievement, attendance and employment) in order to conduct a meta-analysis.

Where the quantitative data cannot be integrated in a meta-analysis, or where the research identified is largely non-numerical, other forms of synthesis are necessary. It is possible to organise the content of the review in other ways, for example, around themes or questions (as is the case with the second mentoring review), around methods (What do all the surveys tell us about the attitudes of mentees to mentoring schemes? What do all the case studies tell us about the ways in which mentoring schemes are set up and run?), or around some sort of taxonomy or model. While these methods do not necessarily call for the same level of integration, they add a degree of organisation to the information presented.

The difficulties of applying meta-analysis and other methods of synthesis developed within a medical context have encouraged social scientists to develop new approaches, including Realist Synthesis and Meta-ethnography. Realist Synthesis is a theory-driven approach (Pawson, 2002) that aims to use the literature to expose and articulate underlying assumptions about how a policy or programme is intended to work. Rather than passing a straightforward 'it works' or 'it doesn't work' verdict on a policy or programme, Realist Synthesis aims to explain how an intervention (such as mentoring) works, why it works and in what circumstances it works. As such, the review involves both theoretical thinking and an empirical testing of this thinking through an exploration of the literature.

First developed by Noblit and Hare (1988), and further developed by Campbell et al. (2003), meta-ethnography uses a qualitative, ethnographic approach to synthesise qualitative research. This method involves identifying key concepts from the individual papers and seeking them out in the wider literature. Noblit and Hare argue that this approach can be used to go beyond individual studies, comparing, challenging and providing new insights.

In the social sciences, narrative descriptions of the research identified remain the most common form of synthesis, and these new methods are still in a relatively early stage of development. Synthesis remains one of the most intellectually challenging aspects of the review process, and one that invites the reviewer to think creatively about how to present the mass of literature in a meaningful way to potential readers.

Reporting

The final hurdle involves the important tasks of reporting and communicating the review findings. Reviewers are encouraged to be as transparent as possible about the process they used to conduct the review. Methodological information does not need to be given in the opening chapters of the report, but should be included (often in detail as an appendix). Furthermore, a full bibliography of papers referenced in the review should be included. Where the reviewer has used data extraction forms, these are sometimes reproduced at the back of the report in an appendix or in a separate volume. One of the advantages of such clear reporting is that the review can be updated by the reviewer or by someone else interested in the topic.

The approach to writing up and sharing the findings of a review will depend on the purpose for which the review was undertaken. For example, some reviews will be conducted for largely internal purposes, such as for a PhD or to inform a new project. However, where a review has been commissioned or has things to say to a wider audience than the review team, it is important to consider carefully the communication of its findings. Reviews can be over-long, turgid documents, as thick as telephone directories (but less accessible). At the very least, the document needs to be navigable and to have a short, well-written summary. The *Findings* series produced by the UK Joseph Rowntree Foundation is frequently cited as an example of good practice (www.jrf.org.uk). Short papers, for example in journals and magazines read by practitioners, can also be a useful method of disseminating the findings of a review.

Often it is difficult to anticipate the future uses of a review. As literature reviews can be invaluable sources of primary literature for future researchers, it is recommended that a copy is sent to the national copyright library (such as the British Library in the UK).

In addition to short summaries and articles, there may be a need to present a review orally to interested parties. Increasingly, formal reports and presentations are also complemented by web-accessible versions. Writing and communicating research findings are discussed in more detail in Chapters 8 and 9.

Management of a review

A protocol is a map or plan of the review process that provides an opportunity to think about crucial issues, such as the resources of time, skills and labour needed to complete the work (NHS Centre for Reviews and Dissemination, 2001). A protocol should not be set in stone and can be revisited and changed as the review progresses. Issues of project management are discussed in more detail in Chapter 6.

While literature reviews have traditionally been seen as a one-person, desk-based activity, they can also be conducted by teams. The advantage of this approach is that a mix of expertise can be brought together. For example, a review team might include an information specialist, a subject specialist and a methodologist with knowledge of review methods. More than one person can be involved in independently appraising the studies in order to try to reduce bias. Like primary research, reviews also often benefit from the support of an advisory group. For example, this was the case for the second review in Table 2.1. Where the review is a lone pursuit, advice from an information specialist, in particular, can be a real advantage.

Case study: A student's perspective on reviewing literature

Adrienne Sidford

I think that most researchers and students can look back on a moment where they got really 'lost' when doing a review. I was looking at evaluation within both policy and public health domains. Before beginning my study I needed to have evidence to support the evaluation method being used, as well as evidence setting the context of previous evaluations.

The review soon became much bigger than me, growing as I was side-tracked. My questions for the review were vague, partly because I had little understanding of the area. The more I read the more I became embroiled in the ongoing debate surrounding evaluation and the views of different researchers' paradigms regarding the discipline/methodology (positivist vs constructionist). I became bogged down in the fine detail and was trying to solve a debate that will continue to permeate through the social sciences. Also, my initial plan for the review was not allowing me to highlight central themes and I became more frustrated. I found I was unable to tease out the story as I was not really sure what I wanted. I had not really accepted that although my main reason for doing the review was to look at how evaluation had been carried out in public health and policy, it was also to provide a rationale for the method that my study was using. Unsurprisingly, my review was going around in circles!

After some discussions with my supervisors, I took a break from the review, reflecting on the problems I had encountered. I came back to it able to see the whole picture, discussed it with colleagues and managed to focus the review to get it to answer all my questions. Writing reviews is both a painful and exciting process, involving a lot of detective work. The reward is a fuller, more powerful argument for the study I am conducting, and a greater understanding of where my study sits within this body of knowledge.

Conclusions

Literature reviewing is a research method and quality considerations apply as they do to all research methods. A review should be conducted in a rigorous and transparent manner and address a clearly defined question or topic. It should be based on a thorough and fully documented search. The reviewer should consider the studies identified in terms of their fitness for the purpose of the review. The reviewer might also appraise the studies and include only those of good methodological quality. A method must be chosen (or devised) of pulling the results of the different studies together to produce a review that is more than an untidy pile of primary studies. Finally, the reviewer must also consider how best to communicate the findings to different audiences. The entire process can be improved by the use of a protocol outlining the proposed review approach, including the search strategy.

This may sound like a lot of work, but well-conducted literature reviews can have something powerful to offer a range of different users, including researchers themselves, policy makers and practitioners. A literature review goes beyond the common reliance on commissioning a new study or relying on one piece of research. Recycling research is likely to be of more and more use to the research community in the future.

Further reading

Davies, H.T.O., Nutley, S.M. and Smith, P.C. (2000). *What Works? Evidence-based Policy and Practice in Public Services.* Bristol: The Policy Press.

Fink, A. (1998). *Conducting Research Literature Reviews: From Paper to the Internet.* Thousand Oaks, CA: Sage.

Relevant organisations and websites

Campbell Collaboration: www.campbellcollaboration.org

Building on the experience of the Cochrane Collaboration, Campbell has been set up to carry out reviews of interventions in the fields of education, criminal justice and social welfare. The website currently includes guidance on protocol construction, specimen protocols and other information. The first Campbell Review on Scared Straight initiatives can be downloaded from both the Campbell and Cochrane websites.

Cochrane Collaboration: www.cochrane.org

The Cochrane Collaboration prepares, maintains and disseminates the results of systematic reviews of research on the effects of health care. The Cochrane Library is a quarterly updated electronic database of reviews. The Cochrane *Manual* and the *Reviewer's Handbook* are available online.

ESRC UK Centre for Evidence-based Policy and Practice:www.evidencenetwork.org

The Centre's EvidenceNetwork website is designed to act as a starting point for accessing key literature and information resources on evidence-based policy and practice. This is a useful site for identifying electronic databases, internet portals and other sources of information for literature reviews, and includes some basic advice on search techniques.

Evidence for Policy and Practice Information and Coordinating Centre: www.eppi.ioe.ac.uk

The Centre was originally commissioned by the Department for Education and Employment to provide a resource for those wishing to undertake systematic reviews in the field of education. A database of systematic reviews, and useful publications on systematic review methodologies are accessible via this site.

NHS Centre for Reviews and Dissemination: www.york.ac.uk/inst/crd

CRD carries out systematic reviews on selected topics in the health-care field and maintains a database of reviews (DARE). A number of useful documents, including *Undertaking Systematic Reviews of Research on Effectiveness* (CRD Report No. 4), are accessible online.

Using the Internet

3

*Nina Wakeford, Kate Orton-Johnson
and Katrina Jungnickel*

- The internet can be used by social scientists as a source of knowledge, as when one looks up an article or data record on the web, but it can also be used as a research site in its own right.

- This chapter explains how the internet can be used as a secondary source for data from databases about social science, and also for primary data collection about respondents using the online equivalents of interviews, observation and surveys.

- The chapter explains and compares chat rooms, web pages, web logs, mailing lists and other ways of interacting with the internet.

- It also considers issues such as data quality and ethics.

In the last ten years the internet has fundamentally changed the ways in which many social scientists undertake research. From the beginning of the literature review, when one can now turn to electronic databases and digital library resources, to the final output of a thesis, which now might include a record of online interactions on a CD or DVD, graduate students must consider when it is appropriate to use the internet to conduct a successful PhD. As we shall explain, the internet is a vast potential resource for data for those doing empirical work. There are several overviews of the technical infrastructures and interfaces that we will not duplicate in this chapter (see Best and Krueger, 2004; Hewson et al., 2003). What we aim to do instead is offer indications of the kinds of question that a researcher should ask when hoping to use the internet to gather or generate primary data. We will illustrate the discussion with examples from recent studies by students.

Using the internet poses many challenges, not the least of which is knowing how to judge its capacity to be a useful tool for social science research. When techniques such as the email interview were first introduced, some predicted that they would create more equality between researcher and research participant. Boshier claims a possible equalising function:

> Email appears to provide a context for the kind of non-coercive and anti-hierarchical dialogue that Habermas claimed constitutes an 'idea speech situation', free of internal or external coercion, and characterised by an equality of opportunity and reciprocity in roles assumed by participants. (1990: 51)

Since these early predictions, researchers have become much more careful about making universal claims for the internet in relation to social research. Pioneers in the field have described the benefits of doing work 'virtually', including the advantages of recruiting participants online, or using online forums to conduct data collection (e.g. Jones, 1999). Certainly there are many cases where online research is appropriate and successful. However, there is a temptation when you have a limited budget for undertaking research, and perhaps limited ability to travel long distances to interview people face to face, to be drawn to using the internet primarily because is it supposedly 'cheap' and 'easy'. Beware! As with any aspect of research design, it is important to have a clear rationale and account of the methodological choices you make. First, when you write your thesis or for publication, you will have to account clearly for the limitations and constraints that this approach has on your study, and explain how your particular discipline (maybe even sub-discipline) judges online research. Second, you will probably find that it is not as simple or cost-free as you imagine. You should investigate both internet-based research *and* the alternatives thoroughly before you assume that internet data collection is for you.

The internet and secondary research

Although this chapter is primarily focused on gathering data using internet interfaces such as the web, chat rooms or web logs, many students may turn to the internet during their initial search for previous work on their topic. Using the internet for secondary research, from databases or web portals, can be useful when you are beginning to refine your research question (see Chapter 5) or during your literature review (see Chapter 2). Electronic library resources should be familiar to every student, including databases such as the ISI Web of Science (www.isinet. com). More specialised resources for the social sciences can be found through Social Science Information Gateway (www.sosig.ac.uk).

You will also be able to keep up with funded research projects in your area by using the search available on the Economic and Social Research Council's website (www. esrc.ac.uk). The ESRC's Society Today, a database of all funded research since 1985, is an invaluable way to understand how your research fits into work currently being done in the UK. The websites of professional associations, such as the British Sociological Association (www.britsoc.co.uk), offer links to specialist study groups and online resources related to particular debates within the discipline. All of these services are more time efficient than simply 'Googling' a selection of your keywords. Having said that, Google has a new service called Google Scholar (scholar.google.com), which is particularly focused on the higher education user.

The speed with which much internet content changes and new services are added or removed can be a source of anxiety for researchers. The Internet Archive (www. archive.org) is an attempt to create a digital library of internet sites and other digital content (including about internet history). It is the place to look up web pages as they were in the past, which could be useful for longitudinal analysis. Other kinds of archive make easier the electronic transfer of secondary data sets over the internet. The largest collection of digital data in the social sciences in the UK is the ESRC Data Archive (www.data-archive.ac.uk), through which students can order data sets from the British Crime Survey and the National Child Development Survey, among many others. Perhaps the real impact for researchers is not so much the ability to acquire such data sets, but the existence of mailing lists on which one can interact with other researchers who are working with the same material or method. One example in data analysis is the CAQDAS mailing list (www.jiscmail.ac.uk/lists/QUAL-SOFTWARE.html), emerging from the collective needs of those using Computer Assisted Qualitative Data Analysis Software.

Understanding the range of online services

To do successful online research, a researcher must understand the range of online services, the different capacities of each one for gathering data, and the specific norms of practice which may dominate each service. Posting a request for research participants to an open web-based chat using a 'guest' login will elicit a very different response from having an email request forwarded by the list owner to a closed mailing list, even if both the web page and the mailing list are on the same topic. Cultures of different spaces vary widely (e.g. contrast Baym, 2000, with Kendall, 2002). As with any other data gathering, it is wise to begin with an exploratory stage and/or pilot.

There is often a variety of specialised software that can be used to collect data, and several packages should be compared. Before setting out to use any online service it is essential to understand what kinds of technological understanding and infrastructure you will need to run it and, if you are setting up a purpose-built service for the project, what kind of technical set-up your participants will need to access it. It is also useful to look at how other researchers have used that particular kind of service. Most internet services are variations on the following.

Early text-based services

In the mid-1990s social science researchers began to undertake studies of interactions over computer networks. Early services did not use the graphical user interfaces (such as Microsoft Windows) to which most PC users today are accustomed. They tended to be based around text-based conversations. Recent guides to internet data collection omit these online services, yet they were a vital early source of data for researchers thinking about what kind of social norms were being created online (Baym, 2000). Furthermore, some early computer-mediated conversation environments persisted for many years, allowing long-term ethnographic fieldwork to take place (Kendall, 2002). Newsgroups, early archives of topic-led discussions, were studied very early on by communication studies researchers (Baym, 2000) and those interested in forms of discourse analysis (Denzin, 1999). Collecting postings to active newsgroups can generate vast amounts of information; Baym collected 32,308 messages in ten months. Bulletin Board Services (BBS), which sometimes operated independently of the internet through dialing up a single computer, allowed researchers access to synchronous text-based chat among individuals who were often scattered over large geographical areas. A persistent theme in these early studies was the existence of very strong group boundaries, and the ways in which outsiders (including researchers) could be barred from membership if basic rules of interaction, or sometimes identity, were not followed. Ethnographic studies picked up the sense of community and shared the social norms that these services often fostered (Correll, 1995). It is useful to remember from this early work that researchers were confronting the ways in which services were treated by participants as new (and sometimes fragile) constructed environments.

Email distribution or mailing lists

A mailing list is a collection of email addresses that are associated with one mailing list address. When an email is sent to that address, all the 'subscribers' to this list receive the email. The software to create and administer these lists is widely available (common programs are listserv, majordomo and mailman). Mailing lists have been very widely used among researchers, not only as sources of data but also as a means of recruiting participants. Indeed, some mailing lists, having been inundated by such requests, now include an explicit direction that the list may not be used by researchers in this way. One of the problems in understanding data derived from mailing lists is that it is often highly contextualised by the local culture of the users (Wakeford, 1998). Another problem is that there is no comprehensive directory of mailing lists, and many are specific to organisations or private intranets. This is significant if you need to know about populations from which to sample. Nevertheless mailing lists can quite easily be set up for a pre-recruited sample and an email list can be used as a way to conduct online interviews or a virtual focus group (Rezabek, 2000).

Chat rooms

Chat rooms are online social spaces for synchronous computer-mediated communication (CMC). Although these first came to attention through the proprietary services of internet providers such as AOL, this kind of interaction, particularly via web-based chat rooms, is an emerging tool for social research. Dedicated chat rooms can be set up within public chat forums. Alternatively, researchers can download software to create an independent chat room on a web page. Using chat rooms as a fieldsite enables the researcher to access geographically dispersed respondents and hard-to-reach populations, and to address potentially sensitive research subjects with an anonymity not provided by face-to-face encounters. Practically, using synchronous chat to collect data requires typing skills to enable effective participation and the researcher may face problems with the recruitment and retention of participants, the nebulous nature of online presence being a key challenge faced by research relying on computer-mediated communication (Mann and Stewart, 2000).

Web pages

Web pages have been integrated into research as objects of study, tools for access or platforms for the collation and exposure of a research project. Some researchers examine web pages focused on a central theme. Hine (2000) provides a concise guide to online ethnographic practice through her study of amateur websites created around the

Louise Woodward case. Other researchers look at specific cultural uses of web pages to understand better the importance of geographical place and global culture for internet-production and consumption (Miller and Slater, 2000). Websites can also be used to connect researchers to notoriously difficult to access cultural groups, such as Goths (Hodkinson, 1993) or drug dealers (Coomber, 1997). Discussion is also emerging about how researchers can engage more imaginatively with web pages for their own projects (Dicks and Mason, 1998) and the number of online hyper-media research websites is growing (Jungknickel, 2003a and b; Wesch, 2003).

Web logs or 'blogs'

A web log, weblog or blog is a web application that enables chronological multi-media publishing. Blogs differ from websites in their diarised format, which delivers a sense of immediacy through frequently updated pages, personal style and interaction with viewers. Blogs are often presented by individuals as being records of a relatively uncensored version of thoughts and feelings, yet they can also be used as a form of fieldwork diary through which the reader may be encouraged to feel involved in the evolving research project as it happens. A feature of blogs is their ability to engage with viewers via a comments facility, allowing responses to each posting which themselves can be analysed. Viewers can directly engage with each other, as well as with the author. While there are an estimated 5 million blogs (Belo, 2004) about specific themes or random responses to everyday life, they are still at an experimental stage for conducting social research, although there is a rapidly growing academic blogging community. Some blogs document the ups and downs of academic life and research projects (Burgess, 2004; Cohen, 2005; Gregg, 2004). Others are directly used to gather data and stories, and universities are increasingly integrating them into teaching (Adenekan, 2005).

New methods, old concerns

Regardless of the online environment, data collection using the internet will involve specifying a research question, developing a sample frame, deciding on a sampling method, determining the sample size and negotiating contact with respondents. Social science researchers have written extensively about the problem of sampling in relation to the demographics of those online (see Best and Kruger, 2004). If your study seeks to generalise to a wider group, this is a crucial issue that must be addressed. However, just as crucial is to understand the ways in which conventional methods frequently need to be adapted to fit the technical infrastructure and the norms of the service which you intend to use. Online research still draws on conventional research techniques, including generating and maintaining rapport (for interviews), and has conventional concerns about sample and response rate (for probabilistic research). Below we describe the potential pitfalls of moving a select set of conventional methods online.

Standardised surveys

The typical standardised survey on the internet is administered via the web, either after embedding a web address in a posting to an email forum or another online space, or by simply posting the survey on a website and then recruiting by other means. Although surveys are one of the most popular ways of conducting social research, most of the work on internet survey methodology is to be found in market research journals, which reflects the attraction of generating very large samples at the lowest possible cost. Social scientists writing about standardised research instruments, both questionnaire surveys and interviews, have emphasised the complications of ensuring an adequate response rate as well as confidentiality (Best and Kruger, 2004; Hewson et al., 2003). Issues such as how to control receipt, or authenticating subjects by access code, must be addressed. How to format the web document itself has also been widely discussed. Best and Kruger (2004: 36–74) show how to make decisions about display configuration, paying attention to the varying size of computer screens; colour and text appearance, pointing out the problems of distinguishing red and green for some users, as well as differing interpretation of colours; delivery and alignment of the questions over single or multiple interactive screens; response style, including the challenges of open and closed questions and, as with any questionnaire, overall length. As well as designing and transmitting the survey, the researcher must plan how the data will be collected and analysed, particularly how to import it into software for statistical or qualitative analysis.

Non-standardised interviews

Online interviews can be held synchronously, through chat rooms or web chats, or asynchronously through email. One of the common themes of researchers writing about their experience using online interviews is the way in which technical expertise, both of the researcher and of the participants, can be a key factor in shaping the kinds of data that are generated. For example, use of the 'Cc' line in a group email to participants led some of Mann's participants to be identified individually and drop out of the study, and others to self-organise into an email list which ran parallel to the official study (Mann and Stewart, 2000: 133). Mann and Stewart emphasise the importance of establishing trust as well as thinking about the impact of mutual self-disclosure. Many online interviews are conducted via sequential one-to-one emails. Unlike face-to-face interviews, such exchanges often extend across days or weeks. The level of rapport that can be generated will depend on traditional interviewing skills, such as listening and sensitivity, as well as the availability of computer access and the willingness of the participant to sustain interest over more than one interaction. One of the issues for a pilot would be whether to send a list of questions at the outset, or to stagger questions in a more unstructured format, using emailed probes.

Focus groups

Face-to-face focus groups have long been established as a mainstream method of qualitative social research used to generate data through group interaction. The perceived necessity for physical co-presence – to facilitate the role of the moderator, to explore group dynamics and establish rapport, and to enable the observation of non-verbal inputs – is challenged by methodological strategies that emphasise the greater equality of discussion in online groups, the reduction in bias, the reduction in research costs, the immediate creation of transcriptions and the interactional benefits of anonymity. However, online groups face technological and methodological problems with recruitment and management of group dynamics. Oringderff (2004) provides some useful practical guidelines for conducting online focus groups, including advice on providing a clear structure for respondents and moderators and on keeping discussions focused. Gaiser (1997) offers an introduction to online focus groups as a methodological innovation, while Mann and Stewart (2000) provide a comprehensive guide to the practicalities and demands of conducting online synchronous and asynchronous groups. They stress the importance of understanding software options and limitations, forms of control and facilitation in an environment which can become 'fast and furious' and quickly drift off-topic, and the benefits of distributing a question schedule in the first few minutes (Mann and Stewart, 2000: 153).

The ethical dilemmas of online research

Ethics have become a major issue in online research. The ease with which covert research can be conducted, the blurred distinction between what is public and what is private and the difficulties of gaining informed consent from research participants have made cyberspace research vulnerable to ethical breaches (Thomas, 1996).

The supposed anonymity and disembodied nature of the online fieldsite provides an arena in which the negotiation of access and consent may be easily circumvented. However, the same ethical guidelines governing covert research in offline settings apply and the likely benefits of engaging in covert research online must be balanced against its ethical ambiguities.

Similarly, the notion of informed consent can be problematic in the online field as a result of the transient and ephemeral nature of certain online environments. This is not to suggest that all research settings do not involve the constant negotiation of access and consent, rather that the transfer of research principles into the online setting can pose particular challenges. Many online spaces have large and fluctuating populations and maintaining informed consent in these environments would require continual and regular posts detailing the nature of the research and requesting participants' consent. This could disrupt the 'natural' flow of the interaction and significantly alter the nature of the fieldsite. An alternative to explanatory messages is the use of a 'signature' at the end of each posting. Signatures are files automatically added to messages containing text or images used as unique, individual identifiers and can be used to provide details of research. However, to condense an ethically appropriate description and summary of research aims and objectives into a couple of lines that do not alienate participants is, in itself, a methodological challenge. Most researchers balance the notion of consent with practicality. Reid suggests:

> It was not practically possible for me to inform all members of a MUD [Multi User Dungeon] of my research interests without disrupting the normal social flow of each system, since the fluctuating member base meant such announcements would have to be made every few days. This meant that if I were to carry out my research some measure of deception or non-disclosure was inevitable. (1996: 170)

The Association of Internet Researchers (AoIR), in its recommendations for ethical research, provides a set of guiding principles which emphasise the ethical ambiguities that internet researchers face and the multiplicity of ethical responses (Ess and AoIR Ethics Working Committee, 2002). Advocating ethical pluralism and cross-cultural awareness, the guidelines provide invaluable assistance in discerning ethically appropriate methodological conduct. Mann and Stewart (2000) also provide a useful summary of the practical, conceptual, legal and ethical issues facing the internet researcher. Chapter 4 reviews some additional sources for guidelines.

Case study: Online fieldwork

Kate Orton-Johnson

As an illustrative case study of some of these issues, I will draw on my doctoral research which was concerned with student use of new technologies in higher education. My desire to focus on a student perspective prompted my choice to become an online student for an academic year and to conduct a participatory 'virtual' ethnography of an online distance course.

The Open University (OU) was selected as a site for fieldwork as an institution which, while not striving to become a 'virtual university', is committed to developing its e-learning activities. I completed an undergraduate web-intensive course, in which the internet was used to provide all teaching and learning resources and support. The ethical deliberations began when I signed up for the course and needed to make analytical and methodological clarifications about what my role was. I was simultaneously a student on a course studying an unfamiliar topic in an unfamiliar environment, and a researcher taking the course to understand the experience of being an online student. I made the decision to contact the course directors and to explain my research interests and ask their permission to draw on my experience of completing the course and on the web-based materials provided. On the basis that I would not be directly contacting students or using student data, the course directors had no difficulty with my participation on the course in this dual role.

A second layer of ethical concerns centred around my fellow students on the course. In addition to the online course materials, students at the OU are

(Continued)

(Continued)

supported, academically and socially, through the conferencing software FirstClass, an electronic mail and bulletin board technology which enables synchronous and asynchronous communication through online 'conferences', synchronous real-time online chat and email messages. Students use FirstClass by installing the software provided by the OU on their own computer or by accessing the FirstClass server via the internet. Messages are organised into conferences and folders, and students then access the conference and read and respond to postings at any time. For synchronous chat sessions students must be logged on to their specific FirstClass server simultaneously to participate in the discussion.

As a student I was assigned to a tutorial group with its own dedicated conference area. I felt that it was ethically appropriate and important that as a member of this intimate and collaborative working group I was open and explicit about my dual role. The initial conference in the tutor group area was oriented towards 'getting to know each other' and this gave me the opportunity to post to the conference that I was a PhD student who was participating in the course to find out what it was like to do an online course, thereby identifying myself as both 'student' and 'researcher'.

I spent considerable time constructing this introductory post and was anxious about what responses I would receive, but, far from being concerned about my dual status, the other students in the group accepted my roles as student and researcher without comment and shared similar stories of conflict and duality in role and identity and the problems of juggling being a student with multiple other responsibilities, commitments and interests.

In contrast, the course-wide conferences, which contained thousands of students and hundreds of postings each day, were environments in which gaining informed consent was difficult and, I have argued, ethically unnecessary as my presence there was overwhelmingly one of 'student' rather than 'researcher'. The course content was new to me and the conferences were used as an arena to clarify knowledge, ask questions and reflect on current work.

The large populations of the conference and the hundreds of messages posted each day meant that maintaining a presence as anything other than onlooker and

(Continued)

(Continued)

occasional participant was a highly demanding activity and my presence as a researcher and my impact on the fieldsite were minimal.

Conducting an online or virtual ethnography had several significant practical implications for research. Ethnography in and of virtual spaces shifts fieldwork to deskwork as the online setting also becomes a primary research question. The obvious advantage of the online field is in the removal of the requirement for physical (co)presence in the setting and the accompanying burden of travel time and costs. The asynchronous nature of much of the OU course allowed fieldwork to be conducted at any time and in any location where access to a networked PC was available.

However, this 24-hour ability to access the field was not entirely without problems and the ethnography was characterised by technical, practical and conceptual obstacles and pitfalls. Technical problems resulting from computer failure, poor network connections and difficulties installing software, were a continuing and frustrating feature of the fieldwork and, in the shift from fieldwork to deskwork, the static geography of the fieldsite and the lack of physical participation in the field often resulted in feelings of isolation and boredom. The 24-hour nature of the fieldsite also increased the danger of one of the key problems of ethnographic enquiry – 'going native' (Fielding, 1993). Becoming a part of the setting that is being researched is an important element in gaining detailed ethnographic understanding. The demands of doing the course itself, in tandem with making ethnographic fieldnotes on my experiences, feelings and observations about doing the course, resulted in a process of constant reflection on my role.

The fact that the online fieldsite is always 'on' and always there increases the danger of being unable to remove yourself physically or mentally from the field and of being able to define clear boundaries and stopping points. This is not to deny that many offline ethnographies also have this problem. However, during the nine months of the fieldwork, the continual presence of the fieldsite on my computer, on my desk, in my home, was both a blessing and a curse.

One of the practical benefits of an online field is that fieldnotes can be detailed and lengthy and a lack of physical co-presence means that strategies for the surreptitious taking of notes which may disturb the research setting are unnecessary.

(Continued)

(Continued)

However, this physical separation also had important implications for how the fieldsite was defined. The embodiment and participation in the field, which is a feature of many ethnographies, is, in many ways, absent from the virtual ethnography. The 24-hour fieldsite enables the engagement with the field which ethnography requires, yet the lack of physical co-presence often led to a sense of isolation from the field.

These conceptual and practical difficulties of defining and managing the virtual field extend to, and have analytical implications for, the production of the ethnographic account. For Hine (2000), textual ethnographic accounts have traditionally relied on the concepts of travel, experience and interaction for their authority. Hine argues that through an account of travelling physically to a fieldsite, experiencing the culture of that site and interacting with members of that site, the ethnographer can claim authority. This poses some interesting challenges for the virtual ethnography and the production of an ethnographic account: without a physical presence in a disembodied fieldsite, how can ethnographers claim authority and authenticity?

Case study: A student view of online research

Katrina Jungnickel

I recently undertook a research project into the use of technology on the No. 73 bus in London. The study built on a much larger study that investigated the consumption of digital content in specific locations in London. The central research question was the relationship between the use of technology (e.g. mobile phones) and the sense of place in urban settings. My focus was predominantly on the bus itself, those who rode it and those who worked on it. In my part of the project I wanted to find out how people used technology and consumed digital content on the move. I also wanted to track my own personal use of technology to narrate and present an ethnography and understand the challenges of gathering people's responses via an online channel. The project was specifically aimed at innovating methodologically through technology.

(Continued)

(Continued)

During the fieldwork I spent time on the bus, with passengers and conductors, undertook historical and cultural research on and offline, interviewed respondents and visually documented the process. I produced a 100-page website (www.73urbanjourneys.com) and managed two weblogs (73bus.typepad.com/73stories/). The first blog documented my everyday personal narration of the project and the second encouraged people to submit stories to the website that were 73 words long about the No. 73 bus.

Because I wanted to narrate my own experience as well as encourage people to respond and engage with my work, my first questions were: Should I start a web log? Should I produce a website with an email address? Should I join a chat room? Should I manage a notice board? I chose a website and web logs since I hoped that they would provide the space and structure to document my process (via the website), narrate my experience and gather data (via the web log).

The decision to expose the ongoing ethnography rather than launch a finished product at the end was crucial and intrinsic to the developmental process. My first task required a simultaneous immersion in both internet design and ethnographic fieldwork. It was surprisingly exhausting at first as it felt like two distinct activities: design application and analytic investigation. I had to learn to integrate these two dimensions creatively and allow them to inform and reflect each other. I did this by thinking about ethnography as a methodology for 'creating and representing knowledge' rather than as separate tasks of gathering and presenting data (Pink, 2001: 18). I was influenced by approaches which suggest that the product of an ethnography need not be a text monograph (Alexander, 2001; Becker, 1998; Berger, 1972). 'Imagination is often successfully invited', writes Wright Mills, 'by putting together hitherto isolated items, by finding unsuspected connections' (1959: 201).

Maintaining focus was sometimes challenging. There are times when 'creating so much information tricks one into thinking one has created knowledge' (Harper, 1998: 34). Despite the short duration of the project, I created a lot of material and it was a useful warning. Sometimes you need to stand back from your project to re-affirm your direction and identity, a point aptly articulated by the title of Hagaman's research study, 'How I learned not to be a photojournalist' (1996).

I chose to construct the website in DreamWeaver and used Photoshop to create the key typographic elements and visual palette. I applied my knowledge of design from my

(Continued)

(Continued)

MA in Visual Culture and years of media and design industry experience, thinking through how the visual identity of the site reflected the objectives of the research, its potential audience and context. During the initial weeks I also started my ethnography. I regularly travelled on the No. 73 bus, I visited the London Transport Museum for their historical archives and searched related bus online sources. I gathered textual and non-textual, on and offline, static and dynamic materials to feed into the design process. Likewise, the design process fed into the ways in which I viewed and gathered data.

I drew creatively from my field experiences. For example, I was inspired by the visual language of the bus stop LCD sign imagery for the web page banner (Figure 3.1) and the route mapping motif for my navigation design (Figure 3.2). I also referenced my street photos in the production of the backdrop design. In this way I tried to bridge the distance between sociology and the topic of my study (Chaplin, 1994). I wanted my images, text and illustration to dominate on alternate pages of the website. I also placed ethnographic notes and other people's stories into experimental reconstructions of the bus floorplan or the bus route, depending on how and where they were gathered (Figure 3.3). I used these ethnographic tools as ways of bridging the distance between individual storytellers on the blog and the collective narrative on the website, and my research as a whole.

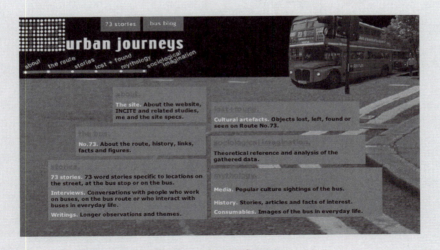

Figure 3.1 LCD sign imagery for the web page banner

(Continued)

(Continued)

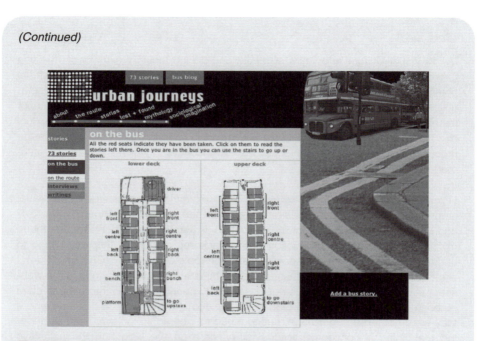

Figure 3.2   Route mapping motif for the navigation design

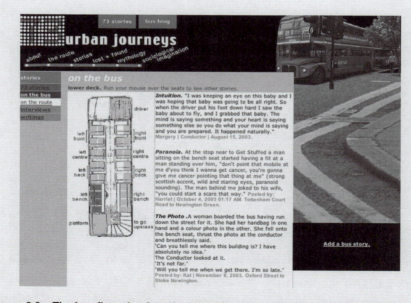

Figure 3.3   The bus floorplan for ethnographic notes and other people's stories

(Continued)

Strong visual and multi-media skills are essential in interactive research projects. To undertake an online project that involves the production and management of a website or a web log requires access to and knowledge of key technologies. I found programs such as DreamWeaver, Flash and Photoshop essential for the construction, design and ongoing maintenance of an aesthetic website and web log. Getting the project online requires embracing another field of knowledge. Some researchers might already be familiar with the minutiae of online publishing, such as registering domain names, choosing a host server, and negotiating webspace, as well as avoiding pitfalls (such as ads on your site unless you pay to have them removed). I wasn't. I started with a basic blogger account (www.blogger.com) which was free and simple to use but had restricted comment and image enablement (only permitted via external providers). However, to get all the multi-media features I wanted on an independent host server with a simple interface, I now use Typepad (www.typepad.com).

Conclusion

Gathering primary data over the internet is increasingly regarded as a legitimate part of research projects in the social sciences. As the number of methodological papers on online research grow, it will be easier to assess the ways in which data collected from the internet compares to that generated by traditional methods. Whichever internet service is used, researchers must keep in mind the ways in which their technical skills will impact on their research design. Partly, as always in research, it is a question of time. For example, if you are unfamiliar with web page construction, you will have to invest time learning the software that helps you construct a successful questionnaire. Unlike the traditional paper form, an online survey may require you to understand many technical infrastructures. Static, single-page web instruments are relatively easy to implement. Any form that is interactive will require server-side programming, and will become more complicated when you want automatic skipping of sections (Best and Kruger, 2004). If you use email for interviews, the set-up time will be far less in terms of data collection, but you will still need to consider how you construct and contact your sample and how your data relates to your research question.

If there is one golden rule of internet research, it is to acknowledge that online services are newly constructed environments with their own codes of practice. The more you understand the technical infrastructure and social expectations, the less time you will spend developing content that is rejected or techniques that just don't function. It is worth bearing in mind that many online services, particularly high-profile websites and chat spaces, have been heavily researched, either by academic researchers or market research companies. In the past, newsgroups and mailing lists have been inundated by students seeking to collect quick and cheap data. If you want to post a link to an online forum, be sure to search the 'Frequently Asked Questions' section to see if this is permitted. Many only accept such postings with the permission of the list owner or web page administrator. As the scourge of spam increasingly dominates email services, it is even more important to distinguish legitimate projects from mass postings. Using a Hotmail address, for example, may severely decrease your response rate, particularly among people whose internet service providers automatically block email from domains associated with spam.

On a more positive note, using or developing an internet service for data collection can be a source of excitement and methodological development. In her student viewpoint, Katrina Jungnickel describes how her project evolved using a web log both for her own fieldnotes as well as to stimulate interaction around her website. Even though she had to immerse herself in several software packages for handling images and web page design, the result was an innovative set of data resources, which she continued to maintain well after the official project ended. If you want to use your PhD as an opportunity for methodological experimentation using the internet, you will probably be drawn into debates which are being conducted by a growing number of interdisciplinary internet researchers as well as colleagues in your own field of study.

Further reading

Best, S.J. and Krueger, B.S. (2004). *Internet Data Collection*. London: Sage.

Coomber, R. (1997). Using the Internet for Survey Research. *Sociological Research Online*, 2(2), http://www.socresonline.org.uk/socresonline/2/2/2.html

Hewson, C., Yule, P., Laurent, D. and Vogel, C. (2003). *Internet Research Methods: A Practical Guide for the Social and Behavioural Sciences*. London: Sage.

Hine, C. (2000). *Virtual Ethnography*. London: Sage.

Mann, F. and Stewart, F. (2000). *Internet Research and Qualitative Research: A Handbook for Researching Online*. London: Sage.

Research Ethics

4

Mark Israel with Deborah Hersh

- Questions of ethics arise throughout the research process and one needs to be prepared for them.
- This chapter considers the main areas where ethical dilemmas may occur and what the principal issues are.
- It also describes the rules governing ethical consent and how to submit an application for approval to a research ethics committee.

Social scientists confront ethical issues throughout their research work. They may have to tackle ethical questions when deciding what relationships they will forge with research participants, sponsors and colleagues, or how they are going to collect or analyse data or report their findings. They will certainly have to think about the ethical consequences of their work if they seek approval from research ethics committees, although in that process purely ethical questions may be swamped by the need to meet bureaucratic demands or assuage the fears of those responsible for risk management.

This chapter considers how social scientists approach research ethics. First, we discuss crucial areas in social scientific research where ethical dilemmas occur, focusing on matters of consent, confidentiality and privacy, harm, and relationships with subjects, organisations and institutions. The second section reviews the current structures of ethics governance in the United Kingdom. Finally, we consider how to prepare a submission to a research ethics committee. Some British practices are either new or are still evolving – regulatory structures in North America and Australia are of far longer standing. As a result, where helpful, this chapter draws on the greater experience of social scientists in those countries to suggest ways of negotiating research ethics.

Basic ethical dilemmas in social science

While ethical issues arise in many guises, four of the major ethical matters that confront social scientists are: confidentiality; informed consent; harms and benefits; and the relationships that researchers have with colleagues, sponsors and institutions. We deal with them briefly here but further information can be found in Israel and Hay (2006, in press).

Informed consent

Other than under exceptional circumstances, guidelines for ethical research require that all participants need to agree to research before it can be started. The consent granted by participants should be both *informed* and *voluntary* (Faden and Beauchamp, 1986). In most circumstances, researchers need to provide potential participants with information about the purpose, methods, demands, risks, inconveniences, discomforts, and possible outcomes of the research, including whether and how the research results might be disseminated. What is going to happen to them and why? How long will it take? What are the risks? What are the potential benefits? Who is funding the work?

In practice, many researchers have found it extremely difficult to gain informed consent and have argued that the need for such consent in some situations (such as passive observational studies carried out in public spaces) has damaged the research and has not been in the best interest of research participants.

Standard approaches to informed consent often require participants to have high levels of literacy and linguistic ability. The written consent form can be difficult to follow and may not be helpful in guiding queries. In an effort to combat this, investigators engaged in participatory research have involved research participants in both the construction of information sheets and the brokering of access to peers. Several researchers have argued that consent should not be limited to the beginning of the research project but, rather, should be dynamic and continuous (El Dorado Task Force, 2002), reflecting changes in the research, the status of participants or the social or political context.

It is unlikely that anyone can offer informed consent in the face of coercion or, in many cases, manipulation. However, researchers may find it difficult to assess whether potential participants do have freedom of action, particularly in the context of research on or in institutions. Many British researchers have relied on consent from institutional gatekeepers, often senior management, and have not gone to the same lengths to obtain informed consent from other people present at the research site, whether the organisation is a school, a prison or the police. For example, Norris (1993) undertook participant-observation with British police officers on patrol. He was assigned to specific officers by their sergeants and felt that the issue of informed consent may have been 'fudged'. Special procedures are often adopted when attempting to obtain consent or assent from children. The British Educational Research Association urged that 'Children should be facilitated to give fully informed consent' (2004: 7). However, Homan (2001) observed that many British educational researchers have been deeply reluctant to seek informed consent from children.

One area of heated debate among social scientists is the degree to which deliberate manipulation of information – deception by lying, withholding information or misleading exaggeration – might be warranted in research. In psychology, several researchers have claimed that the integrity of the research design may be compromised if participants are not misled in some way. Two significant American psychology experiments where informed consent was compromised, one by Milgram (1977) and another by Zimbardo (Zimbardo et al., 1999), have been particularly controversial. Other researchers have argued that covert strategies may be justified in limited circumstances. British sociologists such as Ditton (1977) and Fielding (1982) have defended the use of covert methods on the basis that they reduce disturbance of research subjects and potential risks to researchers in work on extremist political organisations and illegal activities.

The principles of informed consent have been adopted slowly and unevenly by different parts of the social sciences. Part of the resistance has been directed towards the method of obtaining informed consent prescribed by institutional research ethics committees. This, some qualitative researchers have claimed, has been biased towards quantitative research, and in particular that based on formal hypotheses. Van den Hoonaard (2002) attacked the way anthropological fieldwork had been distorted by the 'hard architecture' of ethics forms imposed by ethics committees. For example, some willing participants may be unwilling to sign a form. In other contexts, it is difficult to introduce consent forms into the interaction for either logistic or social reasons, turning an exchange based on trust into one of formality and mistrust.

Confidentiality

When people allow researchers to investigate them, they often negotiate terms for the agreement. Participants in research may, for example, consent on the basis that the information obtained about them will be used only by the researchers and only in particular ways. The information is private and is voluntarily offered to the researcher in confidence in exchange for what will possibly not be very much direct benefit.

While not every research participant may want to be offered or even warrant receiving assurances of confidentiality, it seems that most do and social scientists regularly assure participants that confidentiality will be maintained. Working in the field of bioethics, Beauchamp and Childress (2001) identified three different justifications for confidentiality:

- Consequentialist arguments examine the results of an ethical practice and may consider what would happen if the practice did not exist. So, interviewees might be reluctant to reveal secrets if they thought that the information might be freely disseminated to third parties.

- A rights-based justification is based on respect for autonomy and the contention that everyone has a right to limit access to his or her person and should therefore be able to maintain secrets.

- Fidelity-based arguments rest on the view that researchers owe loyalty to the bonds and promises associated with research and should be faithful to the obligations relating to respect for autonomy, justice and utility that are imposed by their relationship with research participants.

Obligations of confidentiality cannot be considered absolute and in some situations we should contemplate disclosing to a particular person or group information that we had received under an implied or explicit assurance of confidentiality.

Some researchers are able to operate in relatively predictable contexts where standardised assurances may be included in a covering letter with a questionnaire. However, other work takes place in informal and unpredictable environments, where agreements may need to be negotiated with individuals and groups and renegotiated during the course of lengthy fieldwork. In addition, other people, organisations and government agencies may be keen to see what information researchers have gathered. As a result, social scientists have developed a range of methodological precautions in relation to collecting, analysing and storing data as well as strategies to respond to legal challenges to the confidentiality of their data (Israel, 2004a). These include:

- not recording names and other data at all, or removing names and identifying details of sources from confidential data at the earliest possible stage;

- disguising the name of the community where the research took place;

- masking or altering data;

- sending files out of the jurisdiction, and avoiding using the mail or telephone system so that data cannot be intercepted or seized by police or intelligence agencies.

Some Canadian, Australian and American researchers may receive statutory protection for their data. In the absence of statutory protection, researchers may be found guilty of obstructing the police in the execution of a warrant or even of contempt of court if they refuse to disclose information when ordered by a court. One way that researchers have responded to demands by third parties to see their research data has been to offer redacted material, that is information where the identity of study participants has been removed. In some cases, such as those involving short questionnaires, redacting data may be quite easy. On other occasions, it may place an enormous burden on researchers, either because of the sheer volume of data or because identities are embedded in the data.

Recognising that full confidentiality may not be assured, some Canadian and Australian institutional research ethics committees have required researchers to offer only limited assurances of confidentiality, indicating to participants that they could be forced to hand data over to courts (Lowman and Palys, 2001). Adler and Adler (2002) suggested that this might have a 'chilling effect' on research. On the other hand, several British researchers have warned that they would breach confidentiality in order to protect children from abuse (Barter and Renold, 2003; Tisdall, 2003).

Harm and benefit

Researchers are normally expected to minimise risks of harm or discomfort to participants in research projects (the principle of nonmaleficence). In some circumstances, they may also be expected to promote the well-being of participants or maximise the benefits to society as a whole (the principle of beneficence). Although the influence of bioethics means that harm is most often thought of in physical terms, in social science research it is more likely to involve psychological distress, discomfort, social disadvantage, invasion of privacy or infringement of rights.

Most research involves some risk, generally at a level that is greater in magnitude than the minimal risk that we tend to encounter in our everyday lives. Nevertheless, researchers should try to avoid imposing the risk of harm on others, though the extent to which they must avoid risks may depend on the value of the action that causes the risk and the degree of the risk (prevalence) as well as the weight of the consequences that may flow from the risk (magnitude). Consequently, researchers are normally expected to adopt risk minimisation strategies which may involve monitoring participants, maintaining a safety net of professionals who can provide support in emergencies, excluding vulnerable individuals or groups from participation where justifiable, considering whether lower-risk alternatives might be available, and anticipating and counteracting any distortion of research results that might act to the detriment of research participants.

Debriefing has been used extensively within deception-based experimental research as a risk minimisation strategy. Once the data has been collected, the researcher explains to participants the true nature and purpose of the research. However, the effects of manipulation may extend well beyond a debriefing. Indeed, in some cases the debriefing may exacerbate any harm caused. Another way of responding to the possibility of harming research participants is by incorporating in the planning and running of the research, members of those communities who form the focus of the research.

The principle of beneficence requires not only that we avoid harming others but that in some circumstances we also act to benefit others. Researchers often claim that by contributing to a general body of knowledge, the class of people who make up the participants might eventually benefit from the research. Scheper-Hughes (1995) maintained that researchers also needed to take an active stance towards social suffering. Various researchers have asserted that such responsibilities exist when working with intravenous drug-users, survivors of domestic violence, people with disabilities or with indigenous groups. Contemporary debates in anthropolgy, however, suggest that we should be cautious (D'Andrade, 1995; Gledhill, 1999). It may not always be easy to know how best we might support vulnerable populations, nor is it 'always obvious that the oppressed constitute a clearly defined class with an unambiguous shared interest' (Kuper, 1995: 425).

Many research projects do provide some benefit but at some cost. As a result, researchers may find that they have to assess the relative weight of a variety of potential harms and benefits. They may also discover that these harms and benefits have different impacts on and different meanings to different parts of a community.

Some social scientists have been concerned that the goals of beneficence and non-maleficence overstate the ability and resources of researchers to achieve meaningful change in the lives of the groups that they study (Graves and Shields, 1991). Others have noted that attempts by researchers to help are likely to be judged paternalist, misguided, partisan or simply incredibly stupid (Kovats-Bernat, 2002). In addition, those researchers who research more powerful parts of society, uncovering social harms caused by state and corporate misconduct, may find themselves having to justify not only their failure to promote the interests of these groups but also the possibility that their findings might be intended to undermine the privileged positions of such organisations.

Relationships

Kellehear suggested that ethical conduct was at its root 'a way of seeing and interpreting relationships' (1989: 71). The relationship on which attention is conventionally focused is the one between researcher and participant. Yet, researchers owe a professional obligation to their colleagues to handle themselves honestly and with integrity.

Threats to research integrity can stem from relationships that researchers maintain with corporations and governments. Conflicts of interests occur when various personal, financial, political and academic concerns coexist and the *potential* exists for one interest to be illegitimately favoured over another interest that has equal or greater legitimacy in a way that might make other reasonable people feel misled or deceived. Although the chances that social scientists may have a financial stake in the area that they are studying may be less than in biomedicine, there are still many issues that are relevant (Israel, 2000). These include:

- what sort of financial arrangements should academics have with corporations or government agencies;

- should academics disclose corporate or government affiliations when giving advice to the public or publishing research;

- how is an academic society to deal with 'huckstering' by members who 'tart up or adulterate the goods in their shop windows' (Ziman, 1991: 54) to secure funds or support their sponsors (Israel, 2000)?

In 2000, the US Office of Science and Technology Policy published the *Federal Policy on Research Misconduct* (www.ostp.gov/html/001207_3.html). Its threefold definition of misconduct as fabrication, falsification and plagiarism has been adopted in the UK

(Economic and Social Research Council, 2005). Some of the most serious allegations in British social sciences have involved Cyril Burt, a prominent British psychologist. After his death in 1971, he was accused of fabricating data obtained by studying pairs of twins in his work on the inheritance of intelligence (Hearnshaw, 1979). The argument has not been settled (Mackintosh, 1995).

Plagiarism is one of the more prevalent forms of academic misconduct in qualitative social science research. Over the last few years, accusations of plagiarism have led to the resignation of senior academics in Australia and the USA. In 2002, David Robinson, the Vice-Chancellor of Australia's largest university, Monash University, came under pressure to resign after the university discovered that he had been found guilty of plagiarism on two separate occasions while working as a sociologist in the UK.

Issues of authorship can extend beyond plagiarism. In many environments, leaders of research teams may be in a position to exploit the labour of their colleagues. Medical journals have had long-standing concerns that the names that appear at the top of an article do not reflect the true authors, either because someone who has insignificant involvement has been added – gift authorship – or because junior staff who made significant contributions have been omitted – ghost authorship (International Committee of Medical Journal Editors, 2001). Attempts to develop a uniform approach within parts of the social sciences have not been successful.

The role of ethics in social science

There is a story told about the emergence of research ethics. After the Second World War, horrified by the medical experimentation undertaken by Nazi Germany (Annas and Grodin, 1992), the West developed the Nuremberg Code (1947), which, coupled with the World Medical Association's Declaration of Helsinki in 1964, became the cornerstones of bioethics. Slowly, concepts developed in bioethics have been extended to research endeavours across the research spectrum, including social science.

Of course, nothing is ever this simple. First, regulations governing medical experimentation existed before the war in, of all places, Germany. Second, the Nuremburg Doctors' Trial was an American initiative – Britain distanced itself from it. Third, both American and British medical researchers engaged in dangerous experimentation without seeking the consent of research subjects before and during the Second World

War. Far from putting a stop to these activities, Nuremberg marked the beginning of a utilitarian approach to human experimentation on prisoners in the USA (Hornblum, 1998). Finally, the spread to social science of regulations based on bioethics has been neither uniform nor uncontested.

Until recently, in the UK the responsibility for conducting social science research ethically lay largely with the individual researcher. Unlike the USA, Canada and Australia, the UK has no national code for research ethics, nor does it have a network of research ethics committees for the social sciences. Instead, social scientists found themselves surrounded by an uncoordinated patchwork of professional codes, institutional requirements and governance frameworks, many of which were not designed to meet the needs of social scientists (Lewis et al., 2003). In short, the governance of research ethics in the UK is messy. Several institutions have contributed to the current situation.

In 2001, the Department of Health published standards to apply to publicly funded research in health and social care (revised in 2003). The major reason for social care to be included appears to be that it falls within the responsibilities of the same minister as health. In the National Health Service, all research proposals are assessed by Local Research Ethics Committees (LRECs), which employ the Department of Health standards. Researchers undertaking fieldwork at different sites can also apply for Multi-Research Ethics Committee (MREC) Review. While their remit may already extend to parts of social science, including qualitative research on health or involving health professionals within the National Health Service, LREC membership is heavily biased towards people with medical expertise and may contain no one with experience in social science research.

Most British universities now have codes of practice or offer ethical guidance on research. However, a survey conducted in late 2003 suggested that perhaps only about 80 per cent have established research ethics committees (Tinker and Coomber, 2004). Some of these committees are quite new – between 40 and 50 per cent had been set up since 2000. About one-third of universities have a single university Research Ethics Committee (REC) that covers the whole of the institution, while others have committees at both university and school or departmental level. In some cases, universities have no institutional-level committee, and the role of the REC is restricted to particular disciplines such as psychology or medicine. Finally, 'some have no procedures whatsoever for ethical approval' (Tinker, 2004). Although procedures for postgraduate research students are far from standardised, most university RECs have extended their work to cover them.

Lewis (2002: 5) argued that 'if we are serious about raising ethical standards, it has to be across the whole of social research'. In Canada and Australia, research councils have been the major drivers behind the development of national regulatory structures. In both countries, social scientists have expressed serious concerns about the impact of research ethics governance on the future of their work (Israel, 2004b; Social Sciences and Humanities Research Ethics Special Working Committee, 2004).

In 2005, Britain's Economic and Social Research Council (ESRC) released its *Research Ethics Framework* (REF). The REF 'took up the challenge presented by a lack of national co-ordination for social science research ethics, the needs of researchers, and the possibility that inappropriate bioethical regulations would be imposed across the research spectrum' (Israel and Hay, 2006) and sets out the ESRC's expectations for work it is asked to fund.

Israel and Hay (2006) note a clear correspondence between many of the REF principles (beneficence, informed consent, confidentiality, minimising harm) and other national approaches. However, the REF also attempts to work with existing approaches in the United Kingdom. Rather than disregarding other professional and disciplinary standards, the REF offers researchers the opportunity to draw from those standards to decide upon, and justify explicitly, the ethical sensitivity of their project and consequently the extent of institutional review the project receives.

Review may be either a so-called 'light-touch' evaluation by a sub-committee of an institution's Research Ethics Committee (REC) or a full REC review. RECs are expected to comprise about seven members and should be multidisciplinary, comprising men and women, relevant research experts, and lay representation. They are required to be unbiased and independent. The ESRC Framework came into force at the beginning of 2006 and marks a significant change in the British approach to governance of social science research ethics.

British researchers may also be subject to European guidelines. The European Union seeks to develop a European Research Area with common research standards. As part of this, the RESPECT Code of Practice for socio-economic research was published in 2004 with the intention that it becomes the basis of a voluntary code. The Code (RESPECT, 2004) is 'aspirational rather than prescriptive' and covers the need to uphold scientific standards, comply with the law, and avoid social and personal harm (details of the website can be found at the end of the chapter).

How to prepare your application

Several writers give fairly straightforward advice to researchers preparing ethics applications (see, for example, Oakes, 2002). They recommend that applicants think strategically in completing the application form, drawing on skills in research, networking and negotiation.

Consider the ethical aspects of your study from the very beginning, identifying, within your search for the appropriate methodology, the ethical difficulties associated with various approaches.

Identify the regulations that govern your work. Examine the websites and documentation developed by your department, university, professional associations and research councils for the statements that regulate social science ethics in the countries both where you are studying and where you will be researching (the ESRC in the UK, the National Health and Medical Research Council (NHMRC) in Australia, Tri-Council in Canada, for instance) for examples and specific directions. The same study may be dealt with very differently by various committees, even those that operate under the same regulatory framework, let alone those in different countries.

Find out how your local research ethics committee works. Work out whether you need to apply to a university REC or to a departmental one, or to both. If you are working with National Health Service records, clients or employees, do you also need to apply to a LREC or MREC? Talk to other researchers in your discipline who have completed the process, particularly if they have used a similar methodology to yours. Some committees make available copies of successful applications. Many committees provide sample letters of introduction and consent forms that you can adopt or adapt. Check, for example, to see whether your committee has opposed particular kinds of practices that you might have intended to adopt. It may be too early to predict how some university RECs will act in Britain. However, several Australian universities have refused to allow active snowball sampling to be used to recruit participants while others have required all participants to sign consent forms (Israel, 2004b), a Canadian university required researchers to tell participants that confidential material would be handed over if researchers received a court order (Social Sciences and Humanities Research Ethics Special Working Committee, 2004), and covert fieldwork is unlikely to be allowed by many Australasian or North American institutions.

Answer all their questions in a simple and straightforward manner. Filling in forms can be a significant burden. It is particularly difficult if you have to complete applications for several different committees, each of which uses a distinct form and requires different information. Nevertheless, members of research ethics committees have reported that some applications by social scientists are under-prepared. In particular, researchers need to improve their ability to justify their methodologies and articulate the benefits of their research in terms which fit forms that may not be designed for the purpose, and which recognise that research ethics committees may have little experience in such methodologies. Qualitative researchers may groan each time they are asked questions about their 'human subjects', 'interview schedule' or 'experimental hypotheses', but it is still generally worthwhile for us to answer such questions fully and courteously.

Some of Oakes' (2002) hints are worth considering:

- Ask yourself if you would honestly want someone you love to participate in your study.

- Work hard to ensure that recruitment materials yield equitable and non-coercive results.

- Write consent forms so that someone who has completed only a year or two of secondary school can understand them.

- Overestimate risks and underestimate benefits.

- Educate and debrief subjects on the nature, purpose and findings of your study.

- Establish procedures to unlink identifying information from main data sets and sources.

- Establish procedures to encrypt any and all identifying information and destroy it as soon as possible.

Be prepared to educate your committee. Find out what kinds of expertise your committee has – are you writing for social scientists or for medical researchers, or both? In your application, explain why the research is necessary, justify your choice of methodology and explain how other researchers have used it without causing harm. The committee may know very little about the methodology that you propose to use, the topic or the population that you are studying, or the site for your research. Locate your research within past practice – who has used this methodology before – and explain to the committee why your proposal makes sense given the context within which you will operate.

Talk to your local committee. If you have questions, telephone and talk to your research ethics committee administrator or chair. Find out how often the committee meets and when applications are due. In some cases, you may be allowed, or asked, to appear before the committee and answer questions. If you disagree with a research ethics committee decision, read their regulations and then ask for a meeting.

Be prepared for delays. Some committees take a very long time to reach decisions. Australian social scientists and British health researchers reported waiting for almost two years for approval (Israel, 2004b; Nicholl, 2000). In some cases, this can be because committees meet infrequently or proposal submission dates do not coincide with committee meeting dates, because committees raise objections to unaltered parts of submissions that had already been modified to meet an earlier set of objections, or because researchers have to shuttle between different committees. If you need approval from outside agencies, be prepared to wait. Some government agencies use delays in the processing of applications as a way of maintaining control over work in their institutions by external researchers. All this can be very distressing for students who are trying to complete their degrees.

Be prepared to adapt your work. Few research proposals are rejected outright by committees (Webster et al., 2004). For example, according to the Australian National Health and Medical Research Council (2004), only 232 out of 18,323 proposals were rejected by committees between 2002 and 2003. However, some projects have been abandoned in the face of conditions that researchers felt could not be accommodated. The more usual outcome is a process of negotiation between committee and researcher – sometimes protracted, and at times fraught – after which approval is given, conditional upon modifications to the scope and/or methodology of the research.

Case study: A viewpoint

Deborah Hersh

I have been working as a speech and language therapist since 1989 in the United Kingdom and Australia. Much of my clinical work has been with adults who have suffered a stroke and have acquired aphasia, language disorder following brain damage. My doctorate was based on qualitative semi-structured interviews and investigated clinician and client perceptions of how therapy for aphasia ended. This research raised several ethical issues, some of which I discuss here.

(Continued)

(Continued)

In Australia, all research – including non-medical work – is governed by an ethical code established by the National Health and Medical Research Council which, as a condition of funding, requires universities to subject research to a formal process of ethical review. I gained ethics approval to talk to clinicians and their discharged clients in a range of institutions. Despite gaining approval through the Clinical Ethics Committee of the hospital attached to my university, I also had to apply to the ethics committees of three other hospitals, a rehabilitation centre, and two community health centres. Given the difficulties other researchers have faced in obtaining approval for multi-centred research, I was fortunate that once the project had been approved by a teaching hospital, the process was relatively smooth – I was able to use the original format for all committees with only minor modification.

Part of my application to the ethics committee involved clarifying how I was to obtain informed consent of participants. In line with university requirements, I offered clinicians information about the study so they could make an informed choice as to whether they wished to be involved. They read and signed a consent form and were told that they could withdraw from the study at any time or refuse to answer questions. For people with aphasia, it would have been inappropriate to use standardised consent forms which require intact language skills. So, based on the work of Kagan and Kimelman (1995), I developed a tailored consent form, clearly set out, with symbols, enlarged print and short sentences (reproduced in Braunack-Mayer and Hersh, 2001) and discussed the meaning of the form with them face to face. This allowed people with aphasia to demonstrate their understanding of participation in the study, essential for truly informed consent (Beauchamp and Childress, 2001; Faden and Beauchamp, 1986) as well as their competence and decision-making ability. As a clinician who had worked as an advocate for this group, I believed that I had a responsibility to use procedures that preserved participant autonomy.

Confidentiality emerged as an important issue with interviews, in which I linked the perceptions of treatment termination by obtaining particular professional and client views of how therapy ended. These linked stories were most meaningful when presented in my thesis as case studies, in which the narratives of the discharge event could be compared. I had prepared for this by gaining permission from each to speak to the other, by ensuring removal of identifying information and assuring both sets of participants that what they said would not be passed on to the other party. In some cases, clients said that they did not mind if their previous therapist found out their opinion, but in others this was an important assurance. However, when I came to publish my first case study, I was concerned that the therapist might

(Continued)

(Continued)

recognise herself and therefore discover the views of her client. This could have occurred the other way around except that clients with aphasia were less likely to read the professional literature. I sought advice from a bioethicist, further altered identifying information about the subjects and obtained permission from participants specifically for the publication of the article. The research ethics literature was hopelessly under-developed on this point – a subsequent paper simply calls for a 'careful and critical fictionalizing of accounts' (Forbat and Henderson, 2003).

Although I have focused on informed consent, many other ethical issues arose in my study: considering potential harms, being aware of the power differences in interviewing colleagues and clients, giving people access to their transcripts for consideration, leaving the field as a researcher when one continues to work in it as a clinician, data storage and how best to present and disseminate the data.

Further reading

Several British professional organisations have published ethical codes and guidelines (for example, 3, 4, 10 below). Other relevant, though not always helpful, material can be found on ESRC (6), COREC (5) and RESPECT (9) websites. British researchers may find that material created by Canadian (11, 12) and Australian (7, 8) agencies and American professional associations (1, 2) are better developed than their British counterparts. They may also offer a useful insight into the kinds of concerns that British research ethics committees might raise. Not surprisingly, I would also recommend Israel and Hay (2006, in press) from which part of this chapter is taken.

1   American Anthropological Association (1998). *Code of Ethics*, http://www. aaanet.org/committees/ethics/ethics.htm

2   American Sociological Association (1997). *Code of Ethics*, http://www.asanet. org/members/ecoderev.html

3   British Educational Research Association (2004). *Ethical Guidelines for Educational Research*, http://www.bera.ac.uk/publications/pdfs/ ETHICA1.PDF

4   British Sociological Association (2002). *Statement of Ethical Practice for the British Sociological Association*, http://www.britsoc.co.uk

5   Central Office for Research Ethics Committees (COREC) – covers NHS LRECs, http://www.corec.org.uk/index.htm

6   Economic and Social Research Council, United Kingdom (2005). *Research Funding Guide*, http://www.esrcsocietytoday.ac.uk/ESRCInfoCentre/opportunities/research_funding/index.aspx and (2005) *Research Ethics Framework* http://www.esrc.ac.uk/ESRCInfoCentre/Images/ESRC_Re_Ethics_Frame_tcm6-11291.pdf

7   National Health and Medical Research Council, Australia (1999). *National Statement on Ethical Conduct in Research Involving Humans*, http://www. health.gov.au:80/nhmrc/publications/synopses/e35syn.htm

8   National Health and Medical Research Council, Australia (2001). *Human Research Ethics Handbook: Commentary on the National Statement on Ethical Conduct in Research Involving Humans*, http://www.nhmrc.gov.au/publications/hrecbook/01_commentary/contents.htm

9   RESPECT, European Union (n.d.) *Professional and Ethical Codes for Technology-related Socio-economic Research*, http://www.respectproject.org/main/index.php

10 Social Research Association, United Kingdom (2002). *Ethical Guidelines*, http://www.the-sra.org.uk/ethicals.htm

11 Social Sciences and Humanities Research Ethics Special Working Committee, Canada (2004). *Giving Voice to the Spectrum*. Ottawa: Interagency Advisory Panel on Research Ethics, http://www.pre.ethics.gc.ca/english/workgroups/sshwc/SSHWCVoiceReport June2004.pdf

12 Tri-Council (Medical Research Council of Canada, National Science and Engineering Research Council of Canada, Social Sciences and Humanities Research Council of Canada) (2003). *Policy Statement: Ethical Conduct for Research Involving Humans*. Ottawa: Public Works and Government Services, http://www.pre.ethics.gc.ca/english/policystatement/policystatement.cfm

Developing and Writing a Research Proposal

5

Keith Punch with Wayne McGowan

- Almost all empirical social science needs funding if it is to be conducted effectively and this can only be gained by writing research proposals to the bodies that fund research. A research proposal is also commonly needed before obtaining approval to start a doctorate.

- This chapter considers what should go into a proposal. This includes a clear and logical statement of the research question, the research strategy to be used, the sample design, the analytical method and a justification of the costs of the research that are to be funded.

- There is an art to writing a convincing proposal and this chapter offers some valuable advice to maximise your chances of success.

The focus of this chapter is the research proposal. Typically, its presentation and approval are required before a piece of research can proceed. This applies to the graduate student in a university, for whom the research dissertation (or thesis) lies ahead, and for whom the approval of a research proposal is required in order to proceed. It applies also to applications for funds to support research, where the proposal is the vehicle by which the proposed research is assessed and decisions made about its funding.

While there is some variation in nature and function, depending on the context and type of research involved, there are important common elements that apply to all proposals. This chapter is written with empirical research, the most common type of research in social science today, in mind. It is written primarily for the university context. The first part of the chapter deals with the logical foundations for this type of research proposal. The second part describes the proposal itself. The third part gives some tips for developing and writing it. The fourth part reports the proposal-writing experience of a recent PhD graduate.

No major distinction is made here between writing for quantitative and qualitative empirical research, for three reasons. First, the logic of these two types of empirical enquiry is similar, in terms of generating research questions and planning the collection and analysis of data to answer these questions. In this respect, some of the research methodology literature has made too much of the differences between quantitative and qualitative research, ignoring the important similarities. Second, both types of research often proceed in much the same way. Third, readers' expectations for the two types of research proposal are similar. Undoubtedly, proposal writing for some types of 'unfolding' qualitative research is harder than for carefully 'prespecified' quantitative research (Punch, 1998: 23–27). But the model described here is useful in all cases.

Logical foundations

Empirical research

The central idea behind empirical research – quantitative, qualitative or mixed-method – is to use real-world data to answer questions or test hypotheses. This chapter emphasises the answering of research questions, rather than the testing of hypotheses. This is because the logical and empirical operations for answering research questions are the same as those for testing hypotheses.

Once we know what data will be needed to answer the research questions we have set up, we can plan the methods we will need. The methods will tell us how to get and analyse the data to answer the questions. Thus the research questions indicate *what* data will be needed in the research. The research methods describe *how* the data will be collected and analysed to answer the research questions. This provides a robust framework for organising the development of proposals. It places research questions at the centre of research, and of research proposal development work. It also places research methods in a derivative or consequential position – they follow from the research questions.

Readers' expectations

It is important for the proposal writer to understand the proposal reader's expectations. In a university higher degree setting, proposals normally need to be approved by several readers before the research can proceed. In a competitive funding setting, a panel of readers will typically decide on which proposals are funded.

The research proposal reader will normally seek clear answers to three overarching questions:

1. *What* is the proposed research trying to find out (or achieve)?
2. *How* will it do that?
3. *Why* is this research worth doing?

The 'what' question is effectively answered by showing clearly the research questions (general and specific) that the research is designed to answer. The 'how' question is answered by describing the methods the research will use. The 'why' question is answered in two ways: by the logic of the overall argument constructed to present the proposal, and by direct consideration of the significance or contribution of the proposed research, especially in relation to 'value for money'.

The proposal writer also needs to understand that the finished proposal will need to be a stand-alone document. This means that it needs to make sense to a reader (sometimes a non-expert) who has not discussed the work with, and may not even know, the writer. The proposal should not need the writer's presence to interpret or make clear what is being said. It should be a self-contained document.

Research questions

Stressing the central role of research questions means that a good start has been made when a clear set of research questions has been formulated, all of which meet the empirical criterion described below. Getting to this point takes time. Once developed, the research questions become the organising framework for the research and for the proposal. They also organise and simplify the writing of the proposal and make communicating the proposal easier and more effective. Once established, they lead logically to methods. By stressing the direction of influence from questions to methods (while also acknowledging some reciprocal influence of methods on questions), we can maximise the fit between the questions the research seeks to answer and the methods it will use. This question–method fit is an important component of the internal validity, both of the proposal and of the subsequent research. A proposal that has internal validity, which is internally consistent, has coherence and hangs together, is much more convincing than one whose different parts do not fit well with each other.

General and specific research questions

General research questions are phrased in general terms and are not themselves specific enough to be answered. Specific research questions make the general concepts specific and enable direct connections to data. Because a general concept usually contains several more specific concepts or aspects, there are usually more specific research questions than general research questions.

This raises an important point about empirical research. Because it depends on real-world data, empirical research must ultimately deal with data and data-indicators at a very concrete, tangible and specific level. However, the concepts and ideas which drive empirical research, and which are used for describing and discussing the research and interpreting it in a broader context, are at a much more general or abstract level. This means that logical connections are required within the research across different levels of abstraction, in order for more abstract concepts to be connected to specific data indicators. Making distinctions between general and specific research questions and then linking them are central parts of the process of connecting the different levels of abstraction.

A five-level 'hierarchy of concepts' can be used to show this process of abstraction. The five levels, listed here from most general to most specific, are:

1. Area

2. Topic

3. General research question(s)

4. Specific research questions

5. Data collection questions

A *research area* is a very broad description, usually in one word or only a few words, identifying a general area for research.

A *research topic* is a slightly more specific, but still very general, identification of a possible theme for research within an area. Any research area contains many possible topics.

General research questions bring things down to the next level, further narrowing the focus of the proposed research. They identify the general concepts that will shape the research and usually ask about relationships between these concepts. A study may have one general research question or several, and any research topic would typically contain many general research questions. But they are too broad to be answered directly and do not yet satisfy the empirical criterion described below.

Specific research questions make the general concepts more specific, usually by specifying their aspects, components or dimensions. They also develop the relationships between concepts further and point directly to what data will be needed. They are therefore essential in satisfying the empirical criterion.

Data collection questions are the very specific questions that respondents will be asked, for example in a questionnaire or interview. Their function is to enable the collection of the data necessary to answer the specific research questions.

An example of this question development and specification process is given in Punch (2000: 23–27). It is important to realise that it is the specific research questions which are answered directly in the research, using the data generated by the data collection questions. Together, the answers to the specific research questions enable answers to the general research questions.

Making logical connections between these levels, and especially between the general research questions, specific research questions and data collection questions, are all important to the internal validity or internal consistency of a piece of research. It is often useful to plan research with this five-part hierarchy of concepts in mind. An important benefit of organising ideas this way is that it becomes easier to write the proposal. Just as important, it becomes easier to read and understand the proposal.

The empirical criterion for research questions

This criterion is that a well-developed and well-stated research question indicates what data are needed to answer it – 'a question well asked is a question half answered'. Empirical research is not ready to proceed until research questions, at the specific level, satisfy this criterion. Only when the questions tell us what data are needed can we proceed to design the research and plan the methods we will use. This criterion should be routinely applied to research questions as they are being developed. When a research question does not satisfy the criterion, further question development work is usually needed. Although unfolding and exploratory research may well proceed initially with general questions only, aiming to identify and sharpen the questions for investigation as the research proceeds, a proposal for this type of research needs to point this out and to indicate why this strategy has been chosen.

Methods

With general and specific research questions in place, research methods can now be identified to describe how the data will be obtained and analysed in order to answer the questions. It is logical that methods should follow from, and fit in with, questions – how we do something in research should depend on what we are trying to find out. This provides an answer to the question beginning research students so frequently ask – 'Should I do a quantitative or a qualitative study?' The answer is: 'It depends on what you are trying to find out'. The students' question puts research methods (quantitative or qualitative?) before research questions. The answer (it depends…) puts methods after questions.

It is convenient to describe research methods under four subheadings:

- *Strategy and design* – any piece of research requires an overall strategy by which it will proceed. Strategy describes the logic of the process by which the research questions will be answered. The design implements that strategy.

- *Sample and sampling* – all empirical social research involves sampling, usually of people, but also often of situations or events. The central issues here are who and what will be studied. More specifically, from whom will the data be collected?

- *Data collection* – how will the data be collected? What data collection instruments (if any) and what data collection procedures will be used?

- *Data analysis* – how will the data, once collected, be analysed to answer the research questions?

Table 5.1   Checklist of headings for a research proposal

Title and title page

(a) Abstract
(b) Introduction

  – Area and topic
  – Background and context
  – Statement or purpose (or aims)

(c) Research questions*
  – General
  – Specific

(d) Conceptual framework, theory, hypotheses (if appropriate)
(e) The literature
(f) Methods

  – Strategy and design
  – Sample and sampling
  – Data collection – instruments and procedures
  – Data analysis

(g) Significance
(h) Ethical issues
(i) Costs

  – Salaries
  – Travel
  – Equipment
  – Consumables
  – Overheads

(j) Risk management
(k) References
(l) Appendices

*In some types of research, the research questions would come after the literature section.

Proposal structure and sections

Based on these foundations, Table 5.1 shows a set of headings for organising and writing the proposal. Each section is now briefly described.

Abstract

The abstract, written last, is a brief summary of the proposal. It is not an introduction to the proposal, nor to the area and topic of the research. Rather, it should simply summarise what the research is trying to find out and how the research will proceed. That is, it should summarise the objectives (it can use the general research questions for this purpose) and it should summarise the methods. Description of the background and context for the research is not required, and referencing is not needed or appropriate in the abstract. A good discipline is to try to restrict the abstract to 100 words or less. A good test is whether an independent reader can understand the purposes and methods of the research just from reading the abstract.

Introduction – area and topic, background and context, statement of purpose

A strong introduction is important to a convincing proposal. It is part of the answer to the 'Why is this research worth doing?' question. It should introduce the reader both to the area and topic of the research, locating these in the appropriate background and context, and to the logic and the argument of the proposal. There are many ways any topic can be introduced, so formulas are not appropriate and judgement is required. But a widely applicable strategy is to work from the general to the specific. This is why the previous five-part hierarchy (p. 62) is so often useful. The introduction can clearly state the area and topic for the research, and can point ahead to the research questions. Indeed, a useful way to summarise the objectives of the research is to show the research questions at the general level. It is a mistake for the introduction to go on too long, especially about the background to the research and the importance of the research. Remembering the reader's expectations, it is better to get to the point of the research, stated as the objectives and leading on to research questions, as soon as possible.

Research questions – general and specific

If the research planning process has proceeded in terms of the hierarchy shown earlier, writing this section becomes quite straightforward. Once clear and effective wording for the research questions has been achieved (and the empirical criterion satisfied), that wording should be used consistently. Because research language should be precise and consistent, changing the wording unnecessarily only creates doubts and confusion for the reader. It is worth keeping in mind that the reader will often go to this section of the proposal first to find out what this research is all about.

The most common problem in this section is the lack of logical connection between research questions at the general and specific levels. This goes back to the careful planning required in making this connection. If general concepts are 'defined downwards' in terms of their components or dimensions, making the link from general to specific research questions is quite straightforward. The specific questions are bound up in, or implied by, the general questions. They are not something quite different. It follows from this that specific research questions should not introduce something totally new. Any concept or idea used in the specific research questions should be anticipated or implied by the general research questions.

Conceptual framework, theory, hypotheses (if appropriate)

There are two questions here. First, will the proposed research test hypotheses? If so, it is important both to state them and to show the theory from which they follow. Second, is it helpful to show – usually as a diagram – the framework of concepts behind the study? In many quantitative studies, the answer is yes. Qualitative studies will vary and judgement is required, keeping in mind the overriding criterion: Will what I am writing here be clear and convincing to the reader?

The literature

Whatever position the proposed research takes in relation to its relevant literature, it is important for the proposal to identify the relevant literature, the nature and scope of that literature, and to connect the proposed study to that literature. With word limits typically imposed, the proposal is not the place for a full literature review. However, if a full literature review has been conducted as part of proposal development, a summary may be included. But all proposals should identify the literature that is relevant to the topic and how the proposed research relates to this literature.

Methods

Strategy and design

As used here, strategy means the internal logic, or rationale, by which the research will proceed. An important part of a convincing proposal is an explicit and effective description of this strategy. Such a description is usually quite short. Quantitative research has some typical strategies (the experiment, the quasi-experiment, the correlational survey, etc.), as does qualitative research (single or multiple case studies, ethnography, grounded theory, etc.). Mixed-method studies also need a clear description of the logic and strategy of the enquiry: What is the quantitative strategy? What is the qualitative strategy? In what way, in what order, and why will quantitative and qualitative data be brought together to answer the research questions? It is often helpful to indicate which research questions will be answered using which parts of the strategy. Once the strategy is clear, it can be formalised and operationalised in the research design. The importance of research design is well understood in quantitative research, where the design usually follows naturally from the strategy. But design is required in qualitative research as well, as this quote makes clear:

> In general, terms such as *ethnography, participant observation, grounded theory,* and *fieldwork* are not useful to a reviewer unless they are described procedurally, in relation to the specific proposal. For example, participant observation is perhaps the most pervasive technique used in ethnographic designs, yet we know that the investigator cannot participate and observe everywhere at the same time. Methodological choices must be made about where and when observations take place. Although some of these decisions necessarily are made in the actual process of the research, from the emerging data, the investigator should be able to provide reviewers with a general outline of observations that is consistent with the problem being researched. (Dreher, 1994: 289, original italics)

Sample and sampling

The general question here is 'Who or what will be studied?' Very often, this question reduces to 'From whom will the data be collected?' Empirical research typically involves studying a sample drawn from some larger population. The proposal should therefore define the population from which the sample will be drawn and describe the sampling strategy. In all research, there needs to be a logic behind the proposed sampling and that logic needs to fit in with the overall logic of the research. Too often, especially in qualitative proposals, there is an absence of logic regarding sampling. In this regard, the table of 16 sampling strategies for qualitative enquiry provided by Miles and Huberman (1994: 28) is very useful and worth consulting.

If the study is quantitative, the proposal should indicate:

- the sampling strategy, especially whether it is purposive, representative or both, and what claims will be made for the generalisability of the research findings

- how big the sample will be, and why

- how it will be selected, and why

Similarly, if the study is qualitative, the proposal should indicate:

- the sampling strategy, including what intention (if any) there is for the generalisability of findings
- the extent of the proposed sample, and why
- how sample units will be chosen, and why

If mixed-method research is proposed, both sets of considerations above are relevant. In addition, the relationship between the quantitative and qualitative samples is important and should be logically based.

Data collection – instruments and procedures

How will the data be collected? Answers to this question need to be differentiated according to the type of data. The answers need to deal with both data collection instruments and data collection procedures.

Instruments

Most quantitative social science data are produced by questionnaires, standardised measuring instruments, *ad hoc* rating scales, or observation schedules. Whichever of these is proposed, a recurrent issue is: Will I use already existing instruments, developed by someone else? Or will I develop my own instruments for use in this research? In the first case, the proposal should include some background on the instrument chosen, including who developed it, when and how, where it has been used in research, and what is known of its properties, especially its reliability and validity. In the second case, the proposal should explain why existing instruments are inadequate, and should then outline the steps that will be taken to develop the instrument(s) to be used.

Qualitative data may come from interviews, open-ended questionnaires or unstructured observation, but may also include documents, journals and diaries and other written materials. In the case of interviews, qualitative questionnaires and observation, an important issue concerns the degree of structure and standardisation proposed for the data. The use of already existing 'instruments' is unlikely here, so again the proposal should outline the steps to be taken in preparing questions and interview schedules for the data collection.

Procedures

In quantitative research, the usual question is how the questionnaire will be administered (mail, face-to-face, telephone, internet, etc.). In qualitative research, the question usually focuses on interview procedures. After the degree of structure and standardisation of the interview have been settled, numerous methodological issues arise regarding such issues as access, the interview timetable and setting, opening the interview, establishing rapport, closing the interview, recording, and so on. Together, these represent the data collection procedures for interview-based qualitative research. For the collection of both quantitative and qualitative data, the data collection procedures used will have a powerful impact on data quality. The proposal should therefore indicate how the proposed procedures will attempt to maximise the quality of the data.

Data analysis

How will the data, once collected, be analysed in order to answer the research questions? Here again, differentiation by type of data is required. For quantitative data, the proposal should indicate what statistical techniques will be used. Technical assistance may be required if statistical methodological expertise is lacking. For qualitative data, the matter of analysis is much more complicated, since there are several alternative approaches to analysis. Once again, it needs to be stressed that the type of qualitative data analysis proposed should fit in with the overall logic of the study and should be integrated with that logic. The method of analysing qualitative data should not be an afterthought, to be considered only when the data have been collected. Planning for the data analysis should be an integral part of the overall planning of the project. Finally, for both types of data, the proposal should indicate any proposed use of computer software packages.

A common question from students about this section is 'How can I describe my data analysis when I haven't yet collected the data and don't know what there is to analyse?' One useful piece of advice here is to visualise the data – perhaps even to simulate a small amount of data – and to think through logically (as distinct from methodologically) what would be involved in the analysis. For example, start out with the raw scores in quantitative analysis and figure out how you would construct tables to summarise the variables, and how you could use these to look at relationships between variables or differences between comparison groups. Similarly, imagine interview responses in qualitative research, and ask how you would begin summarising and coding the responses, thinking mainly of the logic behind what you are doing and of your research questions. In addition, it is also useful to read carefully through the data analysis section of previous research reports, especially dissertations, which normally describe in detail how the analysis was done. While the assistance of experts may be required and is always valuable in connection with the data analysis, there is also great value in thinking through the logic of proposed data analysis operations.

Significance

Earlier it was said that the 'why' question ('Why is this research worth doing?') could be answered in two ways. First, the potential relevance, significance and contribution of the study should be clear in the way the proposal is introduced and written. These things can be explicitly dealt with in the literature review, where the relationship of this study to the literature is described. The introduction also offers the opportunity to set up the argument behind the proposal in such a way that the significance and contribution of this research follow logically. Second, the issue can be dealt with directly and explicitly in this section. The proposal can indicate the possible contribution of the study to knowledge in the area, to policy considerations and to practitioners. The first of these, contribution to knowledge, is closely tied to literature in the area and is often interpreted as a theoretical contribution.

Ethical issues

The principal issues here are consent, access and participants' protection, and together they cover the range of different ethical issues which might arise in a piece of social research. The proposal writer needs to identify which particular ethical issues are relevant for this project, and how they will be dealt with (see Chapter 4).

Costs

Proposals to organisations for funds for research support will always require you to specify the costs you expect to incur, but even for doctoral research the proposal writer needs to have a clear idea about what the project will cost and where the money will come from. The main costs incurred in social science research are:

- salaries
- travel

- equipment
- consumables
- overheads

Salaries

If the research is to be carried out by paid staff, the basic salary costs will need to be calculated, including employers' pension contributions, health and other insurance charges and annual increments in salary. In most places there are national agreements about the salary scales that you will need to follow. It is essential to get advice on these matters, which may come from your employer or university. In addition to the researchers, you may need to employ clerical or technical assistance, either on an annual or monthly salary, or freelance, paid by the hour. If you need to provide respondents with honoraria to persuade them to participate in surveys, or to thank them for their contributions, this also needs to be added in.

Travel

If your research involves travelling to see respondents or to examine documents, you will need to allow for the costs of travel, and meals and accommodation ('subsistence'). Organisations often have standard rates for subsistence which you should use. The travel cost will be the rail or bus fare, or a standard rate per mile for car journeys.

Equipment

Depending on your sponsor, you may be able to claim for equipment such as laptop or desktop computers, professional grade cassette recorders, and transcription machines for transcribing interviews, but you should certainly justify the need for these purchases.

Consumables

This heading includes all the minor expenses involved in carrying out the research, such as postage (which can mount up if you send questionnaires to many respondents), printing and copying charges, purchase of books and documents, computer supplies such as ink cartridges, computer maintenance, the cost of phone calls and so on.

Overheads

In addition to those costs which are directly attributable to the project, there will be other costs borne by the organisation. For example, someone has to pay for the heating and lighting of the office. Rather than try to divide up these costs precisely, the custom is to charge projects a percentage of their total expenditure (or sometimes, a percentage of the salary bill). These are called the indirect costs or overheads and can be anything from 20 per cent to 120 per cent of the direct costs. Your organisation will tell you how much they charge.

What you can claim will vary according to the organisation that you are in and according to the rules of the funder. It is important that you familiarise yourself with the funder's regulations if you are making a proposal for research support, so that you claim all that you are entitled to and no more. Even if you not requesting funds, but just approval to proceed with research, you need to satisfy your reader that you have the resources to carry out the research effectively.

Risk management

What could go wrong in the research? In other words, what are the risks, and how would they be managed? This section of the proposal, which is increasingly required by research funders, is another chance to demonstrate that you have carefully thought through your proposed research, that you can anticipate possible problems, and that you can suggest contingencies for dealing with them. The nature of the risks will vary with the context and setting of the research, but it is especially important to assess realistically any risks involved in gaining access to the data your study will need.

References

This section lists the references cited throughout the paper. These should show full bibliographic details, and be listed alphabetically, by surname of author (or first author).

Appendices

These may include any of the following: a timetable for the research, further budget details, letters of introduction or permission, consent forms, measuring instruments, questionnaires, interview guides, observation schedules, and example of pilot study or other relevant work already completed (Maxwell, 1996).

Developing and writing the proposal

Getting started

There are many possible sources for research ideas, including personal experience, curiosity based on something in the media, the state of knowledge in a field, solving a problem, issues which are topical and offer opportunities, personal values and everyday life (Neumann, 1994: 110), clinical or professional experience, professional literature, interaction with others, societal trends, legislative initiatives, public documents, and agency goals and priorities (Gitlin and Lyons, 1996: 36). To these, we can also add reading research journals and previous dissertations. Many research students find it easy enough to identify an area and a topic within that area. While this is an important first step, it is only a beginning. As soon as possible after this, it is important to confront the question 'What am I trying to find out?' It is also wise to begin writing your ideas down.

A useful early exercise in this respect is the 'two-pager' – in no more than two pages, try to describe, as precisely and directly as possible, what the research is trying to find out and how it will do it. At this early point in research planning, too much focus on background or context or literature can be counterproductive. There is value in trying to state research questions, both general and specific, and outline research methods, as early as possible, knowing that nobody gets them right the first time and that several iterations will be needed before closure is reached.

There is also value in using the five-part hierarchy described earlier, working either deductively downwards, inductively upwards, or both. The main benefits of this are that it helps you to organise your thinking, and that it forces concentration on the important logical connections between general research questions, specific research questions and data collection questions. In so doing, of course, it also forces direct consideration of the empirical criterion. When some stability has been reached in this, another useful exercise is the ideas paper or a discussion and concept paper, which can now work with the background, context and perhaps the literature of the research, showing where this project would fit.

The value of discussion

Discussing your developing ideas with others, both expert and non-expert, has several benefits:

- It is a step towards writing things down – both discussing your ideas with others and writing them down force you to think about structuring and representing your ideas so that they can be understood by others.

- It is part of the clarification/communication process – you have to plan and design a piece of research, and communicate that plan to others.

- It brings feedback from others, which is often important in clarification.

- It may suggest aspects of, or perspectives on, your topic that have so far escaped you.

- Discussion with experts may suggest literature you need to consult; discussion with non-experts may suggest aspects of the context or situation you need to take into account.

The value of writing it down

But despite the undoubted value of discussion, there is no substitute for writing the ideas down. This is not only because the proposal, ultimately, will of course have to be a written document. It is also because it involves the structuring and representation of your ideas in a way that communicates them to others. The main value in the concrete activity of writing it down as it is being developed, for others to read, is in clarification.

Focusing on research questions

As already noted, there is great practical value in focusing on research questions, for most students and especially for beginning students. Trying to write the research questions down, from an early stage, is also very valuable. As a supervisor, the most useful question I can ask during research planning is 'What are you trying to find out?' And it needs to be asked repeatedly, since developing and finalising the research questions is an iterative process. Indeed, this point applies to proposal development as a whole – it is iterative, cumulative and progressive.

Departmental or university guidelines

Common sense requires that you should check the departmental and/or university guidelines governing proposals if you are a student, or the guidelines provided by funders if a grant or commissioned project is involved. It is also worth finding out about the process used for proposal evaluation and approval in your situation. Time and length guidelines and restrictions will normally apply, and universities especially are increasingly placing limits on the size of proposals and dissertations. This can present a dilemma, since a full treatment of all issues raised here may well require a proposal which exceeds those limits. In that case, a good strategy is to prepare a full version of the proposal and then to summarise it down to the required size. This preserves the learning value of full proposal development.

Two important ideas to keep in mind when writing the proposal are to organise for understanding, and to write for clarity. Both follow from the extremely valuable practical advice which says: 'Put yourself in the position of the reader. Will this make sense to the reader?' For the university environment, a third important idea is to observe scholarly conventions and requirements.

Organise for understanding

The proposal outline described above is structured to make it easy for the reader to understand. Keep in mind that a proposal is not an essay and that readers will expect the sorts of things shown in the outline to be dealt with. A coherent and interconnected structure is important, remembering that your proposal will almost certainly be read in a stand-alone environment and that the reader will usually want to re-read different sections, cycling between them, in order to assess the proposal, especially its internal validity. It is a good idea to develop a detailed and logical table of contents. As well as creating a favourable first impression, this helps the reader navigate around the proposal and locate the places where feedback comments are most appropriate. In addition, organising in this way creates a modular structure which makes the task of proposal writing seem less formidable.

Write for clarity

Elegance and sophistication of language are not the main objectives in writing a proposal. Clarity is. Aids to achieving clarity are to draft and re-draft sections of the proposal, making the writing process iterative and cumulative (usually this involves shortening), and to break up long sentences into shorter ones. It is important to remember that research language needs to be precise and accurate, using particular words in a precise and consistent way. Thus, when your research questions are effectively phrased (usually after numerous attempts), do not vary their wording.

The scholarly context

In addition to the standard scholarly requirements of correct spelling, grammar and punctuation, and correct referencing (both in the text and in the reference list at the end), good quality scholarly writing shows the following characteristics:

- It is logical.

- It uses internally consistent arguments.

- It is careful, thorough and accurate, with attention to detail.

- It shows the precise and consistent use of language in general and of key terms in particular.

- It prefers conclusions based on evidence, recognising and pointing out when speculation goes beyond evidence.

- It uses sentences and paragraphs, since these are necessary to construct arguments.

Several times throughout this chapter I have used the term 'argument'. The idea of 'proposal as argument' has great merit. It means that the writer works to assemble the different elements of the proposal into an internally consistent chain of reasoning. The goal is an integrated whole whose different sections fit together convincingly.

To what extent does a carefully designed proposal, along the lines suggested here, constrain and limit the subsequent research? What about the possibility that the research itself will open up worthwhile lines of enquiry not envisaged during proposal development?

There is a continuum of possibilities regarding the relationship between the proposal and the finished piece of research. At one end, the research is totally prefigured in the proposal and the task is simply to carry out and report the steps proposed. At the other end, either because the research was unfolding or because serendipitous events dictated change of direction, the finished project may differ markedly from the proposal. In the first case, the contribution of the proposal to the finished project is clear and the finished report will probably show a close structural similarity to the proposal. But even at the other end, where the project goes off in substantially different directions from those originally proposed, there are important learning and other benefits in proposal development. In the case study below, Wayne McGowan reflects on the benefits he found in his PhD thesis proposal development, even though his subsequent thesis differed substantially from what was proposed.

Case study: The best I could do

Wayne McGowan

This section provides my reflections on the task of developing a research proposal at a time when all I had was an idea and a desire. As for the literature and an understanding of the other complexities associated with doing research, that was to come later.

When I started to develop my research proposal I was conscious that approval to proceed would be contingent on two factors. That is to say, the proposal review committee would need to be convinced that I could do the research and that what I wanted to do could be done. With this in mind, I started work on drafting a research plan that reflected social science's belief in the symbiotic relationship between data and theory.

My first task was to prove that I could do research. To this end, I treated the development of my proposal as a mini research project in its own right. The aim was to produce a paper that would demonstrate that I could be scholarly, that I could exercise self-discipline, research skills and, to a certain extent, some intellect. I believed the proposal and its presentation would be evidence of my commitment, integrity and enthusiasm towards the research as well as my capacity to review literature, build an argument and, most importantly, to write. In doing so, I hoped to present myself as someone who could be trusted to do the research. Final approval, however, meant that this perception of me had to be supported by what others would see as a 'doable' project. Even I recognised the futility of sending a trusted person on an impossible mission.

(Continued)

(Continued)

My efforts to communicate what I wanted to do and to convey a sense that it could be done, however, underlined my dilemma. To develop a convincing argument meant I really did have to know exactly what I wanted to do and how to do it, whereas, in reality, I only had a vague idea of what I wanted to do and very little understanding as to how to convert a fuzzy notion into a tightly conceived and organised research project. To wriggle out of this tight spot, I needed to come up with a proposal that offered the review committee something that at least looked feasible. To do this, I sought the security of a conceptual framework for writing a research proposal because I needed the support and guidance it offered if I was to get the job done within a reasonable time period.

On this basis, I started by putting together what I had so far. First, there was the topic. I knew I was interested in power in society and I was definitely curious about how the law, in the form of the recently proclaimed *School Education Act 1999 (Western Australia)* (the Act), used a combination of knowledge and power to do things. Second, I had the data: the Act itself, volumes of *Hansard* recordings of the Parliamentary debate on the Act and a number of other official documents. What was missing, however, was a theory that would help me make sense of all these data. After discussing this gap with my supervisors, it was suggested that I try discourse analysis. This led me to explore the literature and to discover rhetorical theory as an intellectual framework that would support the analysis of the Act and associated Parliamentary debate as persuasive discourse aimed at protecting and reproducing a particular ideological position.

In the end, my proposal was approved. After all, I had presented myself as someone who could be trusted to do the research and, besides, I had a topic, a theory and some data. And so, the proposal review committee and I now had a written agreement – a research proposal – that said I would deliver a dissertation that would use rhetorical theory and the data I had to analyse the ideological effect of the Act. While I started this research assignment in good faith, what I eventually delivered did not fully comply with the contractual terms of the approved proposal. As a result, one could legitimately question the extent to which the process of writing a research proposal was a success. It seems reasonable to ask whether the process was worth the time and trouble. If the product delivered is not what was agreed, why would one adult student and a number of busy academics give time and energy to its development? In response to these questions I still believe the process of developing a research proposal was definitely worth the effort.

(Continued)

(Continued)

For me, the research proposal did three essential things that were invaluable to the overall success of my project. First, it gave me a framework for writing. Its headings and questions provided a systematic approach that meant I could concentrate on filling in the details in an already accepted and acknowledged style. This provided the support and guidance I needed for organising and communicating the logic that connected what I wanted to do with how I would do it in a way that made the final proposal document coherent. Second, it gave me an identity. Developing the proposal and presenting it introduced me to the faculty and said this is who I am, this is what I am interested in, this is what I am doing. For me, this was an important element in building my esteem and a positive working relationship. I felt that significant others were not only interested in what I was doing, but also its quality. This gave me a strong sense of collaboration with critical friends who valued me and what I was attempting to do. Third, it gave me a problem to solve. Although I did not use rhetorical theory in the end to explain the data I collected, it was the best I could do at the time. Nevertheless, it was the literature on this theory and its connections to cultural studies that were to see me, at a later stage, investigating the complex interrelationships between thoughts, knowledge, power and discourse. After the research proposal had been approved, it was discourse analysis that propelled me into the philosophical thinking that had me seriously questioning the traditional approach to social criticism. This put me on a path that led me away from the destination that my proposal identified as the outcome of my research. It was rhetorical theory, as the best option at the time, that oriented me in this new direction.

The discussions I had and the writing I did at this initial stage influenced my later decisions which changed the way I would interpret my data. While the conceptual plan for my research was not perfect, the process of researching, writing and presenting what I saw as the best I could do at the time had an important and significant effect on shaping the final outcome.

My thesis supervisors were Dr Felicity Haynes and Professor Keith Punch and the full reference details are: McGowan, W.S. (2004) *Thinking about the Responsible Parent: Freedom and Educating the Child in Western Australia.* Unpublished PhD thesis, The University of Western Australia. I expect the thesis to be published, as a book, by Edwin Mullen Press in 2006.

Further reading

Bell, J. (1993). *Doing Your Research Project: A Guide for First-time Researchers in Education and Social Science.* (2nd edn). Buckingham: Open University Press.

Brink, P.J. and Wood, M.J. (1994). *Basic Steps in Planning Nursing Research: From Question to Proposal* (4th edn). Boston, MA: Jones and Bartlett Publishers.

Kelly, M. (1998). 'Writing a research proposal. In C. Seale (ed.), *Researching Society and Culture* (pp. 111–122). London: Sage.

Locke, L.F., Spirduso, W.W. and Silverman, S.J. (1993). *Proposals that Work* (3rd edn). Newbury Park, CA: Sage.

Punch, K.F. (2000). *Developing Effective Research Proposals.* London: Sage.

Project Management

6

*Linda McKie and Jonathan Tritter with
Nancy Lombard*

- This chapter provides advice on how to manage small-scale research projects.

- Carrying out research requires skills in managing people, resources and time –
  in short, in project management.

- Vital skills include keeping adequate records, budgeting, managing a team
  (unless you are sole researcher), deciding ahead of time when and what will be
  the 'outputs' of the project, and planning regular meetings and opportunities for
  communication with the sponsors.
- You also need to make contingency plans in case things go wrong.

Skills in project management are invaluable and critical to the development, running
and successful completion of a research project. At its most fundamental, project
management is about how to bring a research proposal to life and that process is likely
to involve negotiation and compromise with participants, supervisors, advisory group
members and funders. Many of these skills in the administration and management of
research are embedded in the process of 'doing' the research project. These are often
taken for granted and yet critical to the planning, progress and completion of projects.
They are also crucial to future careers in research in all sectors of the economy and the
academy, not least as funding bodies expect projects to be completed to schedule with
the content reflecting the agreed proposal, and the resources effectively managed. For
example, the Economic and Social Research Council (ESRC) regulations on postgraduate research stipulate that 'students will acquire research management skills'.
The regulations go on to propose that these skills might include how to:

> set appropriate timescales for different stages of the research with clear starting and fin-
> ishing dates; present a clear statement of the purposes and expected results of the research;

and develop appropriate means of estimating and monitoring resources and use of time. (ESRC, 2005 D11)

In this chapter we explore these and a range of related issues. Case studies are offered to illuminate points and provide examples for developing project management skills. These are drawn from our experiences as lone researchers, Master and doctoral supervisors, and as members and leaders of research teams. Examples are also drawn from the experiences of a doctoral student and a research team. Throughout the chapter we illuminate the joys and tensions of multidisciplinary, multi-agency and cross-national working.

Chapter 6 provided information and advice on developing and writing a research proposal. By contrast, in this chapter we consider what to do on receipt of the news that you have the go ahead to start your research. The skills and ideas we offer are relevant to managing research in a range of contexts and projects, including Masters and doctoral studies. Much of what we suggest may seem obvious, but in the excitement of getting started it can be all too easy to skip or forget crucial elements of planning, reviewing and resourcing the research. Time taken at this point to establish ways of working will pay off in the long run, especially during periods when communication or research difficulties become apparent.

In general a research project receives funding on the basis of peer or agency review of a proposal. In drafting a proposal applicants are asked to provide a number of details, including the research problem, aims and objectives, project design and budget (see Chapter 6). In the design section it is likely that a reasoned explanation of the scale, timing and resources necessary for the research will have been provided. Funding bodies often ask applicants to consider how realistic they are about timing, and how relevant is their approach and the choice of methods to the problem or topic under investigation. How will the design relate to and deliver the objectives? Methods, data collection and analysis, potential difficulties and dissemination will all have been considered. However, actually putting research ideas and plans into practice raises issues and problems that require resolution, often necessitating changes to the original plans.

One tip we offer at the outset – *keep records of all aspects of the project*, especially agreements on roles and responsibilities, minutes and action points, from supervisory and other meetings with external or funding bodies. These records should be backed up (on paper or disk) and include, as a minimum:

- the proposal as submitted

- all correspondence from funders and referees

- referees comments, if received

- any amended proposal(s)

- dates of supervisory meetings, agendas, minutes and action points

- publication and dissemination plans, including conferences and publications

- copies of all outputs, including virtual as well as paper-based items

Record keeping can ease working relations and promote scheduling and planning. Agreeing what records to keep, how to do this, and who is responsible for these, creates an atmosphere in which colleagues are reminded of the various stages of any project. This also establishes the need to reflect upon and work towards achieving appropriate processes and outcomes from the research. Further, while everyone hopes for a smooth and positive experience, if there are issues or disputes, records can prove invaluable.

Getting started

In the wake of enthusiasm provoked by acquiring funding for a project or the go ahead for a postgraduate degree, the day-to-day realities of undertaking research can seem distant. Yet there are some academic and practical issues to tackle almost immediately. Most importantly, if there are *comments from referees*, then you need to consider these. These are likely to come from more than one source and can, on occasions, be contradictory. Nevertheless, if academic colleagues, or users, have given their time to review your work and these comments have had an impact on the decision to proceed to fund your project, then they are worthy of some reflection. Deciding whether to act on them is best taken in conjunction with the research or supervisory team. If nothing else, critical comments may alert you to issues that you are likely to encounter in academic and user communities, and the research arena, as the project takes shape.

Securing funding is one thing, knowing how to allocate and access funds is another. First, review what the budget will pay for. Consider what the contract or award provides in terms of *resources*. For example, will it include office accommodation, access to libraries, budgets for materials, data collection, analysis and dissemination? Will the resources be adequate to cover the research project and, if not, can you renegotiate now or must you consider ways to curtail expenditure and manage resources if the funders have provided less than you requested? Planning your budget early allows you to reorganise your project and reallocate some funding to better fit the views of the referees and any constraints in the resources provided. While the sums allocated to some budget categories cannot be altered, others can be changed. In the case of some projects this may mean considering hiring more junior staff or allocating fewer days to data collection.

It is also worthwhile considering the relationship between the status of the *funding* organisation and the amount of funding provided. Some high-status funders, for instance the ESRC, tend to provide lower levels of funding for organisational over-heads than others, although this is set to change in the coming few years. There is a trade-off, however, for both the researcher and his/her organisation between the level of funding and the status of the funding body. This may create opportunities to nego-tiate with your department or organisation about obtaining additional resources for a project funded from 'high-status' sources.

Establishing budgetary accounts and learning to manage these is critical, as is ensur-ing early and easy access to library, computing and administrative services. Become acquainted with *key people in research and financial services* and nurture these relation-ships. In the long run knowing who does what, when and how, and establishing good working relations, can save time and heartache.

Acquiring knowledge about university or organisational libraries is invaluable and helps to ensure that you are part of an academic and research community whose work informs policy, practice, research and teaching developments (see Chapter 1). Depending on the topic there may also be relevant *information sources* or *background literature* and data in public and private sectors (see Chapter 2). If gathering literature was necessary for the writing of the proposal, reviewing this material and undertaking further searches of relevant publications or data sources are worthwhile in the early phase of the project.

In the writing of a proposal you will have considered *outputs*. Depending on the fund-ing body and the context, this might range from the production of an 80,000-word PhD thesis to a 3,000-word Final Project Report. For all these outputs there is guidance avail-able on what to aim for in terms of content (section headings or chapters) and this should be consulted early on (see Chapters 8 and 9, and Becker, 1986). The classic problem that many researchers encounter in analysis and writing up is the collection of too much data. If nothing else, regular reminders of what you are aiming for should help to keep the overall project within the required – and manageable – dimensions. Also familiarise yourself with the guidance on conducting research that some bodies, such as the ESRC, provide, including ethics (see Chapter 4) and research training. Learned societies and professional associations, such as the British Sociological Association (www.britsoc.co.uk), British Psychological Society (www.bps.org.uk) and Social Policy Association (www.social-policy.com), among others, provide information on aspects of establishing projects such as ethics, publications, report writing, etc. Establishing who will be responsible for producing the different forms of output and writing up the research and publications is a must. This is a tricky area in which those less powerful – the graduate student or research assistant or fellow – can feel especially vulnerable. The British Sociological Association has guidelines on the authorship of publications that can be consulted (http://www.britsoc.co.uk/new_site/index.php?area=publications&id=20), as do many professional journals (see for instance bmj.bmjjournals.com/advice/article_submission.shtml). These should be consulted and inform the negotiations within the research team concerning writing, responsibility, authorship and dissemination plans (Nardi, 2003).

Becoming a team player

While teams of researchers, some or all of whom may work full-time on a project, conduct much research, in Masters and doctoral research the student is guided by a supervisory team but retains overall responsibility for the management and production of the primary research outcome: the thesis. Masters, doctoral and undergraduate dissertation research are essentially one-person projects. Yet no student is allowed to proceed without a *supervisory person* or *team*. In these projects the student, with appropriate guidance, must address the array of factors and issues that come under the broad heading of project management. For many, postgraduate research is the first opportunity they encounter to develop team skills in research work, albeit that the final thesis is their responsibility (Pole and Lampard, 2002).

An increasing number of PhDs involve *multidisciplinary work* funded from the combined resources of research councils, public, private and voluntary sectors. These highlight the need to reflect upon the opportunities and challenges of working within a multidisciplinary research team. Funded research, beyond doctoral study, almost always involves a team of researchers from different backgrounds and often different institutional and sometimes national contexts. The challenges that this raises are also apparent for students pursuing research degrees focusing on international or cross-national issues or those who are studying for all or parts of their degree abroad. This section highlights some of the issues that have proved problematic in relation to the complex forms of joint working needed in international multidisciplinary research.

A common issue in research teams involving participants drawn from different disciplines and from different organisations is *expectations and experiences of very different patterns of working*. Much applied research is based on collaboration with non-research staff who typically have little experience of research and whose expectations may be very different from those of the project team and funders. The lack of knowledge about work cultures, responsibilities and styles of working can lead to confusion, disagreements and inefficiency.

Case study: Academia meets the NHS – a clash of working cultures

I (JT) was the academic lead on a Department of Health funded project. The research team was based in a Cancer Network housed by the local health authority. I would spend a week on site working with the local researchers undertaking the data collection and attending numerous meetings, some with the project workers, some with the Advisory Group and some with clinical staff and managers in the Cancer Network. Typically, I would arrive at my hot-desk in a large room shared by the administrative staff in the Cancer Network around 8am. Most of the staff, used to NHS working hours, arrived around 8:30am and left by 5pm. Often I worked later, being more used to looser academic timetables.

One night, I finished a piece of writing, looked at my watch and decided 8pm was late enough. Having turned off the computer I went out in the hall and down the unlit stairs to the main entrance, only to find it locked. I walked around the building but nobody was there and all the external doors were secure. I finally called one of the researchers who gave me the name of the security company and, eventually, some one came and released me from the building.

Such difficulties were symptomatic of broader differences that related to working culture. There was an insecurity on the part of the NHS researchers that if I, and other academic partners, was not visibly working in the Cancer Network, we were probably not working at all. This led initially to a directive and bureaucratic form of

(Continued)

(Continued)

project management and a vetting of publications and reports. In addition, meetings with the Department of Health coordinator permitted the project's academics an opportunity to engage critically in dialogues about the direction and process of the project. However, this was felt by the NHS researchers to be tantamount to rebellion and there was pressure to accept unquestioningly any points about content, dissemination or research practice raised by the Department coordinator.

Over time, we learned about each other's sensitivities and work practices and found the trust that was needed to allow difference of opinion and working style. In the end, the NHS researchers realised the value and opportunity offered to them by project members who had the 'right' to comment critically, without vulnerability, to the Department of Health. We realised how much networks internal to the NHS and the trust that came with being an insider created opportunities to access and study.

Most projects establish an advisory group that includes members of user groups, funding bodies and *representatives from other interested parties*. Many supervisory teams for postgraduate degrees may be required to liaise and meet with university postgraduate review and advisory groups. These can be useful sources of advice and data for a project but can also add layers of communication that can increase the administrative workload and may slow down decision-making. It is important to establish roles and responsibilities at the start.

In summary:

1. From the outset of the project, establish 'ways of working' and communication.

2. Organise timescales for regular meetings and reporting to funding bodies. Establish who has responsibility for organising meetings, keeping notes and circulating these. Might these tasks revolve around the group or team?

3. Know from the outset what the output will be (e.g. thesis or research report) and what is expected in terms of length, style and review. At every meeting it is worthwhile reminding everyone what they are working towards.

4. Consider what to do if things do not go according to plan with, for example, supervision, access to data sources, and access to software for data analysis.

Communication – agreeing how and when to communicate – is critical. Space precludes us from doing more than proposing a structure around which different forms of communication should be organised. The 'project manager' must negotiate and record individual responsibilities, timetables and meeting schedules as well as establish communication mechanisms that do not always rely on face-to-face contact. Email and telephone conferences are likely to be ingredients of any successful communication strategy, as well as being essential to data collection and the evolution of the project design (Ezzy, 2002). While the graduate student or research fellow may undertake the practical tasks around communication, there are differentials in power and access to resources that must be addressed. For example, the principal grant holder in a research project may chair meetings and have most contact with funders, while the researcher may undertake the practical work of communicating with the team as a whole. Again, reflecting on these aspects of project management from the outset, and recording agreements, aids working relations.

Case study: A student's perspective on getting the team started

Nancy Lombard

When I first began my PhD I brought with me my own fears, needs and expectations of how it would all develop. I had been working for three years and had recently had a baby. It was therefore important to me that my PhD was structured around my domestic commitments without being dominated by them. I have three supervisors, two of whom are based within my university and one who is at another institution in the same city.

I was asked before our first meeting to draft a list of my expectations of my supervisors, including what I anticipated their roles in my PhD to be. They agreed to do the same for me. These were then discussed and agreed upon:

- I felt it was important that even though we had specific roles these should be open to negotiation on an ongoing basis.
- I also wanted a structured timetable to work around and suggested we meet every six weeks. We also agreed that I should initiate meetings between these should I need to.
- My supervisors requested that before each meeting I should circulate one page on my progress to date. I should also email an agenda with items for discussion and write up the minutes from the meeting and send to all.

(Continued)

(Continued)

- I was also asked to keep a research diary.
- As my supervisors were all well established in their fields, I asked that they kept me informed of relevant conferences and networking opportunities where I could raise my academic profile.
- It was suggested that I join the relevant learned society, the British Sociological Association, and subsequently I have participated in the Annual Summer School for Postgraduates and a number of conferences and events.
- I asked that any work I sent to them should be discussed as a group but also returned to me with their written comments.
- I asked for my supervisory team to be positively critical.
- It was decided that any personal or professional problems I had with my supervisors should first be brought to their attention and then if I felt they were not resolved I should approach the Head of Department.
- It was agreed that we would review this *modus operandi* at the same time as annual review reports were submitted.
- Last, but not least, *records* would be kept of all meetings and correspondence with university committees and research sites and participants. These would be kept by the research student and copied to the supervisory team, as agreed by the team.

The ingredients of a research team

The ways in which various aspects are negotiated and managed must reflect the roles and responsibilities of the person or people involved in the research. Establishing clear roles and responsibilities is crucial. If the project is a PhD study, there is generally a team of one – the research student (Grady and Wallston, 1988). He/she will have overall responsibility for all aspects of the research, although the timing and structure of the study will be framed by university regulations, requirements from the funder and advice from his/her supervisors. Some doctoral students conduct their research as part of a larger research team. For them, the doctoral research is a component of a larger study and the student is expected to undertake some research tasks on behalf of the whole project team and not concentrate solely on his/her personal research. *Negotiating and clarifying the boundary* between the aspects of the study that are solely for the PhD and those that are more general is important and will be an ongoing process as research progresses.

Research assistants and research fellows sit at the heart of any research team. Their responsibility is usually solely focused on one or two research projects. Typically, they will be responsible for data management, which will include data collection, entry and initial analysis. Often literature reviews and obtaining literature are also the responsibility of such staff. Research fellows are usually more experienced than research assistants and will be expected to work more independently. Research fellows may have primary responsibility for a particular aspect or phase of a study.

The *research director or principal investigator* is the public face of the project and has primary and ultimate responsibility to the sponsor for the research. His/her agenda will focus on maintaining the integrity of the research questions and ensuring that the deliverables (interim reports, meetings, conference papers, articles, etc.) are produced on time and in a consistent and appropriate form. Typically, the principal investigator is a senior academic who is involved in a number of different research projects and so his/her management will be through regular meetings, in addition to relying on email and the telephone.

Often a research project will rely on *specialist expertise and draw on consultants*. Typically, consultants will have a small but essential part to play in the research and will have limited time. For example, it is not unusual for the statistical expertise needed for analytical design or power calculations to be 'bought in' from an external consultant. These members of the research team also add to the disciplinary diversity of the project but rarely play a major role in the writing up or presentation of research findings.

Another category of consultants increasingly being required by sponsors are *'users'*. Users are typically thought of as laypeople, or at least non-researchers, who are directly affected by the issue being studied. In educational research, for instance, users might include pupils, parents, teachers, educational managers, school governors, members of the local council and representatives of local educational authorities, sixth-form and further education colleges, universities and employers. Users can be involved in a variety of ways in the research: setting the research agenda, designing research tools, collecting data, commenting and contributing to analysis and presenting findings (de Koning and Martin, 1996). Users can also be drawn from, for example, a voluntary organisation that is seen as having specialist and appropriate knowledge of an issue connected to the research topic (see, for instance, www.invo.org.uk). Their participation will need to be negotiated and, sometimes, paid for. Often users (it is good practice to have a minimum of two users) will be invited to be members of the Research Advisory Group. Increasingly, engagement with users at all stages of the research process is good practice. This also increases the chance that more valid and applicable research is funded and has a broader impact.

Relationships with sponsors

A key skill that all researchers must learn is keeping funders content not only by meeting their requirements but also by *engaging with them* (Arksey and Knight, 1999). PhD research can be part of a larger research project and so the researcher must find ways of dovetailing his/her specific research interest with the agenda and timetable of the overall project.

Most bodies that choose to pay for PhD research do not do so altruistically: they require an *output*. Sometimes it is the process of the research and the development of a methodology, in addition to anticipated outputs, that is of interest to funders. In other cases the research may generate further work or policies that might also form an aspect of employee recruitment or retention. Often part-time PhD students who are sponsored to do their research must make a commitment to stay with their employer for some period of time following the completion of their degree, and to undertake specified dissemination activities. One funding model that seeks to capitalise on both altruistic and instrumental justifications in the UK is the ESRC Collaborative (CASE) Studentships.

An example: ESRC Collaborative (CASE) Studentships

This programme is part of the ESRC's commitment to promote collaboration between academics and the public, commercial and voluntary sectors. An academic is responsible for approaching a potential partner organisation and agreeing a research project. This may relate to a currently 'hot' topic, build on previous collaboration or develop student work at undergraduate or Masters level. The collaborating organisation agrees to pay an additional stipend to the student (a minimum of £2,000 a year in 2004/05) and £2,000 to the collaborating academic department. This model of PhD research funding benefits the student by exposing them to an environment where research findings are applied. For the collaborating organisation this approach is a way of accessing expertise not usually found in their organisation and getting high-quality research focused on an area of particular need (see http://www.esrcsocietytoday.ac.uk/ESRCInfoCentre/opportunities/jointfunding/business/index1.aspx).

Regular meetings and briefings with your funder help to demonstrate that you are working and the research is progressing. It is possible to have a series of specially arranged 'funder meetings', but a better strategy may be to invite a representative of your sponsors on to an advisory group. Such a group will usually meet around twice a year. At these meetings you will be expected to give a presentation and discuss an interim report that you will have circulated in advance. It may be a good idea to have identified a number of key issues that you then ask the group to help you with. For example, circulating and seeking comments on a draft questionnaire or interview schedule ensures that members have a task that they can undertake. This also helps to keep the group focused on what is realistic and relevant to the overall project. It is worth noting that we have termed this group an 'advisory' and not a 'steering' group. Membership of the latter may imply that the group is expected to set the agenda for the research while advisors are typically seen as more responsive to the leadership of the researcher. Engaging with your funders in a constructive manner helps to ensure that they feel a sense of connection and ownership of the data, but such relationships need to be managed if the researcher is to retain a measure of independence (Patton, 2002).

You also need to consider a variety of ways to *ensure that your funders feel that they are aware of what you are doing*, secure in the knowledge that your progress fulfils agreed plans, and that they have a sense of participation and 'ownership' in the project. Maintaining good communication links with your sponsors will help to ensure that the research is grounded and has both utility and validity and, most importantly, is likely to lead to a willingness to fund you again in the future.

Objectives, timescales and monitoring

Translating research questions into *objectives* is a process that requires regular review. At the design stage of a project the objectives are generally drawn from moulding a combination of the available literature and reports, and the experiences and ideas of members of the team, to what seems possible within the proposed timescale and resources. An early focus on these objectives may bring to light issues around access to research sites and participants as well as the overall viability of the project. An advisory group, combined with good working relations with sponsors, can be invaluable in helping to translate the objectives in the proposal to those of the actual project.

An example: Work–life balance in Scottish food retail companies

This three-year project, funded by the European Social Fund, considers women's experiences of combining paid work in food retail companies with caring for family members and other dependents. A particular interest of the research team, and one written into the research proposal, was to explore issues for women in their 20s and women in their 50s. This was intended to provide a life-course perspective as women in their 20s are likely to be planning future employment and care responsibilities while women in the their 50s might reflect back upon experiences as well as projecting forward to retirement.

When the project got underway and nine companies were recruited, it became apparent that companies interpreted the UK data protection legislation in such a way as to make it impossible to offer the research team guidance about the age groups of potential survey respondents. The previous experience of the research team, the review by the funding body and initial advice sought from companies had given no indication that this might pose a problem. Thus a key empirical and theoretical objective had to be changed. The team addressed this problem through seeking advice and held a series of meetings with a range of experts. Central to the ongoing project was the need to retain the goodwill of both the companies and the women.

It was agreed to increase the number of women contacted to take part in the survey and to request that respondents identify their age group. The team could then extract information on age categories. After debate with the advisory group and colleagues working on similar topics, the team recognised that we could also gain from exploring perspectives across a broader age range from the early 20s to 60.

Planning your research and keeping to an agreed *timetable* is a central aspect of successful management. Your proposal is likely to contain a timetable and this may already be out of date as a result of delays in making funding and project decisions. A series of issues must be considered:

- reviewing referee's comments
- the need for further literature or design work
- ethical issues and ethics committee clearance, if required

- negotiating access

- sampling

- the collection of data

- analysis of data

- interim reports and updates

- scheduling advisory and team meetings

- writing up

- publications and dissemination

Be realistic, especially about the time required for negotiating access, data analysis and writing up.

Embedded in your timetable should be a number of '*milestones*' that mark the end of particular phases of research, such as completion of interview data collection or of a case study. It is good practice to mark each milestone with a brief report that summarises the nature of the task completed and, if appropriate, provides an account of the methods, data and initial findings. These interim reports might also be sent to the funder and participants, together with a brief letter explaining how they mark a particular phase of the whole project. Such practice also makes the final write up and development of publications and dissemination work much easier.

Keeping a *research or project diary* is also useful. The main reason for keeping a research diary is to provide both material for reflection and data on the research process, while recording the development and history of the project. Write down what you did, why you did it, including the pros and cons, and critically reflect on the process. Keeping a diary, alongside regular updates and report writing, allows for detailed exploration of research practices and opportunities for critical reflection, and can aid confidence as you chart how issues and problems have been identified and tackled.

One pitfall many projects encounter is a *shortfall in resources*, especially in the later stages of the research. Here, software can help to maintain good records on financial matters. Seek advice from experts in financial planning and monitoring at the design stage and again on receipt of funding. Advice may also be useful if you encounter any timetable changes or have to seek additional resources to collect or prepare data for analysis (for example, the need to employ additional staff to transcribe interviews in order to keep to schedule). There may be ways to save money if resources need to be reconfigured to take account of additional needs. For example, a conference call or tele-conferencing might save travel costs. Most universities and organisations supply monthly and quarterly information on budgets and an ability to understand these is a useful skill to take through your career. If you encounter problems that might impact on the research design and schedule, inform funders. Explain how the problems emerged and suggest ways of overcoming them. Funders and advisory groups can offer ideas and, on occasion, additional time or resources, especially if problems could not have been anticipated. For example, organisations may have changed their policy on access to data sets or to potential participants after the project started (Wallis, 1977). In addition, recent changes in procedures for ethical consent have resulted in time delays for some projects.

The sponsors will want to be assured that the project is progressing and that it remains in line with the programme that was agreed. It is also a good idea to *make sponsors or supervisors aware of any problems* that emerge that may impact on the quality or timing of research products. It is far better to tell them early on, giving them an idea of a plan to overcome the problem, than to wait until deadlines have passed or the initial research aims become impossible. A number of methods provide appropriate mechanisms for keeping your funders aware and informed of the progress of the research: interim reports, project meetings, and briefings, and research advisory groups (see above).

Project management into the twenty-first century: continuity and change

In this final section we reprise one common issue for many projects – methodological approaches – and identify two emerging topics, namely, cross-national and cross-cultural projects, and software that can aid project design and management.

Methodological approaches

A common issue that can arise in multidisciplinary research teams and with funders is assumptions about the appropriate theoretical and methodological framework and types of data needed to draw conclusions. This emerges as a polarisation between quantitative and qualitative data and between theory- or hypothesis-driven enquiries and those that are more exploratory. In reality, most research is a mix of methods, theoretical exploration and hypothesis testing. This mixture can sometimes provide an appropriate strategy for managing methodological disagreements. Those phases of the research that adopt a particular methodological approach can become the responsibility of those team members who are committed to them. This has the added benefit of matching expertise to research method. The downside is that unless a lot of work is done to synthesise the results, the research can be rather 'bitty' as it is composed of distinct mini-projects.

These issues also highlight the different forms of collaboration and distinctions between multidisciplinary and interdisciplinary research. The latter is premised on working through the differences in perspective and arriving at a consensus on an approach that is acceptable methodologically to all team members. The resulting research will be far more integrated and coherent and has greater potential to yield methodologically interesting results. However, interdisciplinary research requires a great deal of time and contact early in the project, in order to learn about and from the different members of the research team.

Cross-national and cross-cultural issues

Research that has an international aspect, either because the study draws data from different countries or involves researchers from different national backgrounds, presents particular challenges. Language differences may make communication or comprehension difficult. If data are sourced in different languages, the implications of translation must be considered. These implications include both cost but, perhaps more importantly, interpretation, which is always an aspect of translation and may hide rather than reveal different underlying cultural assumptions.

An example: *Globalisation and citizens in healthcare – exploring the role of users, choice and markets in European health systems*

This research, funded by the Academy of Finland, is an analysis of policy content and the policy-making process related to health-care reforms in Finland, Great Britain and Sweden, focusing on competition, marketisation, patient choice and user involvement. The research also explores the international legal and regulatory spheres in the relation to the European Community and three international organisations: the Organisation for Economic Cooperation and Development (OECD), the World Health Organisation (WHO) and the World Trade Organisation (WTO), because of their role and relevance in the context of globalisation and public policy reform.

(Continued)

(Continued)

The nature of the research required that the majority of the research team was fluent in three languages: Finnish, Swedish and English. The language of the funder is Finnish and the language used within the team is English. The composition of the Advisory Group, too, reflects the international character of the research and includes Finnish, Swedish and British experts.

But differences of language also hide more significant cultural and social differences. The approach to policy making is very different in the three countries and this is particularly true of the amount of publicly available documentation. Similarly, the rate at which policy is made varies and therefore tracing the impact of the same piece of EU legislation on policy making in the three countries leads to different results at different points in time.

These substantive differences are part of the research itself but it is other cultural differences that add complexity. Scheduling project and Advisory Group meetings and interviews with key policy makers and stakeholders must be sensitive to different social and cultural practices. While August may be the most common month for holidays in Britain and France, making it impossible to arrange interviews or observations during this time, in Finland and other Nordic countries it is the beginning of autumn and the month during which people return to work and school following the summer. Gaining an understanding of these underlying differences is one of the necessities and rewards of international research.

Software

The introduction of project management software over a decade ago was hailed as a solution to a range of issues, not least those of scheduling and budgeting. There are two broad categories of software available:

- Packages that concentrate on objectives, timescales and monitoring by listing tasks, meetings and deadlines.

- Packages that both address the above and the management and organisation of projects.

In the former category are programs that provide a graphical representation of the duration of tasks against time. These are termed Gantt charts, and include Excel Spreadsheets and Microsoft Project. The latter category includes tools that allow for collaborative working on and offline. This means that charts and tables can be accessed, read and amended by members of the project team at different points in time and at different locations. This can help to spread knowledge and share responsibility within the team. However, without agreed terms for the use of these facilities, they also have the potential to blur roles and limit progress.

Software allows for a range of tasks to be monitored by the team, including project timetables, task allocation and status, risk assessments and reviews, resources and finances, discussion sites and email notification. Many programs, such as Microsoft Project, pose questions and provide structures taking teams through, for example, establishing goals and tasks and considering the work required to achieve these. Programs can also generate reminders to the researcher or team of the need to address an aspect of the project work and management.

An example: *Multi-site project management – the evaluation of community arts projects*

Many multi-site projects require teams to work across a number of organisations and locations. Communicating schedules for tasks to all members of a team, updating these, and monitoring progress poses challenges for any project manager. This can be acute when team members have a range of duties and projects. Often the project that is controlled from another site or organisation is the one that slips down the work schedule.

In this multi-site project a series of small grants were awarded to community projects for arts work. Resources for evaluation were limited but it was a requirement of the funding that an evaluation report be submitted to release the final 20 per cent of funds. For many community projects those funds were critical to ongoing sustainability. Project facilitators were asked to lead these evaluations but most had little or no research and evaluation experience. It was agreed that the final evaluation report should emerge from a central point and that local projects be asked to collect information on a regular basis on the plan of activities, participation, content of events and participants' views of these.

The use of software proved invaluable. At the outset tasks and schedules were established during a one-day meeting involving representatives from each of the eight project sites. These were entered into the software and local project facilitators received automatically generated email reminders on data collection and

(Continued)

(Continued)

submission. They were also able to access a project and evaluation timetable. Some colleagues were keen to receive support on using the software and there were some concerns about the level of IT skill required. By the end of the project all agreed that online access to information combined with regular alerts about stages in the collection of information had taken pressure off local projects and promoted the development of computing skills.

In addition, there are 'structured' methods that provide projects with a 'standard approach to the management of projects', such as PRINCE2 (www.ogc.gov.uk/prince2), *Projects in Controlled Environments*. This provides an overarching approach to project management from initiation, across planning and management, to the final outputs. It has been adopted in the UK by the Office of Government Commerce as standard for project management in the public and private sector. However, researchers have to generate the ideas, tasks and schedules, and input these data to the system. So while the software can generate timetables and reminders, suggest areas you need to address, and provide access to this information for everyone in the team, it cannot do the fundamental thinking and decision making.

Conclusion

Project management is a key role composed of a range of skills. It is essential that it is done consciously and conscientiously. Like other research roles, the level of activity will wax and wane over the course of a project. Project managers are responsible for delivering project outputs and will be held to account by the funder and the other members of the team. Ideally, they must help to bring together and integrate the different forms of data, experience, expertise and disciplines that members of the research team bring to the project. The moulding of a group of individual researchers with distinct agendas into a team with collective aims and shared responsibilities brings benefits far beyond the life and findings of a research project.

Further reading

Lock, D. (2003). *Project Management*. Aldershot: Gower.

Maylor, H. (2002). *Project Management* (3rd edn). London: Prentice Hall.

Sapienza, A. (2004). *Managing Scientists: Leadership Strategies in Scientific Research*, (2nd edn). New York: Wiley-Liss.

Intellectual Property

7

Alison Firth

- The result of social science research is intellectual property.
- You have rights over your own intellectual property which you may want to defend.
- You also need to respect other people's intellectual property.
- This chapter defines intellectual property, explains what intellectual property rights are, and indicates what are permitted and infringing uses of intellectual property.

In this chapter, we consider how researchers create intellectual property and how intellectual property affects their use of other people's work. These are linked to proper citation (Chapter 9), research ethics (Chapter 4) and the communication of research results (Chapter 8).

What is intellectual property? It is a form of property that protects *creations of the mind*, such as literary works (books, but also tables of results or computer programs), artistic works (such as drawings or sculptures), films, photographs, inventions (new products or industrial processes, including biotechnology), designs (two-dimensional designs, patterns or logos, three-dimensional designs), trade marks (for example, McDonald's 'golden arches'), confidential information (such as unpublished research), databases, new varieties of plant, and so on. Different types of intellectual property are important in different types of research and attract different types of right.

We shall use two case studies to investigate the various kinds of intellectual property, based on the experiences of real researchers. I am grateful to the individuals for allowing details of their studies to be included.

Case study: Florian

Florian took his first degree in France, followed by postgraduate attachment at a university in the Far East. While there, he worked on a laboratory project to improve the extraction of DNA from dried plants, in support of a larger government programme to monitor traditional pharmacology. This kind of research can be expected in the long run to lead to inventions, for example, new and improved processes for extracting DNA or new kinds of DNA identification kit. Florian's work was recorded in laboratory notebooks in the form of notes, tables, graphs, diagrams, machine print-outs and photographs. He wrote up his results as a formal report.

Florian went on to take a Masters degree in the management of intellectual property. He then became a law research student and embarked on a PhD project studying the research exemption in patent law. He has written articles for publication, quoting from legislation, from case-law and from the published work of other scholars. He has delivered papers orally at conferences and contributed short pieces to an intellectual property information website. Recently he has started giving lectures and tutorials.

Case study: Delioma

Delioma is a geographer investigating risks to the human and natural environment in the vicinity of an active South American volcano. In support of her research she has been developing a geographical database, with a variety of data types. These include topographical elevation data (heights above a reference level) and satellite images.

Within the class of elevation data, there are elements of discrete data, from existing sources (maps, survey information, existing data sets) and from fieldwork conducted by Delioma herself. She selects specific locations as relevant to her thesis. There are also complex data inputs, such as surface models.

The sources of Delioma's discrete data include public domain material, such as old maps, modern data from publicly available sources and also data from commercial providers (e.g. distributors of NASA products). Satellite images also come from commercial providers. These are automatically generated (sensors on satellites transmit information to processing centres which work them into final products for end users, who apply them to their own researches). Full permission for use of the images is given by the providers as part of the commercial supply arrangement.

(Continued)

(Continued)

Delioma uses software which provides the main framework or architecture for her database. However, the structure is not standard – Delioma has selected fields and functions that she is using to construct her database. These have been chosen to suit the analysis that she wants to carry out upon the data, to test her hypothesis. Thus she selects the fields and what goes into them, the best to further her research. She will use the software to analyse the data and possibly she will have to modify the structure and arrangement of her database as her research progresses.

Creating intellectual property

Table 7.1 sets out different kinds of intellectual creation and shows what kinds of intellectual property can arise. There are basic minimum criteria for each type, shown in the third column of the table.

Registered rights

Some kinds of intellectual property, such as patents, registered trade marks and registered designs, are brought into being by filing an application at an intellectual property office. This is shown by the column headed 'Is registration needed?' The office has to examine and approve the application to bring the rights into force. Registers of intellectual property can be searched to find out what earlier rights and registrations exist. Each intellectual property office grants rights for a specific country or region, so that many applications would have to be filed to patent a product or process worldwide. To make this easier, there are filing arrangements which enable international applications to be routed centrally through the International Bureau of the World Intellectual Property Office. (The Paris Convention, the Patent Cooperation Treaty, the Madrid Arrangement for the international registration of marks and the Hague Agreement for the international registration of designs all assist applicants to protect registered rights internationally.)

Advantages of registration

The registers provide a repository of information which can be searched. For example, a company wishing to adopt a new trade mark can search the trade mark registers to check that the mark has not been registered by another trader. A research laboratory wishing to engage a research team for a specific project can look at registers of patents to discover what related work has been patented and to identify creative individuals who are named as inventors. Registration usually gives stronger rights. An invention which has been patented in a given country can only be used there by the patent owner or with their permission. If someone subsequently makes the same invention, they will not be able to use it in the face of an earlier patent. If the other person made the invention first, they may continue to use it and perhaps invalidate the patent.

Unregistered rights

Other kinds of intellectual property, such as copyright, come into existence automatically, when a work is created. Although each country confers rights only for its own territory, almost every country in the world belongs to the Berne Convention for the protection of literary and artistic works. By this treaty, the member countries agree to give copyright protection to works created by nationals or residents of the other member countries, or works first published in one of those other countries. So a work which is protected by copyright in one country is usually protected in most countries of the world. The Berne Convention covers many works of authorship, not just literary works and works of fine art:

> Art 2(1)   The expression 'literary and artistic works' shall include every production in the literary, scientific and artistic domain, whatever may be the mode or form of its expression, such as books, pamphlets and other writings; lectures, addresses, … dramatic or dramatico-musical works; choreographic works …; musical compositions …; cinematographic works …; works of drawing, painting, architecture, sculpture, engraving and lithography; photographic works …; illustrations, maps, plans, sketches and three-dimensional works relative to geography, topography, architecture or science.

Other rights, such as unregistered design right or database right, are only available in a few territories (including the UK and other European Union countries).

Advantages of unregistered rights

Rights which come into being automatically are useful to their owners because they do not have to do anything to obtain them and only have to worry if things go wrong – if their work is copied. However, it is difficult for other people to know that the rights exist. For this reason, unregistered rights are usually weaker than registered rights, protecting their owners from copying but not from independent creation of a similar work or design.

Duration of rights

Table 7.1 also shows how long the rights last. Rights of authors last for many years after the author's death, while the community unregistered design right lasts only for three years from publication of a design. This right is intended to protect short-lived designs. Longer-life designs will need to be protected by registration.

International agreements concerning intellectual property

There are many international treaties concerning intellectual property. Most of them are administered by the World Intellectual Property Organisation (WIPO) in Geneva and deal with specific aspects of protection or procedure. Details of these are available at www.wipo.int/treaties/en

The World Intellectual Property Organisation divides the treaties into three groups:

1. *Intellectual Property Protection Treaties*, which lay the ground rules for national protection worldwide or harmonise aspects of national registration procedure.

2. *Global Protection System Treaties*, which create international filing systems.

3. *Classification Treaties*, under which schemes of classification of goods, services, designs elements, fields of technology, etc. are drawn up. These enable intellectual property registers to be structured in a uniform way, to enhance efficiency and facilitate searching.

None of these treaties provide for global rights; rather, they are intended to streamline and strengthen national systems.

There are regional systems, including:

- European Community trade mark, design and plant variety right regimes
- The European Patent Convention

Table 7.1   The intellectual property characteristics of a range of media types

Intellectual creation	Intellectual property right (IPR)	Basic minimum criteria, or ingredients	Is registration needed?	Typical maximum duration	International agreements
Literary work (book, journal article, table of data, words of a speech or song, computer program)	Copyright (known in some countries as 'author's right')	Original (in the sense of a personal intellectual creation, not copied) Recorded in material form (This requirement is also known as 'fixation', and is not necessary in all countries)	No	From creation until 50 or 70 years after the author's death Sound recordings are protected for 50 years from creation or release	Berne; Universal Copyright Convention; TRIPs; WIPO Copyright Treaty
Databases	Copyright (in the selection and arrangement) Database right in Europe in the contents of a structured collection of independent data	Originality for copyright; substantial investment in the obtaining or verifying of the data for database right	No	Copyright – from creation until 70 years after the author's death; database right – 15 years from creation, publication or last substantial investment	
Artistic work (such as drawing, painting, map, photograph, sculpture, work of architecture)	Copyright	Originality, fixation	No	From creation until 70 years after the author's death	Berne; Universal Copyright Convention; TRIPs; WIPO Copyright Treaty
Musical work and dramatic work	Copyright	Originality, fixation	No	From creation until 70 years after the author's death	Berne; Universal Copyright Convention; TRIPs; WIPO Copyright Treaty

Table 7.1 (Continued)

Intellectual creation	Intellectual property right (IPR)	Basic minimum criteria, or ingredients	Is registration needed?	Typical maximum duration	International agreements
Film	Copyright (there may also be a so-called 'neighbouring right' in the medium on which the content is recorded)	Originality, fixation	No, although many in the industry would like a register because of the difficulty of identifying and tracing all contributors	From creation until 70 years after the author's death As many people may contribute to the making of a film, this calculation can be difficult (50 years from creation/release for neighbouring right)	Berne; Universal Copyright Convention; TRIPs; WIPO Copyright Treaty; Film Register Treaty
Sound recording or phonogram; broadcast	Copyright or neighbouring right	Not copied	No	50 years from creation or release	Rome Convention; Brussels; WIPO Performers and Phonograms Treaty
Live performances	Performer's right	Live	No	50 years	Rome Convention; WIPO Performers and Phonograms Treaty
Invention – a product (such as a jet engine or a new chemical) or a process (such as a chemical process)	Patent	Industrially applicable, new, non-obvious Not available for mathematical methods, scientific theories	Yes	20 years	Paris; Strasbourg; Patent Cooperation Treaty; Patent Law Treaty; European Patent Convention; Budapest

(Continued)

Table 7.1 (Continued)

Intellectual creation	Intellectual property right (IPR)	Basic minimum criteria, or ingredients	Is registration needed?	Typical maximum duration	International agreements
Pharmaceuticals and agro-chemicals				Note that in the EU, 'Supplementary protection certificates' extend patent term for medicines, etc. where there are long regulatory delays	
New kind of plant (in the sense of a plant not commercially available before)	Plant variety right	Distinct (from earlier varieties), uniform (across a generation), stable (variety breeds true)	Yes	10–25 years, depending on the type of plant	International Convention for the Protection of New Varieties of Plants (UPOV)
Small invention (such as garden tool)	Utility model	Novelty	Yes	Typically 6–10 years	
Layout of a semiconductor chip	Semiconductor topography right	Original (not copied, not commonplace) [check regs]	No	10–25 years in the UK	Washington Treaty
2-D or 3-D design	Registered design; unregistered design right available in Europe; designs may be protected by copyright as works of applied art	New and having distinctive character	Yes	25 years for registered designs; 3 years for European Community unregistered designs; 10–15 years for UK unregistered designs	Paris; Locarno; Hague

Table 7.1 (Continued)

Intellectual creation	Intellectual property right (IPR)	Basic minimum criteria, or ingredients	Is registration needed?	Typical maximum duration	International agreements
Trade mark (usually a word, product name or visual device. Might be a slogan or a sound)	Registered trade mark or passing off/unfair competition	Capable of distinguishing goods or services connected with the owner from other goods or services; not objectionable on public policy grounds; not too close to existing marks on register or in use	Yes for registered trade marks Passing off/unfair competition protection does not depend upon registration Nor does the international protection of very well-known marks	Trade mark registrations usually last for 10 years but can be renewed indefinitely if the mark remains in use	Paris; Vienna; Nice; Madrid Agreement concerning international registration and its Protocol; Madrid Agreement for the Repression of False and Deceptive Indications of Source on Goods; Nairobi
Geographical indications of origin	Geographical appellation	Indicates qualities of products, such as foodstuffs, dependent on place of origin	Various recordal systems exist; No registration needed for passing off/unfair competition protection	Indefinite	Lisbon Agreement
Confidential information, sometimes called undisclosed information	Breach of confidence or unfair competition	Secret (not generally known), substantial (not trivial) and identifiable	No	Until information passes into the public domain	TRIPs

- ARIPO, the regional intellectual property system of English-speaking Africa

- AIPO, the regional intellectual property system of French-speaking Africa

- The Andean Community in South America

Last, but not least, the Agreement in Trade-related aspects of Intellectual Property rights (TRIPs) of the World Trade Organisation lays down minimum standards for the protection and enforcement of many types of intellectual property. The TRIPS agreement is unique in having a serviceable mechanism to resolve disputes between states about compliance with obligations. There is an agreement for cooperation between the World Trade Organisation and the World Intellectual Property Organisation.

The influence of these treaties depends upon their membership. Some have been outstandingly successful, such as the Berne Convention for the Protection of Literary and Artistic Works, which had 157 signatory states as of November 2004. Others have proved less popular, such as the Treaty on the International Registration of Audiovisual Works (Film Register Treaty), which had 13 adherent countries as of October 2004.

Some of the more important treaties are listed in the final column of Table 7.1. Many are named after the city hosting the diplomatic conference which concluded the treaty and the names are shortened accordingly. Full titles may be found in the list of references.

What has Florian created by way of Intellectual Property and who owns it?

Florian's laboratory report on the DNA project, as well as his notes and the tables of results recorded by him, are original literary works. His graphs, diagrams and photographs are original artistic works. Because of the Berne Convention, we can expect these to be protected by copyright in many countries. This does not mean, however, that only Florian can use his results. As we shall see later in this chapter, once his results have been published, other people can quote from them, provided Florian's contribution is properly acknowledged. Second, ownership of copyright may have passed from Florian to the university where he did his laboratory research. As it was part of a large project, the university may have agreed to share intellectual property with the government funding body. All this will depend upon the relationship between Florian and the university. Until published, the information will remain confidential to Florian and the university. In his legal research he has been generating mainly literary works – conference papers, articles, chapters of his thesis, lecture guides. As Florian's own intellectual creations, these are original copyright works.

(Continued)

Continued

Many universities do not lay claim to copyright in works created by staff and students, apart from things such as examination papers. Florian's research student handbook states that his college owns the results of research but only refers to patents, knowhow, designs, computer software and data. There is a system for notification of inventions and other creations with commercial potential. Research students are entitled to share in royalties from successful exploitation.

Florian's comments

Florian says that he worked as a volunteer in the research laboratory and was not paid as an employee. Therefore he feels that he remains owner of copyright in the works he created. However, he was glad to gain experience in the laboratory and he left the results with the university for their use. Florian feels that he contributed to the laboratory's research effort and that his results did show practical promise. However, as to whether he made any inventions while working in the laboratory, Florian considers that he did not go so far as to make an invention in the time available. He generated new scientific information but he did not take an inventive step, in the sense of providing a non-obvious solution to a technical problem. On its own, his work did not lead to an industrially applicable product or process, although he showed what could be done.

As his research student handbook makes no mention of copyright, Florian has looked at the terms of employment for staff. These state that the employee is the owner of all copyrights. Florian believes that the same applies to him, so that he is owner of copyright in his original writings. He will check if it becomes an issue. Florian does not think he will be writing any computer programs or databases, but the copyright situation is not so clear with these because the student handbook asserts the university's right over them.

What is Delioma creating by way of Intellectual Property?

Delioma, like Florian, is generating literary works and confidential information from her fieldwork. However, she is integrating this into another kind of work, a database. Delioma's database contains some elements that are her own copyright creations. Other elements are taken from works in which others have copyright. (For the moment we shall assume this is permissible.) Some elements are taken from copyright-expired works, such as old maps, and some elements are not protected by copyright at all.

(Continued)

Continued

The Berne Convention for the protection of literary and artistic works requires collections of literary and artistic works such as anthologies and encyclopaedias to be protected by copyright if they are original by virtue of the selection and arrangement of their contents. This is in addition to any copyright in the works forming part of the collection. Delioma's collection is certainly original in its selection of data and in the way she has chosen to arrange it. So her database as a whole may be protected as a copyright collection in the many countries who have signed up to the Berne Convention. In the countries of the European Union, Delioma has a further right – database right. European legislation defines a database as:

- *a collection of independent works, data or other materials*: this describes Delioma's database exactly
- *arranged in a systematic or methodical way*: this is certainly the case
- and *individually accessible by electronic or other means*: again the software that Delioma is using enables her to do just this.

Because the selection and arrangement of the data is Delioma's own intellectual creation, there is copyright in the database as a whole. She is the natural person creating it, and will be regarded as the author. The database right is available where there has been substantial investment in obtaining, verifying, or presenting the contents. This condition is probably satisfied – Delioma has invested substantial time and her university has invested in the satellite and other data from which she is constructing the database. Database right entitles Delioma to object to the extraction or re-use of substantial parts of the content, or to the repeated and systematic extraction or re-use of insubstantial parts.

Delioma has not yet consulted her student handbook to find out whether her university lays claim to any rights over her database. There would be some justification for the university taking this view – it has invested in the licences which allow Delioma to make use of commercial material.

Infringing and permitted uses

Copyright

Nearly all researchers rely upon the works of others, citing and reproducing other people's publications, research results, satellite images and so forth. How does copyright affect the use of such material?

Copyright legislation gives an author or copyright owner exclusive rights over a work – to reproduce (copy) it, to publish it, to broadcast it and so forth. In principle, any unauthorised copying or dissemination of a work, or a significant part of a work, can infringe copyright. Whether there is infringement or not depends on several factors.

First, there is the *copyright status* of the work used. Assuming that it is original, a work may be in copyright for up to 70 years after the author's death. After that, the work will be freely available for use, at least if it has been published while in copyright. Some countries have perpetual copyright in unpublished works, or give a publication right if a work is published after expiry of copyright term, so care must be exercised even when using old material. The Berne Convention does allow countries to deny copyright protection to works of public interest, such as news of the day, individual political speeches and legislative texts. Again, the local position should be checked.

The second factor is whether the use made of the work is *restricted* by copyright. Some activities, such as reading a book or looking at a picture are not restricted by copyright. Nor is independent generation of a new work, without copying. But acts of reproduction and communication to the public (performing, broadcasting, dissemination over the internet) are generally restricted. However, infringement involves use of a *substantial part* of the source work. Use of an insubstantial part will not infringe.

Third, even a restricted use of a substantial part may be *permitted*, by the copyright owner, by statute, or by convention.

The laws of countries that have signed up to the Berne Convention *must* allow for quotation of lawfully published works. Article 10 stipulates that the quotations must be compatible with fair practice and of an extent justified by the purpose of quoting the material. There must be mention of the source and of the author, if identified in the source.

The USA has a very general 'fair use' defence to copyright infringement. The effect of extensive case-law on fair use has been encapsulated in section 107 of the US Copyright Act, which sets forth relevant factors – the purpose and character of the use (including whether such use is of commercial nature or is for non-profit educational purposes), the nature of the work, the amount and substantiality of the portion used in relation to the work as a whole, and the effect of the use upon the potential market for or value of the copyrighted work. As the US Copyright Office puts it:

The distinction between 'fair use' and infringement may be unclear and not easily defined. There is no specific number of words, lines, or notes that may safely be taken without permission. Acknowledging the source of the copyrighted material does not substitute for obtaining permission.

In the UK and other Commonwealth countries, fair dealing with copyright works for *specific purposes* – private study, non-commercial research, criticism, review and the reporting of current events – is permitted. It is usually necessary to acknowledge the source, either because the statute says so, or to ensure that the use is fair. Note that both the requirement of fairness *and* that of permitted purpose must be satisfied.

Furthermore, authors have moral rights. There are two main moral rights: the right to be identified as the author of a work, sometimes called the paternity right; and the right to prevent the publication of mutilated versions of a work, often called the integrity right.

Copyright statutes usually permit certain uses in the cause of education, public administration, scientific abstracting, and so forth. The Berne Convention allows the reproduction of works in special cases, provided the use does not conflict with normal exploitation of the work nor unreasonably prejudice the legitimate interests of the author.

Examples

(a) Insubstantial part of the source work

It is easy to see that use of one or two choice words from a book, or a single item of data from a set of experimental results, is unlikely to form a substantial part or the source work. In *Geographia v Penguin*, a case involving maps, copying of choice of colour was held to be insubstantial. Use of insubstantial parts will not infringe copyright, although courtesy or academic propriety may require attribution. (Note that systematic and unfair taking of insubstantial parts of a database could infringe database right.) It is difficult to know exactly at what point a part becomes substantial, so very often it is wise to look at the next categories.

(b) The part used may be substantial but the use is
permitted by statute

Usually a researcher will be able to rely upon the exceptions for fair dealing for the purposes of private study, non-commercial research, criticism or review. For example, photocopying a journal article for private study or circulation among a research team is likely to be fair dealing. Conversely, photocopying every article in this year's volume of a favourite journal is unlikely to be fair dealing. This undermines the publishers' interest in selling subscriptions. Nor would it be fair dealing to photocopy the same article for 100 colleagues. In *Newspaper Licensing Agency v Marks & Spencer*, it was not fair dealing to make multiple copies of newspaper cuttings for distribution.

As for the condition that research be non-commercial, it is the type of activity that counts, rather than the nature of the organisation. As recital 42 of the EC directive on copyright in the information society puts it:

> the non-commercial nature of the activity in question should be determined by that activity as such. The organisational structure and the means of funding of the establishment concerned are not the decisive factors in this respect.

Where the purpose is criticism or review, that commentary can relate to the source work itself, another work (e.g. in a comparative critique) or to the ethos behind the source work. For example, in *Hubbard v Vosper*, criticism related to the cult of scientology rather than to the literary merits of its founders' books. In *Pro Sieben Media v Carlton TV*, excerpts from a television programme were used in a critique of the practice of 'cheque book journalism'. In these cases, the source work must be published.

The courts judge fairness 'by the objective standards of whether a fair-minded and honest person would have dealt with the copyright work in the manner in question' (*Hyde Park v Yelland*). However, there may be circumstances in which the users' motives are relevant. If the motive is to compete with the source work, the taking is unlikely to be fair. Whether the work is published, unpublished or confidential will also have a bearing. In *Beloff v Pressdram*, publication of 'leaked' information was held not to be fair dealing.

The UK also recognises a residual defence of public interest to the unlicensed use of copyright material. Usually the specific provisions will be enough, but occasionally important considerations like the exposure of wrong-doing, the liberty of citizens (*Lion Laboratories Ltd v Evans*) or freedom of expression (*Ashdown v Telegraph*) may justify other uses of copyright works. Although freedom of expression will generally be used to interpret, rather than override, intellectual property legislation, cases such as *Esso v Greenpeace* have shown that it is a useful defence.

Certain classes of work are excluded from the scope of permitted acts. In particular, the copying of photographs is not permitted for the purpose of reporting current events. This enables professional and amateur news photographers to charge for the use of their images. Sheet music is another category of work for which copying is more restricted.

(c) Use is substantial but permitted by a licensing scheme

In the UK, the Copyright Licensing Agency operate various photocopying licences. Note that different rules may apply to the copying of text and the copying of artistic works. The Copyright Licensing Agency's scheme specifically exclude maps, charts, books of tables and printed music (including the words). There are other schemes for some of these works and for newspaper cuttings.

(d) Use is substantial and express permission has been obtained

The process of obtaining permission to use copyright works is often referred to as 'copyright clearance'. There is no central agency for this. The first port of call is the publisher. The identity of the publisher of a book or journal and their city are usually displayed inside the front cover or on the reverse of the title page. Even where the author has retained copyright, it is necessary to get permission from the publisher if the typographical arrangement of the published edition is copied, by scanning or photocopying. Many publishers are extremely helpful and will contact authors on behalf of applicants. This is not invariable; you may have to be persistent. The UK Authors' Licensing and Collecting Society may be able to help.

(e) Use is substantial; it falls outside the statutory permitted acts and no permission has been obtained

In this case there will be copyright infringement. For example, the author Alan Sillitoe sued the publisher McGraw-Hill for unauthorised use of his writings, which had been nominated as set books for school exams (*Sillitoe v McGraw-Hill*). The publishers issued study guides, which reproduced many excerpts from the books, together with commentary for students. They argued that as there was criticism and buyers of the books would use them for private study, they could rely upon fair dealing defences. The court did not agree – the publishers were not engaging in private study but in commerce. Furthermore, so much of Sillitoe's writing was reproduced that students might well buy just the study guide and not bother to get a copy of any of Sillitoe's books. The use of his work was not fair: it conflicted with his own book sales.

From all this we can see that copyright is unlikely to prevent fair, accurate and properly attributed citation of other people's work. However, unacknowledged copying or inaccurate use can infringe copyright as well as academic convention.

Access or copy control of digital works

Publishers can protect their work against unauthorised copying by technological means. Sometimes this restricts access to a work to those who have obtained a contractual right to use it (access control). Sometimes access is not restricted, but the work cannot be copied (this form of copy-protection is often used on music CDs and video games). Sometimes the work can be copied, but there is embedded software to track and charge for use (digital rights management). In order to deter circumvention of these technological measures, many countries have introduced laws which make it a criminal offence and/or a civil wrong. This is worrying not only for commercial music pirates and those who share music over the internet, but also to academic researchers. Although in principle, governments are committed to allowing access to works in order to engage in fair dealing activities, such as research, quotation and criticism, in practice, arrangements for this are not as well advanced as the technology or the criminal sanctions.

Database right

This right, which protects the contents, as opposed to the structure or arrangement, of a database is available under the laws of countries in the European Union. Database right allows its owner to prevent unauthorised extraction (temporary or permanent transfer to another medium) or re-utilisation (commercial re-use) of substantial parts of a database. Exceptions to the right include private use, teaching and research for a non-commercial purpose. Unfortunately, these exceptions are not wholly uniform across Europe. Insubstantial parts may be extracted and re-used by any lawful user of the database. Rental of databases is restricted by the rights but not public lending by libraries. Once a copy of a database has been sold with the rightholder's permission, it may be resold freely in the European Union.

Delioma's use of material from commercial databases is permitted because she is a lawful user under her department's contractual arrangement with providers, because many of the data items will be insubstantial parts of the databases in question and because she is engaged in non-commercial research.

Patents

A patent gives its owner the right to prohibit use of the invention by manufacturing, using or selling products or using processes. Copying is irrelevant: a patent owner can object to the use of her invention even by someone who has devised it independently. Acts which are both private and non-commercial do not infringe. Most patent laws allow the use of patented inventions for experimental research, provided the research relates to the subject matter of the invention. For example, if the patent were for a new type of thermometer, experiments to see whether the thermometer worked, or to improve upon it, would not infringe. But making and using the thermometer to take temperatures in a completely unrelated experiment would require permission from the patent owner. Of course, if the researchers had bought a thermometer from the patent owner, they would have implied permission to use it to measure any temperature. There are also special defences relating to pharmaceuticals.

Plant variety rights

Plant breeders' rights over registered plant varieties confer exclusive rights to propagate the plants and sell them. Farmers have the right to save and sow seed, but otherwise the rights extend down generations of plants. As with patents, acts which are private and non-commercial do not infringe. The defences are wider than under patent law – experiments generally do not infringe, nor do acts carried out for the purpose of breeding another variety.

Registered designs

Designs registered in Europe confer absolute protection, against all-comers, if registered. There can be infringement without copying. There are various permitted uses, including:

- private use for purposes which are non-commercial
- use for experimental purposes

- fair reproduction for teaching or citation, providing there is acknowledgement of source

- using a component to restore the appearance of a product

There are two ways in which a design can be registered in Europe. Registered Community Designs are recorded at the Office for Harmonisation in the Internal Market and are protected in all countries of the European Union. National registrations are subject to similar laws but are registered at national offices and protected locally.

Unregistered design right

Unregistered designs are protected only against copying. Again, there are two legal regimes in Europe. Regulation (EC) No 6/2002 of 12 December 2001 on Community Designs creates protection for unregistered designs for a period of three years from publication of the design. Unregistered Community Designs are subject to the same defences as registered designs. The UK also protects unregistered designs by design right which begins earlier (on creation of a design document or prototype) and lasts longer (10–15 years depending upon speed of marketing) but has more exceptions; during the last five years of UK design right, infringers will not be ordered to stop if they undertake to obtain a licence.

Registered trade marks

Registration gives exclusive rights to use a mark in the course of trade. For this reason it is rare for a researcher to infringe a trade mark. The rights may be infringed by using an identical or similar mark, on identical products, on similar products, or (if the mark is well known) in dissimilar products. Trade mark or unfair competition laws may be used to restrain cybergriping websites, that is, those that are devoted to the denigration of trade marks and their owners. However, the authorities will bear in mind the importance of freedom of expression. For example, Greenpeace in France opposed activities of the oil company Esso and published critical material and slogans referring to Esso as E$$O. Esso sued for infringement of its trade marks, but Greenpeace contended that their material was protected by the principle of freedom of speech. Esso's case was rejected by the Court of Appeal in Paris at the preliminary stage and ultimately dismissed.

Passing off/unfair competition

Likewise, passing off rights and unfair competition are usually invoked in commercial situations. The most generally recognised principle of these laws is to protect traders from acts which confuse and divert their customers or which unfairly tarnish their reputation.

Breach of confidence

Confidential or undisclosed information is often protected by general principles of equity or fairness in competition. In Commonwealth countries, the legal action for breach of confidence is recognised as protecting non-trivial information of various kinds:

- personal information (which may also be protected by privacy or data protection laws)

- commercial information, often called trade secrets

- government information, which may also be protected by Official Secrets Acts

Information will only be protected as long as it remains secret. If it enters the public domain, it will no longer be protected generally. However, someone who obtains or publishes information in breach of a duty of confidence may be restrained from using it, under the principle that a citizen should not profit from wrong-doing.

Very often, information is passed on in confidence for a specific and limited purpose. An example would be a confidential curriculum vitae or reference for a candidate being interviewed. The interviewers may refer to the documents in conducting the interview, but should not use or disclose them without permission for unrelated purposes.

The most important defence to breach of confidence is the public interest. This may coincide with the freedom of expression, especially where publication is in the public interest. However, there may be a public interest in more limited disclosure, for example in informing the relevant authorities about a breach of the law.

Although information may be protected by confidentiality agreements, very often the circumstances and nature of the information will demonstrate that it is confidential. Great care must be exercised, for example, in using information about patients in medical research. It may be proper to use scientific information, but in a way that does not reveal the identity of the patient. Ethical committees are often available to advise or rule on this. Researchers who are in doubt should seek advice before disclosing confidential information. In the United Kingdom, the Economic and Social Research Council spells this out in its *Key Conditions For ESRC Studentships*, under the heading 'Research Ethics and Confidentiality' (see Chapter 4):

2.112   Should any ethical considerations arise in the design or conduct of your proposed postgraduate study, you and your supervisor(s) should address these explicitly. Full consideration should be given to such ethical implications drawing on any ethical standards which are appropriate to your discipline. In particular, you should ensure that:

- you are aware of any published material on research ethics relevant to your discipline or field of study, such as guidelines published by Learned Societies;
- potential ethical issues are identified and built into the design of the research at an early stage;
- you are open and honest about the aims, methods and intended use of results from your postgraduate studies; and
- that confidentiality of data on individuals is maintained within the limits of the law.

Intellectual property and research contracts

Contracts are made between specific parties – individuals or bodies such as companies and other corporations. Most universities, but not individual departments, will be corporations with legal personality – they enjoy legal rights and incur legal obligations independently of members, shareholders, academics or other persons.

Contract between student and university

Enrolment of a research student at a university involves a contract or bargain between the student and the university. This will be on specific terms – a research student studying for a doctorate or Masters award will have rights and obligations *vis-à-vis* the university. In many cases these terms are set out in a student handbook and/or on the university's intranet. If you have a question on intellectual property which is not covered by this information, you should seek out the university's intellectual property officer. He or she may be contactable through a licensing office – sometimes called 'technology transfer' or 'knowledge transfer' department or 'industrial liaison office'. Often copyright issues are dealt with separately and you may find that the university library is the best starting point.

If you are employed by the university, then the conditions of service for research staff will apply to you. These are usually the province of the personnel or 'human resources' department.

Contracts with funding bodies

There may be other contracts relevant to your work. For example, if your research is funded by a studentship from a government funding organisation, you will need to refer to the terms of that studentship. These will usually include guidance or conditions about data deposit, publication of research results, ownership of intellectual property and exploitation of intellectual property. For example, the UK's Economic and Social Research Council states:

> Students are advised to refer to the ESRC data policy that is available on the ESRC Website. As an ESRC-funded student, you are strongly encouraged to offer copies of any machine-readable data for deposit at the Data Archive, or, if your dataset is qualitative, you should offer a copy to the Qualidata archival resource centre: both archives are located at the University of Essex and you should contact whichever is more appropriate. (Key Conditions for ESRC Studentships, para 2.108)

> The ESRC leaves decisions on whether the results of a student's work are published to the discretion of the student and supervisor. However, if a decision is made to publish any of your work, as an ESRC-funded postgraduate student it must include an acknowledgement of ESRC financial support. Details of any published papers, including those published jointly with your supervisor(s), should be sent to the ESRC. (Key Conditions for ESRC Studentships, para 2.110)

Although the UK Economics and Social Research Council does not claim rights in the intellectual property generated by the students it funds, it encourages students to ensure they do not enter into other agreements which might involve suppression of results and it encourages universities to make provision for exploiting students' results and sharing the rewards.

Contracts with university spin-off companies

Some projects are carried out under the auspices of university spin-off companies. Sometimes these have their own premises off-campus, and sometimes their activity is less clearly separated from the university.

Contracts with industrial or commercial organisations

University collaborations with the private sector can benefit research students by funding their projects. The contracts are usually between the outside organisation and the university. In principle, the university can only contract away any intellectual property which it owns, so the effect of these contracts on research students depends upon the relationship between the student and the university as well as that between the university and the commercial sponsor. Your own position may therefore be governed by two sets of terms: (1) the province of the student registry and (2) the province of the industrial liaison or knowledge transfer department.

Contracts subject to specific legislation

Finally, you should be aware that many countries have specific legislation governing the ownership of inventions made by employed or academic researchers. This may set out matters such as a duty on researchers to disclose inventions to the university, a duty on the university to claim or disclaim its rights, to file for patents and to share net income after the payment of patent fees. Such specific laws are less common for other forms of intellectual property.

Your intellectual property audit – a checklist

1. Subject matter

    -   Consider what original material you are producing as a result of your research and try to match it up with the subject matter of intellectual property rights summarised in Table 7.1

    -   Note whether the rights arise automatically or whether you would need to seek help in registering rights

2. Relationship with the university

    -   Check the terms of your enrolment

    -   Identify the university departments you may need to contact for advice, help, or disclosing of inventions

3. Relationship with funding body or company

    -   Check the terms of any funded studentship you receive

4. Specific laws

- You may need to consult the laws of the country in which you are based for your research. These can often be found on the website of the World Intellectual Property Organisation

5. International treaties

- National laws should conform to any international treaty which that country has signed and ratified (put into effect). The most important for researchers are listed below.

Further reading

Intellectual Property – International Conventions and Treaties

(Details of these are available at www.wipo.int/treaties/en/)

Agreement Between the World Intellectual Property Organisation (WIPO) and the World Trade Organisation (WTO)

Berne Convention for the Protection of Literary and Artistic Works

Brussels Convention Relating to the Distribution of Programme-carrying Signals Transmitted by Satellite

Budapest Treaty on the International Recognition of the Deposit of Microorganisms for the Purposes of Patent Procedure

Convention for the Protection of Producers of Phonograms Against Unauthorised Duplication of their Phonograms

Hague Agreement Concerning the International Deposit of Industrial Designs

International Union for the Protection of New Varieties of Plants (UPOV)

Lisbon Agreement for the Protection of Appellations of Origin and their International Registration

Locarno Agreement Establishing an International Classification for Industrial Designs

Madrid Agreement Concerning the International Registration of Marks

Madrid Agreement for the Repression of False and Deceptive Indications of Source on Goods

Nairobi Treaty on the Protection of the Olympic Symbol

Nice Agreement Concerning the International Classification of Goods and Services for the
Purposes of the Registration of Marks

Paris Convention for the Protection of Industrial Property

Patent Cooperation Treaty (PCT)

Patent Law Treaty (PLT)

Protocol Relating to the Madrid Agreement Concerning the International Registration of Marks

Rome Convention for the Protection of Performers, Producers of Phonograms and
Broadcasting Organisations

Strasbourg Agreement Concerning the International Patent Classification

Trademark Law Treaty

Treaty on the International Registration of Audiovisual Works (Film Register Treaty)

Vienna Agreement Establishing an International Classification of the Figurative Elements of
Marks

Washington Treaty on Intellectual Property in Respect of Integrated Circuits

WIPO Copyright Treaty (WCT)

WIPO Member States

WIPO Performances and Phonograms Treaty (WPPT)

WTO Trade Related Agreement on Intellectual Property Rights (TRIPs)

Books on UK and EC law, with relevance to Commonwealth jurisdictions

Cook, T. (2002). *A User's Guide to Patents*. London: Butterworths.

Davis, J. (2003). *Intellectual Property Law* (2nd edn). London: LexisNexis UK.

Jacob, R., Alexander, D. and Lane, L. (2004). *A Guidebook to Intellectual Property* (5th edn).
London: Sweet & Maxwell.

Jones, H. and Benson, C. (2002). *Publishing Law* (2nd edn). London: Routledge.

Norman, S. and Chartered Institute of Library and Information Professionals (Great Britain)
(2004). *Practical Copyright for Information Professionals: The Cilip Handbook*. London: Facet.

Padfield, T. (2004). *Copyright for Archivists and Users of Archives* (2nd edn). London: Facet.

Christie, A. and Gare, S. (2004). Blackstone's Statutes on Intellectual Property (7th edn). Oxford: Oxford University Press.

Wilson, C. (2002). *Intellectual Property Law in a Nutshell*. London: Sweet & Maxwell.

Cases

Ashdown v Telegraph [2002] Ch 149

Beloff v Pressdram [1973] 1 All ER 241

Esso v Greenpeace [2003] ETMR 35; [2003] ETMR 66 Cour d'Appel (Paris); [2004] ETMR 90 (substantive hearing)

Geographia Limited v Penguin Books Limited and Others [1985] FSR 208

Hubbard v Vosper [1972] 2QB 84

Hyde Park v Yelland [2001] Ch 143

Lion Laboratories Ltd v. Evans [1985] QB 526

Newspaper Licensing Agency v Marks & Spencer Plc [2003] 1 AC 551

Pro Sieben Media AG v Carlton UK Television Ltd [1999] 1 WLR 605; [1999] FSR 610

Sillitoe v McGraw-Hill [1983] FSR 545

Websites

Authors' Licensing and Collecting Society: www.alcs.co.uk

British Copyright Council (UK umbrella organisation; website contains much useful information on copyright and links to the websites of its member organisations in various creative sectors): www.britishcopyright.org

Copyright Licensing Agency (reprography, UK): www.cla.co.uk

Design and Artists Copyright Society (licensing of artistic works, UK): www.dacs.org.uk

European Commission's copyright pages: europa.eu.int/comm/internal_market/copyright/documents/documents_en.htm#directives

Music Publishers' Association (UK): www.mpaonline.org.uk

Office for Harmonisation in the Internal Market (European Community Trade Mark and Design Office, has good explanatory material): www.oami.eu.int/en

UK Patent Office: www.patent.gov.uk

UK IP portal (these have excellent links to the websites of other intellectual property organisations, including those representing users): www.intellectual-property.gov.uk

United States Copyright Office: www.copyright.gov/fls/fl102.html

World Intellectual Property Organisation: www.wipo.int

Writing Dissertations, Theses and Reports

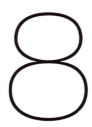

Nigel Fielding with Jonathan Allen

- Writing dissertations and theses is an essential rite of passage in higher education, and represents an important source of new knowledge (Rhind, 2003). Such writing has a dual role: demonstrating a grasp of professional norms and standards, and marking a first foray into the professional literature, to which writers will thereafter contribute reports of their research.

- This chapter profiles the structure of social science dissertations and theses.

- It outlines the process of writing a research report.

- It illustrates this field of professional practice with a case study.

- The chapter also profiles the experience from a graduate student's perspective and provides links to further information.

Dissertation and thesis structure

This section is about writing extended documents as a coursework requirement at graduate level (in the UK, the written product of a Masters research project is often called a 'dissertation' and that of a PhD project a 'thesis', while in the USA the terminology is generally reversed; this chapter uses UK terminology). As with any recipe, readers may interpret the advice in relation to their own tastes and their programme's requirements. What follows are guidelines, not rules. Dissertations and theses are likely to be the most substantial writing projects the learner has yet tackled and can seem forbidding. Clarity about their requirements and purposes helps us keep on target. Such work has three main goals: communicating findings and/or theoretical interpretations, persuading readers that the analysis appropriately relates to the subject matter, and demonstrating mastery of the discipline and medium.

These goals apply whether the project is library-based, analysing existing literature, or empirically-based, involving collecting original data. In either case, clarity of expression is important. Even the most sophisticated material benefits from a clear, direct writing style. Tortuous prose betrays unclear thinking, as examiners know. It is good practice to:

- use necessary technical terms but avoid jargon

- write in short, simple sentences

- organise the argument logically

- offer signposts to readers

- be alert to structure: there should be a distinct beginning, middle and end

Some may prefer to draw on these practices in their first draft while others might apply them at the editing stage. Uncluttered writing style, logical topic sequencing, and attention to the balance between parts, make for effective narratives in any genre. We can thus draw on personal networks to help fine-tune them, even if a peer, partner or parent lacks specialist knowledge of our topic (Becker, 2004). Telling others a story often exposes gaps or haziness in one's argument. Cicero maintained that 'no man truly understands a thing until he writes about it'. Further, study circles formed by trading drafts can establish lasting collegial networks. Mention of narrative does not mean that dissertations or theses must tell the story of the whole research *process*. The main purpose is to communicate results and one's interpretation. This is seldom best done by a blow-by-blow account, although a judicious element of this may be called for in the methodology section.

Any graduate programme worth its fees offers a style guide stipulating the components of the dissertation or thesis. Obtain a copy when you begin planning your dissertation or thesis. A central ingredient is the length requirement. Social science can take many words to report, although this varies between research approaches (quantitative versus qualitative methodologies, conceptual versus empirical pieces). Maximum word limits can be a challenging constraint. Writing to length is a discipline. The first draft of my PhD was four times longer than the maximum. Even though I naturally regarded my topic as the most interesting thing in the world, no one could make such an investment in reading one document. In the UK, a Masters dissertation is often in the range 10,000–20,000 words, and a doctoral thesis up to 100,000 words (with a considerably lower norm). It helps to orientate to length requirements from the outset and remind oneself while drafting. Limits set in the tens of thousands may make it seem like one has boundless space, but the reality is more often constraining.

If you start by brainstorming a rough structure you can estimate how long each main part should be (a rule of thumb is that the Introduction should not exceed 10 per cent of overall length), and this can guide the drafting process. Readers will mainly be interested in what you have found that is new, so reserve most space for the findings and analysis sections. In a 15,000-word dissertation, one might allow 1,500 words for the Introduction (highlighting the research question), 2,000 for the literature review (not everything written on the subject but only literature directly relevant to your research question), 1,500 words for the methodology, and 2,000 for the conclusion (including a modest element of summary but mostly pinpointing the significance of the findings). That makes 7,000 words, which leaves the same amount to report and interpret all your findings. Since postgraduate essays are often limited to 5,000 words, the parts of your dissertation requiring you to come up with something brand new are just a bit longer than an essay.

This is just an illustration and no substitute for planning your document with your supervisor and according to local regulations and norms. Regulations may include in the overall count all or some of reference lists, tabular and graphical material, data extracts, and appendices (containing access letters, research instruments, etc.). Check your programme regulations and if these are unclear, ask. As to the agony of cutting material, there are three solaces: (i) you are in good company, nearly everyone overwrites; (ii) there are lots of ways to save length; (iii) anyone committed to a field can find another use for the material.

How important is it that your dissertation or thesis has a conventional structure and the right number of words in each section? Not very. These things are looked at if the overall quality falls flat and there is an enquiry into what went wrong. So the following conventions are a recipe around which one can be creative. Having said that, the conventions have served many researchers well. Examiners will expect to find something resembling the conventional structure below, but will accept variations better fitting the topic. For instance, qualitative research can require adjustment of the structure to accommodate illustrative data.

Some find outlines a handy way to capture the structure and will elaborate them as their thinking develops. The familiar 'topic outline' encourages an orderly, logical sequence. A '*sentence* outline' takes each line in the topic outline as the first sentence of a paragraph in the final product, which helps writers get started (O'Connor and Woodford, 1978). Planning software for authors (e.g. *Storyspace*) and idea-mapping software (e.g. *Decision Explorer*) can also be useful. Enough of the preliminaries, let's turn to the structure.

Title

This should be brief, exact and descriptive, staking out the topic with precision. Snappy titles may not sell dissertations (or books) but they do not hurt. Titles in active form and/or putting a catchphrase in a new light can excite interest (e.g. 'Joining forces' for a study of police training; Fielding, 1988).

Abstract

Most programme regulations stipulate an abstract, often 100–150 words for a dissertation, 300 for a thesis. Abstracting services use them to compile lists of dissertations and theses in university libraries that other researchers may consult. So dissertations and theses are a first step into the published literature. Abstracts conventionally present conclusions first, then sample and method. They should not include citations to other literature. In research reports, the Executive Summary is the equivalent of an abstract. Research users may read only the summary, which should be self-contained and direct.

Introduction

Introductions specify the research question, show why it is important and how it relates to existing knowledge, sketch how your research addressed it, and profile the dissertation/thesis structure. Introductions position dissertations/theses without trying to be exhaustive. They can be combined with the literature review or may stand alone. Some prefer to write the Introduction last, once they know what they are introducing. A common fault of academic writing is withholding conclusions until last. Research is seldom sufficiently suspenseful to merit a mystery novel format, and such structures leave readers to speculate over what was found for much of the document. Some will turn first to the conclusion or findings anyway, so it is often best to tell readers what the broad conclusion will be in the Introduction. This helps them see why each subsequent part is relevant and builds towards the logic of the conclusion.

It need only be a broad indication, for example, 'based on interviewing teachers and children, this study found that the established link between ethnicity and educational achievement is affected by teacher commitment'.

Literature review

The purpose is to show how your work proceeds from previous work and is informed by promising lines and pitfalls exposed by previous contributors. There is also a pedagogical demonstrator function, showing that one has read the right stuff, signifying one's claim to membership of an intellectual community. Even if a sub-text is to show examiners you've done your homework, it identifies the intellectual scope of the study, so should be grasped firmly. The demonstrator element is not an end in itself. Its main value is to set up the research question and how you will answer it, which requires a targeted review focused sharply on the approach you have taken. Becker (2004) refers to some being 'terrorised by the literature', the intimidating effect of a literature that seems to have no bounds being exceeded only by the fear of finding a study that has already done what you have. Taking a no-nonsense approach can slay these dragons (even studies with similar research designs cannot be identical, if only because the second will inhabit a research universe altered by the existence of the first). There is seldom a case outside librarianship for attempting a comprehensive review of every study there has ever been on your topic. Examiners know that a sign of a refined intellect is the ability to discriminate the key ideas and studies from the also-rans. A keen literature review is an exercise in judgement, not a catalogue. This is so even in doctoral theses, although their intellectual reach is usually more expansive, justifying a more extensive review. Even those following the supervisor's traditional advice to read around the topic should remember that this will expose some dead-ends. Only mention items if they contribute to your enquiry, not just because their subject matter is in your field.

Theory

This may be a stand-alone chapter or be covered in the introduction/literature review. The idea is to declare what theoretical approach(es) you have adopted and why (which may involve describing approaches you rejected, and why). The question is not best answered 'because I like it' or 'because it's the one I understand', although any strong intellectual commitments should be declared. Theoretical approaches are best justified by their fit to the phenomenon (where you draw on the published arguments of others), to the data (where you invoke your own judgement about the data) or because they have not previously been applied to the topic (where you need to address reasons for this). In giving your account of theory it is seldom necessary to think in terms of the kind of 'grand theory' representing major schools of thought, such as Marxism. Unless you are practising to be a theoretician, theory will be applied at the conceptual level, although grand theory may be mentioned as part of the positioning effort. Thus, research into hypnotism workshops might be positioned against a 'negotiated order' conceptualisation (Kidder, 1981) and the concept's derivation from symbolic interactionism noted, but one need not then give a synopsis of symbolic interactionism. At this level anyone likely to read your dissertation or thesis will know what that is. Effort saved in re-hashing grand theories should be invested in introducing the concepts used. You must define them, identify refinements to accommodate your study, and describe the relationships between concepts applied to your research question.

Methods

While some find this boring, it is the basis of your claim to have contributed to the field. Critics who doubt your findings will look here for ammunition to attack your work. You should state the research design – the study's overall strategy – and why it was appropriate to the topic, indicating why other designs were not. It is acceptable to say that a given design was too demanding for a student project, though you may need to show you've genuinely thought it over rather than done what's easiest. You should follow the research design statement with information about some or all of the following:

- access
- instrument design (e.g. questionnaire) and research method
- sampling (size, sample design, respondent characteristics)
- sources of data and when data were collected
- biases and other limitations
- response rate
- data analysis technique(s)

When discussing research instruments you should indicate whether you have applied a previously used instrument (and whether it is a validated instrument, as in much psychometric work) or designed your own. Analysis software can be mentioned here. In empirical projects there should be a statement about research ethics, including any problems encountered, whether you followed the code of a professional association, and any arrangements for fieldworker security (See Chapter 4). In projects based on secondary analysis (analysis of data previously collected by others), you should indicate where the data were obtained, any stipulations on their use, and where the original analysis was reported.

If you have used a standard procedure in a standard way, you do not need to specify it further. For example, a dissertation/thesis is not a place to rehearse how to calculate statistical significance. You should provide detail (including a justification) if you have modified a standard procedure, or pioneered a procedure. For example, if you added to the standard five-point Likert scale, it is not enough to say you used a modified Likert scale, you should say why you needed the extra points. The methods discussion is to show how you reached your conclusions and allow readers to evaluate them, not to enable exact replication. While exceptional and even dramatic things can happen in research, you should only include those affecting the basis or interpretation of results. An untoward proposition by an interviewee may affect the data and your interpretation and therefore merits mentioning. However, being chatted up by the taxi driver before the interview probably would not.

Results

The previous sections have told readers what gap in knowledge your study addresses, and how. With the results section you finally get to say what you achieved. As the genuinely new aspect of your study, readers will likely be most interested in this section, particularly in research reports (where demonstrating mastery is less often a consideration). This means you need to get to the point promptly, giving a brisk account of what has been found. You should place this against relevant analytic points but not let such contextualisation crowd out the findings (the exception being a theoretical piece, where elaboration of your conceptualisation replaces findings).

It is only necessary to present the data required to confirm your findings. Leave out anything not fitting that rule, no matter how interesting or bizarre. Do not include raw data except brief quotations from interviews or fieldnotes that usefully illustrate findings. In quantitative work, findings will be conveyed by tables, statistical coefficients and diagrams. In qualitative work, there is much summarising to do, with extracts confined to those epitomising a given point or contradicting the general run of opinion. Offer an account of what you found rather than how you came to find it. The process of discovery is not for inclusion (but may be discussed in the Methods section, if important in contextualising findings), nor are lines of enquiry that did not pan out. To explain how you reached a finding you must sometimes detail the statistical procedures or the context in which an item of qualitative data emerged. This is the main exception to the rule of only presenting the data necessary to confirm your findings, as you may need to discuss, for example, alternative statistical tests that were tried.

Discussion and conclusion

The Discussion section may be separate, with results analysed against relevant concepts and the research aim, followed by a Conclusion summarising the study and stating what it has contributed, or both functions may be combined in a single Conclusion. Either way the text should relate to the positioning discussion in the Introduction, showing how the research aims were addressed. The Discussion/Conclusion has a different tone from the Results section, because inferences and generalisation beyond the data are allowed. While flights of fantasy should be avoided, having new findings warrants speculation about their significance, and/or identifying defects in previous contributions. Cynics suggest that the near-ritual call for further research appears here simply to justify the next grant application but the legitimate purpose is the measured speculation a researcher informed by these findings can make about their significance. The main text should end with a summary of findings, remembering that, particularly in research reports, readers will look first at the end for what has been found before deciding to read the whole report. The most important point should be the last. Last sentences should not address a specific result and it is better to end with your voice than a data extract.

Notes, references and appendices

Avoid notes if you can. Things sufficiently important to merit mention should be in the main text. Notes divert readers from the main argument. If you feel compelled to include occasional notes, don't mix footnotes and end-gathered notes.

References must be presented consistently, following the format laid down by your programme. Avoid referring in-text to sources not in the reference list, or leaving items in the list that were deleted from the text in re-drafting, by using word-processor search features. See Walker and Taylor (1999) for conventions for referencing online sources. When citing a chapter in an edited collection, the in-text reference need only contain the chapter author's surname, not the editor's as well (thus, 'Fielding, 2006' rather than 'Fielding in Gilbert, 2006'). Even experienced writers sometimes fail to keep references in the detail required. For instance, direct quotation from publications requires page references, but it is easy to forget to record them when making notes. It can take hours to go back to sources; a note-taking template with standard reference elements would remind you what to include.

Even where appendices do not count towards word limits they are not a dump for everything that might be nice to include. Appendices are the place for lists (e.g. field-work sites), supplementary tables, instruments like interview schedules, and access correspondence, but not raw data (e.g. transcripts).

Structure

Each main section needs a beginning, middle and end. The beginning sets up the point to be made in the section, the middle makes the point, and the end says what point has been made and what needs to be considered next. Explicit links between sections convey the sense of an articulated argument held together by a central thread. Each section except the Introduction should have a descriptive title, either conventional (e.g. Findings) or substantive (e.g. Implications of Sex Segregation).

There are other structures than the one described above that address particular purposes and that the more sophisticated writer can pull off (see Hammersley and Atkinson, 1994). For example, the 'chronology' follows the career of an occupational group (from recruitment through training to practice) or temporal processes such as cycles of medical treatment (onset/diagnosis/treatment/outcome). The 'zoom lens' approach varies between events in micro (interaction in one classroom) through meso (the functioning of a school) to macro (the education system). The most prominent alternative format is 'thematic', where findings are interleaved with concepts to which they relate, giving several findings chapters, each on a particular theme (e.g. a study of gangs might have themes of membership, relations with authorities, and relations with other gangs). The main thing is to consider what structure to adopt before you start writing and to stick to the purpose of each section, keeping a watchful eye on the balance between sections so they each do their job without over-developing one at the others' expense.

The writing process

Getting started is often the most difficult step. Preparing an outline, or single paragraph statement of the ground to be covered, helps divide the drafting process into manageable chunks. Such devices also help keep writing consistent. Periodically checking them reminds writers where the current segment fits in the overall scheme and identifies irrelevant material that can be cut.

It is important to know your audience. A dissertation's primary audience is the supervisor and examiners, and similarly with a thesis, possibly supplemented by specialists in the field. Examiners are chosen for relevant expertise so are likely to have relevant publications. It is wise to cite something the examiner has written on the topic! In reports for policy makers it is sensible to refer to related work sponsored by the same body, and/or relevant policy instruments (e.g. consultation papers).

It is general practice to anonymise research participants, and if data extracts name others, to anonymise them too. Unless you have an analytic commitment to the precise way speech was uttered, you can lightly edit extracts, removing ums and ahs, and insignificant self-corrections. Use conventional spelling – don't attempt to transliterate accents. If dialect is used, it should appear as it was said. Only correct grammar if it is essential for intelligibility and indicate which words are yours (often shown in square brackets). Giving extracts an informative but anonymous identifier (e.g. 'Constable, two years service') helps readers tell when quotes are from the same speaker, to see if particular respondents are quoted a lot and build up an impression of particular respondents.

Checking such matters can be helped by trading drafts with peers, which can yield constructive, on-target criticism because it comes from others writing for the same purpose and tackling similar issues in the craft of constructing a persuasive argument. It helps to control the feeling that drafts must be perfect before anyone can see them. Working in research teams often has similar effects. Getting the view of partners, relatives or friends is also useful. They can detect spelling or grammatical errors, and their outsider's view can help check whether your argument is clear. Co-counselling and mutual support help students survive demanding courses.

Other craft skills may be useful. Faults like gaps in the argument can be exposed by working on something else for a while. It can refresh your perspective and spark new thinking, provided one doesn't leave drafts too long. Another trick is reading drafts backwards, starting at the last paragraph, then reading the previous one and so on.

This is surprisingly effective in checking that what is needed to make a point is all in place, but is best reserved for key passages as it is time-consuming.

It can be helpful to prepare a timetable with the deadline at the top and listing key stages (e.g. in an empirical project, research design, data collection, data analysis, first draft, revision and editing, final draft with complete references and appendices). You can then gauge how long is needed for each stage and create a schedule, allowing extra time for difficult elements or other commitments.

These approaches are about construing writing projects as a series of steps rather than one huge task. They avoid the situation where you sit at your desk with a stack of data and pad of blank paper, prime circumstances engendering the famous writer's block. Armed with your timetable, you are in a good position to do some writing every day and progress steadily. Many professional authors set themselves a daily quota of words, having learned how long they can write before creativity and attention lapse (when they turn to other work, such as checking references).

The purpose of first drafts is to get something on to paper about each point on your outline, rather than to be definitive or polished. Some text can simply be a placeholder, reminding you a given point needs to be made when all the data are in hand or you have figured out what you want to say. Some blast through the first draft, taking no great care over any point that would delay them. They then hone the argument and polish the prose during the editing stage. This has several benefits: one briskly achieves a full draft, writing in a sustained effort makes for coherence of argument, and it encourages economy of expression.

Of course, it also elevates the importance of the editing stage. In dissertation projects or sponsored research there is often time only for one main edit following the first draft. Editing is when you have to exchange placeholder tokens for real statements that you will stand by. For example, in first drafting you may recognise that your data shows the effect both of ethnicity and socio-economic status on educational achievement, and that these factors are interrelated. At editing you need to decide precisely how much influence your data suggests each factor has and the extent to which effects are amplified by their different combinations. One has to be as precise as one's data permit without overstating the case. A single study is unlikely to produce the definitive analysis. The best service researchers can perform is to encapsulate as precisely as possible what their particular study contributes, so others can gauge its implications. The professional approach does not over-claim but demonstrates the warrant for material that genuinely contributes and connects it with other work, making for a cumulative body of knowledge.

As well as those lofty aims, careful editing not only improves your argument's coherence but makes it a better read. Scholarly writing is notorious for pomposity, long-windedness and jargon. Some complaints about jargon simply reflect the frustration of interested outsiders who lack specialist knowledge, but it is wise to monitor if you are using special terms because they are apt and necessary or as a badge to signal membership. Attending closely to your wording will expose metaphors that don't precisely apply, stale catchphrases, and overly complicated prose that masks muddy thinking. Reflecting this, many writers make a determined effort to save words while editing. It strengthens clarity and the power of your writing to say the same thing in fewer words; a rule of thumb is to shorten the draft by at least 10 per cent. Remove unnecessary adjectives, repetition and unnecessary explanations.

Also critical are the spelling and grammatical checks associated with editing, such as dealing with split infinitives and ensuring sentences have a main verb. Make good use of the grammar checkers and spellcheckers built into word-processing software, but do not wholly rely on them; remember that spellcheckers just check that the word is a word, not whether it is the semantically right word, and if writing for British English check that the software is not using US spellings. Do not be so perfectionist that you never finish, but remember that examiners and research users are intolerant of spelling and grammatical errors. Unlike publishing, where copyeditors assist, the buck stops on your desk.

Although writing will always be a subsidiary skill, much social science knowledge, and most of its impact, comes from what is recorded on the page. Unlike, say, engineers, whose work is represented by the production of physical artefacts whose quality can be gauged by their function, the social sciences are in the business of having, and testing, ideas, and these are more likely to register with audiences if they are couched in precise but accessible, engaging prose. The essential thing is that writing is about communication. Following a time-honoured structure is a good way of communicating, but not the only one, and the more practise you get the more you can experiment with less conventional approaches.

Writing reports of applied research

So far we have considered the writing of dissertations, theses and research reports, noting occasional variations. However, writing up research for sponsors and policy audiences poses some distinctive requirements. The advice to 'know your audience' holds emphatically here, and it requires shrewd thinking about the applied research audience to gauge how you should pitch your report. This starts with understanding the purposes for which research was commissioned: to determine the contours of an issue around which to develop or implement a policy, to evaluate a policy's workings and effects, or even to delay change when the commissioning body wants to buy itself time (see Fielding, 1999). These purposes need to be taken into account in selecting findings to highlight and the context in which to present them. Researchers will often have met the body commissioning the research and been briefed on the expected level of detail; increasingly in official research this is closely specified, along with the broad structure and length. Researchers need to think themselves into the perspective of the report's primary users: civil servants involved in policymaking? Politicians? Representatives of special interest groups? Clients of a service? Organisational managers? The report needs to be oriented to primary audiences, but not so narrowly that subsidiary audiences will find it irrelevant or partial.

In research for government, civil servants are more likely than politicians to be interested in research because they hold briefs for longer times and specialise in technical aspects, while politicians move on. If aiming to put your research before a policy audience wider than those who commissioned it, find out which legislators are interested in the issue; legislators pay little attention to unsolicited representations. If uncertain how to target people you think should be interested in your research, a good starting point is the Web – government department websites offer ministerial biographies, departmental press releases and consultation papers. In the UK, the *Civil Service Yearbook* and *Whitehall Companion* list senior civil servants and organisation charts showing their policy areas. *Dod's Parliamentary Companion*, available from university and reference libraries, lists legislators according to their policy interests, and officers of backbench committees and all-party groups. The parliamentary website offers transcripts of debates and memberships of select and standing committees. There is canny advice on influencing policy by research in McGrath (n.d.).

Research relevant to official commissions and inquiries may have an opportunity to influence change. The criminologist Ben Bowling conducted a decade of research on 'violent racism' but was initially too busy with academic work to consider responding to the MacPherson Inquiry into the bungled investigation of the racist murder of the black teenager Stephen Lawrence. A colleague asked, 'If you won't submit research evidence, who will?' Bowling submitted his book along with a summary and recommendations. His research was quoted in the Inquiry and contributed to its conclusions.

He also noted 'there were unexpected benefits. My over-priced book was reprinted within months of publication. A revised paperback edition and consultancies followed' (Bowling, 2004). While he had to research the Inquiry's terms of reference to configure his evidence and be ready to defend his views, many may feel with Bowling that it is the duty of those with relevant knowledge to participate.

Writing an executive summary

The Executive Summary is an essential part of applied research reports. The 'executive' word indicates that it is aimed at people in a position to act on the basis of the report, and the 'summary' word indicates that the essential points are presented in the most efficient way for people with little time. Every evening, ministers are presented by their civil servants with cases full of documents (in Britain, they are called red boxes) to read by the following day when decisions will be made. Imagine your report sitting in one of these cases among dozens of draft laws, statistical graphs, draft press briefings and administrative notes by policy advisors. Not all research reports end up in red boxes – probably rather few – but the image offers a good discipline to inform writing the Executive Summary. It should never exceed 10 per cent of overall report length, to a maximum of five pages.

The Executive Summary's prime business is reporting findings with maximum directness and minimum caveats and complications. There may be an initial one-paragraph sketch of the research issue, focusing on aspects connecting most closely with the primary audience, followed by main findings (often shown in list form, e.g. bullet points), or the main findings list may come first, with the one-paragraph sketch of the research issue following it as context. The main findings are then presented in more detail, each item previously listed as a bullet point being the subject of one paragraph. There is seldom scope to report more than ten main findings and the most important must come first; ten is an upper limit and you should aim not to exceed five. Following main findings, there should be up to two paragraphs on their implications. These should not attempt to guide the hand of those with executive responsibility but to inform them. For example, one might say that a given finding indicates that current policy helps a particular group but disadvantages another. It is for those with executive responsibility to settle the balance. There can be a final paragraph connecting the research with other research (several studies of an issue will often be commissioned and rather than treat them as competition it is best to see it as an opportunity for coordination and collaboration). Final paragraphs may also identify necessary further research.

The policy maker's interest is in what was found and what it suggests should be done. How the findings were arrived at is barely of interest. Only if they may have affected the findings should the Executive Summary refer to the methods or research process (say, a major and relevant unforeseen event that occurred during data collection). Executives assume that those who commission research on their behalf will have chosen the best team for the job and it is a sign of their confidence that they do not want to know how you got your findings, just what they are. It is nevertheless important to forewarn sponsors of methodological weaknesses that may limit their validity and reliability. Choosing whether to include such in the Executive Summary or a covering document depends on how clear and serious the weaknesses are, and it is best to discuss such concerns with organisational contacts.

Many official bodies receive reports in draft and circulate them to advisors, giving researchers advice on changes required before formal acceptance. Where researchers seek preliminary advice on difficult points from organisational contacts it smoothes this review process. If there are points about the research process that you feel simply must be in the Executive Summary, they are best included either as a qualifying state- ment following the sentence about the finding to which they most directly relate, or as a stand-alone 'health warning' at the end of the Executive Summary, at no greater length than one paragraph. The problem should be stated in plain, jargon-free terms ('the response rate was significantly lower for Asian females') and precisely indicate the likely effect ('the effectiveness of the recruitment literature could not be firmly established for Asian women').

Writing a press release

The main function of media releases is to grab the journalist's attention. Polished prose is unnecessary but rules of grammar and spelling should be followed to signal professionalism. Press releases should not generally exceed two pages of double- spaced text. Write in such a way that any intelligent reader can understand it at a glance. Work from the most important findings to the least. Text is sometimes used as is, but sub-editors will remove paragraphs from the bottom of the story until it fits the available space. Date the release (at the top) and if you don't want it used before a par- ticular date (e.g. when the main report appears), put 'Embargoed until [time & date]' in bold at the top. There should be a headline spelling out the main finding, in capital letters and/or bold. Journalists and sub-editors enjoy dreaming up catchy headlines so yours can just be descriptive (but succinct).

The first paragraph gives the main finding and why it is significant; aim for a statement that makes sense even if the rest is ignored. The second paragraph provides details elaborating on the first, including subsidiary findings. To personalise the material (which audiences like, as it gives stories a second dimension), include a quote from one of the researchers; effective quotes often mention policy significance. The main text should end by offering contact details to obtain the report. Below this, 'Notes to Editors' lists the research sponsor and any essential details about how the research was done, e.g. a sentence about the way the questionnaire was administered in a survey-based study (e.g. postal, etc.) and one about the sample (e.g. sample sites). An ESRC booklet listed below (see end of chapter) offers further advice, and specimen good and bad press releases.

Case study: controversial policy research

This case study profiles the dissemination of research in a controversial field of policy research. It is followed by a section on writing a dissertation from a graduate student's viewpoint. These sections aim to bring alive some of the principles expounded above, to help you to see how things work in practice, and as an antidote to the inevitable counsel of perfection when writing in terms of general principles.

In 1987, news broke of a major child sex abuse (CSA) scandal at Cleveland in northern England. Eventually, the whole Cleveland detective squad was investigating allegations resulting from the use on children of a controversial diagnostic technique called the anal dilatation test. The allegations implicated dozens of families, friends and relatives in what appeared to be organised and widespread sexual abuse of children. There was enormous public concern, particularly when experts suggested that certain features indicated ritual practices involving 'satanic abuse'. Investigations elsewhere apparently revealed similar circumstances. The immediate question was whether investigators had happened on a hitherto hidden reality that demolished the general public's view that child sex abuse was the isolated activity of deranged perverts. If so, what were the authorities going to do about it? Police and social workers customarily had frosty relations but rising awareness of network abuse compelled inter-agency cooperation. Awareness was fuelled from one side by research into 'recovered memory syndrome' and from another by a backlash against the 'sexual revolution', seen by fundamentalist religious groups as bringing with it opportunities for paedophilia.

(Continued)

(Continued)

A number of interests were thus involved: scientific (doctors), professional (social workers, police), government (health, criminal justice) and the public (including special interest groups). This meant there were flashpoints of controversy at numerous points. For example, the dilatation test divided doctors (leading to research on its reliability), feminist groups saw CSA as a problem of men (leading to research on females as suspect abusers), and two powerful government departments – Health and the Home Office – were divided over who held responsibility for such cases (leading to research on joint investigation). A colleague and I were approached by a charity promoting research on policing issues to evaluate joint training and investigation. We observed training sessions between social workers and police officers investigating CSA in one police force, interviewed participants, observed investigative interviews with suspected victims and suspected abusers, compiled a set of videos of such interviews, and interviewed relatives of suspected victims.

We published two reports. An interim report responding to the wide concern over CSA appeared after we had enough information to say something useful, but far from definitive. The abstract noted that 'findings emerging so far indicate that the project is regarded as a success by all those directly involved in implementing it', speaking of high commitment and morale, but noting the need for better resources (staff time, but also video to allow re-examination of victim interviews without repeatedly interviewing children). The abstract closed by obliquely noting what we had not yet done: fully analyse the specimen video interviews we had obtained (they proved highly problematic in evidential terms; Fielding and Conroy, 1992), and establish what victims' parents thought (they proved reluctant to speak to researchers, ambivalent about the process, and the clearest conclusion was that parental opinion was coloured by trial outcomes). Reviewing the interim report now, it addressed an 'insider' audience of social agencies and researchers, and its conclusions reflected the incomplete nature of the data and the well-known 'treatment effect' whereby nearly any innovation is well-received initially due to novelty and its originators' enthusiasm.

In the final report our eyes were still on the professional audience. The report was 95 pages long, had an abstract like an academic paper, no Executive Summary, and the subheading on page one bore the daunting words 'The sociological context'. This was not a report that would hit the headlines. While that was not its purpose, a detailed report of a local initiative might address the needs of policy specialists and

(Continued)

(Continued)

investigators but risked not engaging the senior policy makers whose support was necessary in adopting the approach nationwide. By now, too, we had analysed the video interviews and knew what the parents thought, both of which qualified the early assessment. The report's real objective was contained in a letter at the back of my file copy. It confirms to the sponsor that the report was intended as the basis of a book (Fielding and Conroy, 1990). The story of this part of the research is one of researchers whose main orientation was academic and professional-oriented, and whose approach to writing-up was to address an insider audience and rehearse for an academic book. This was not a bad objective but a limited one.

The team gained funding for a national study of joint investigation. New policies were in preparation, putting the official imprimatur on joint practice, and we gained access to 94 per cent of social service departments and every police force. This more elaborate study involved statistical analysis, observation of investigative work, more video analysis and more attention to parental perspectives.

With the national survey results coinciding with a dramatic development – the issuing for the first time of a policy direction by two government departments in unison – it was sensible to seek a higher profile and thus more impact. We organised a London conference chaired by a national expert on CSA, with talks on policy and practice by leading investigators, followed by tailored workshops for police, social services, and family rights workers, and a panel discussion. The event advertising was professionally designed, with drawings by child victims, and the delegates pack facilitated networking. Despite happening during a blizzard, the conference was well attended by investigators, children's and family organisations, officials, researchers and journalists. The Executive Summary related the research to the Cleveland Inquiry's conclusion that the crisis spoke to 'a lack of proper under-standing by the main agencies of each others' functions' (Cleveland Inquiry, 1988: 243). Officials told us our work had contributed to the new approach to child protection.

The broad lesson of this case study is that there are both strategic and tactical considerations in reporting research. Researchers need to consider what they want to achieve and what their sponsors expect, and configure their dissemination effort accordingly. For academics, the most familiar modes and styles of dissemination – the dissertation/ thesis, the monograph, the scholarly article – are not best-suited to research that seeks real world impact.

Case study: A graduate student's viewpoint

Jonathan Allen

On sitting down to write this section, I was initially uncertain how to begin. However, I soon realised that this was strangely useful since this was similar to how I felt four years ago on approaching my MSc dissertation. Looking back, I must admit to a degree of difficulty in recalling some specifics (my ability to repress trauma never ceases to amaze), but what is clear is that it was an arduous and time-consuming process, fraught with numerous set-backs and hiccups, but that ultimately it remains one of the most rewarding pieces of research I have undertaken to date.

I decided to study the phenomenon of 'fear of crime', an interest stemming from my undergraduate professional placement. In particular, I wanted to investigate the (somewhat marginalised) concept of male fear, and this led in the process to questions regarding the validity of measurement tools and disclosure difficulties. The choice of topic was, in retrospect, the most important part of the whole undertaking, and I was fortunate that the project's evolution continually stimulated interest, since by the time the deadline drew near, like for many others, the dissertation became my first and last thought of each day. My advice to anyone about to embark upon their own would simply be to ensure that their topic choice was of real and lasting interest to them.

The first step was reviewing relevant literature. It took much reading (some 70 articles and books) to determine relevance, and it was during this time that further gaps in the field of study became apparent. This was invaluable in helping to cement initial ideas and develop new strands to explore. It also emphasised the value of journal articles and lecturers' stockpiles. However, it became clear that given the limited space for the literature review in the final product, and relative to the project's other demands, excessive time was spent on this phase.

I adopted a multi-method approach, partly because I wanted to take advantage of skills developed during the course while they were still fresh in my mind, but primarily because it best suited the research aims. I decided to survey a sample of men and women and through their responses obtain a follow-up sample for (semi-structured) interview, enabling me to compare responses to the two different instruments. Additionally, I wanted to look at nationally representative data so I undertook secondary analysis of the *British Crime Survey* to complement the local-level information.

Given the time constraints, I chose a student sample. This was not without difficulties. Negotiating access with department heads turned out to be a lengthy process,

(Continued)

(Continued)

but eventually permission was given by all but one of the six approached. The practicalities of conducting the survey were time-consuming. Designing and distributing the questionnaire, then constructing the SPSS database, while relatively straightforward, were also exhausting. Response was naturally a problem (from a heavily over-sampled student population) but speaking to groups post-lecture and placing reminders in departments was surprisingly effective. Two hundred questionnaires were sent (100 to each sex) and 115 returned, of which 46 were from men. However, only six of these agreed to a follow-up interview. Securing the qualitative sample through a quantitative method allowed comparison of responses, although finding time slots to interview the students was difficult and the research suffered a number of cancellations, re-arrangements and 'no-shows'. The interviews themselves were a rich source of data, except for the first, which proved virtually useless due to recording quality (subsequently my testing of recording equipment was nearly compulsive). The transcription process was demanding, and I soon became a strong advocate of the selective transcription approach, to which I switched after transcribing four of the total twelve hours of talk.

Once primary and secondary data collection and analysis were complete, then came the challenge of linking the plethora of data from disparate sources and presenting a coherent and concise picture (while keeping it sociologically grounded). The sheer level of exposition that even the simplest analytical table required became increasingly clear. Some ruthless but essential editing needed to be employed (I found that while drafting can itself be painful, editing is worse). Late in the day I also asked my long-suffering girlfriend to comment on the draft, which was very useful in highlighting some obvious omissions (surely the reader should have known what analysis package I was using?).

Finally, fatigue and the deadline conspired to ensure the report was submitted. The topic itself remains of interest, and perhaps the personal value of the exercise is best demonstrated by the fact that in a professional capacity I have repeatedly drawn on the knowledge that the process provided.

Further reading

Publications

Berry, R. (1994). *The Research Project: How To Write It*. London: Routledge.

Cooper, H. (1998). *Synthesizing Research: A Guide for Literature Reviews*. London: Sage.

Cuba, L. and Cocking, J. (1994). *How To Write about Social Sciences*. London: HarperCollins.

Denscombe, M. (1998). *The Good Research Guide for Small-scale Social Research Projects*. Milton Keynes: Open University Press.

Economic and Social Research Council (n.d.). *Pressing Home Your Findings: Media Guidelines for ESRC Researchers*. Swindon: ESRC.

Johnson, W. (2000). *The Sociology Student Writer's Manual*. Upper Saddle River, NJ: Pearson, Education.

McGrath, C. (n.d.). *Influencing the UK Policymaking Process*. Swindon: ESRC.

Oliver, P. (2004). *Writing Your Thesis*. London: Sage.

Peck, J. and Coyle, M. (1999). *The Student's Guide to Writing*. Basingstoke: Macmillan.

Web resources/relevant organisations

American Sociological Association (for publishing guidelines including the ASA style guide): www.asanet.org

British Sociological Association (for guidelines on ethics, authorship, anti-sexist and anti-racist language): www.britsoc.co.uk

Economic and Social Research Council (for guidelines on presentation and dealing with the media, copyright): www.esrc.ac.uk

Social Research Association (for guidelines on ethics and fieldwork security, and commissioning social research): www.the-sra.org.uk

Government offices:

- www.parliament.uk (House of Commons Library Tel. 0207 219 3000)

- www.northernireland.gov.uk

- www.scottish.parliament.uk

- www.wales.gov.uk

- www.london.gov.uk

- www.firstgov.gov (the US government's official web portal)

ESDS (access and support for UK and international social and economic data): www.esds.ac.uk

UK Council of Graduate Education (promotes best practice in thesis/dissertation supervision): www.ukcge.ac.uk

Writing Articles, Books and Presentations

Rowena Murray

9

- This chapter deals with four forms of written and spoken communication for disseminating research to many different audiences, from the academic to the 'general' reader.
- These forms of communication include academic papers, books, writing for the media and presentations.

The previous chapter dealt with formal academic writing for theses, dissertations and reports. This chapter considers other media for disseminating the results of research. Each section will take you further away from purely academic writing: academic papers still address academic audiences, but for the social sciences particularly there is a wide range of papers and journals; writing a book will probably require you to step back from your academic writing and develop a new story line; writing for the media usually demands not only a different style, but a radical 'reduction' of your work; while for presentations, if they are to work well, you need to think in terms of 'visual writing'. The key skill that holds all this together is translating your academic work and research for different readers.

That this means adjusting structure, style and content is obvious, but the specific ways in which you have to modulate your story are not. Which words do you use? What other structures are available? What are the principles of good practice in each of these media?

Perhaps the most contentious point in this chapter is that you have to learn to write about your academic work in quite 'un-academic' ways.

Academic papers

When you are writing an academic paper, targeting a journal is the first and arguably most important step. There is little point submitting a paper to a journal if you cannot accommodate its agenda. Yet some new writers feel that adapting their work to suit a journal feels like 'cloning'. One way of resolving this dilemma is to think of writing for an academic journal as joining a debate that has been going on, in that journal and elsewhere, for some time. This is one of many occasions where, if you want people to notice your work, you will have to write about it in ways that they recognise. Over the long term, you will find several ways to write about your research, each adapted to the sometimes quite subtle, sometimes quite obvious, differences between journals.

Before you start your paper, therefore, become a 'scholar' of your target journal. Analyse the journal's content, types of paper, styles and structures. For example, take the abstracts of several papers – of the type that you want to write – published in the past year in your target journal and ask yourself the following questions.

Analysing abstracts

- What do the first sentences usually say?
- What kind of statement do they make?
- Do they state the problem, begin the rationale, or what?
- Do they start with the literature: 'A literature review of … shows …'?
- In what terms is new work defined?
- Is the word 'new' ever used? What other words are used?
- Does the last sentence spell out the contribution?
- Are the sentences in the abstracts 'matched' with sections of the papers?

Once you have done this level of analysis, on all the sections of the papers, you will have a clear idea of your writing task. You will know not only the required word length for papers – almost always specified in the 'Instructions for Authors' – but also the relative lengths of different sections. You can then begin to design your paper in a way that is 'calibrated' with the journal's conventions. Of course, you will find variation in the papers published in your target journal, but that variation is not infinite.

Most researchers know the journals in their fields very well – you read them all the time. In some disciplines, academics or supervisors mentor researchers and support them in publishing, but they do not always spell out how they make writing decisions. This type of analysis will help you to make these decisions in a way that is likely to 'fit' the journal.

The second important step is contacting the journal editor directly by email. Not everyone agrees with this strategy, but an 'initial enquiry', by email, can bring you an assessment of the relevance of your proposed paper to the journal's agenda. You can send initial enquiries to several journals at the same time. The editors may reply that they cannot give feedback until you submit your paper, but they may give you an indication of significant minor or major adjustments that would make your paper more relevant to their journal. This is extremely valuable: it saves you wasting time writing a paper that they do not want; it establishes direct contact with your new audience; and, more importantly for your career, it gives you more insight into 'publishability' than simply reading the instructions for authors.

Other important issues are not covered here, such as developing productive writing habits, improving your writing style and writing for high-level journals. These, and other issues, are dealt with in Chapter 8 and elsewhere. A reading list is provided in Murray (2005) and in the Further Reading section of the Writers' Group website (www.strath.ac.uk/Departments//CAPLE/writersgroup).

Books

Before you go any further, you should know that the key point publishers assert again and again is 'don't just send us your thesis … or even chapters of it':

> The [thesis] system must have laid at its door an enormous squandering of creativity, youth, time, and money each year upon the execution of prose works that do not communicate significantly and are therefore dysfunctional. The publisher, upon whom depends much of the scholar's success, usually refuses even to look at them. (Harman and Montagnes, 1976 [2000]: 28)

Whether or not you agree with this view, the fact remains that writing a book proposal means starting with a clean slate. This can be quite liberating. Although it might sound like more work, if you analyse the publisher's list (a similar process to analysing your target journals), you can put together a proposal quite quickly. Try to ignore the feeling that you are not making the most of your thesis; your book will be the product of your development in writing a thesis, not the thesis itself.

You may have to think yourself into a different role, a new voice and a different writing identity and this too can be liberating, as well as an important step in your career:

> Tradition has it that rather than being the first act of the scholar, the [thesis] is the last act of the student. The [thesis] is viewed therefore as the work not of a professional but of a pre-professional. (Armstrong, cited in Harman and Montagnes, 1976 [2000]: 25)

You may have to find a way to capture this new voice – and content – in your book proposal, expressing your 'professional' perspective, not just your 'student' knowledge, perhaps using professional language, rather than researcher's language:

> I suspect that the [thesis] uses more conditional sentences than does any other prose form in the language. The worst offenders in this respect are the social scientists. In these disciplines the young appear to learn early in their careers an inviolable relationship between truth and tortuous conditionality. Thus: *all things being equal, it would appear to be the case that, under given circumstances, it may not be uncommon for writers of [theses] to execute certain prose styles which those who seem to like their English straight and strong might conceivably call a perversion of the language.* (Armstrong, cited in Harman and Montagnes, 1976 [2000]: 29, original italics)

In addition to a shift in language, there are other shifts in moving from thesis to book.

Thesis-to-book: cut the following

- Display of knowledge
- Writing to impress
- Demonstrating ability to handle research
- Detail on methods
- Emphasis on content, not communication
- Pointing out, reminding, referring back and forwards
- Signposts, signals and repetitions
- Apologetic openings
- Warm-up pages
- Detailed literature reviews
- Extended definitions, justifications and reference lists

Arguably, some of these are features of good writing in any context – for example, 'signposts' tell readers where they are going in your text – but you have to use them differently in a book for a wider audience. Compare Nigel Fielding's definition of the 'dual role' of a thesis (Chapter 8) – 'demonstrating a grasp of professional norms and standards, and marking a first foray into the professional literature' – with the purpose of your book: it will not be to demonstrate your grasp of norms, standards, issues or literature, which it will be assumed you already have. Of course, your proposal has to show these qualities, but that is not the purpose of a book. Similarly, the concept of 'originality', fundamental to your thesis, will have a different meaning for your book. What can your book provide that existing books do not? Arguably, therefore, you have to transform every aspect of your thesis: audience, purpose, structure and style.

There are four main steps on the way to writing your book, each giving you an important opportunity to develop your idea: (i) establishing contact with commissioning editors; (ii) writing a book proposal; (iii) revising the proposal in light of reviewers' feedback; and (iv) securing a contract. Only at this last stage, it could be argued, do you have an actual audience and a fixed focus for your book.

The first step is considering who will publish your book. Start by thinking about who publishes the kind of book you want to write. Look at several publishers' websites. Contact more than one commissioning editor. Are they interested, at all, in your idea for a book? Have you made it clear to them how you see it fitting in to their current lists? Have you done the work – briefly, by email – of making that connection for them? If so, do they agree or disagree? Can you go back and make the case to them, perhaps in different terms, now that you know more about their perspectives and priorities? Can you, and are they willing to, develop and sustain a dialogue? If they want to end the conversation, they will soon tell you so.

Perhaps the key choice you have to make is whether your proposed volume will be an academic book or undergraduate textbook. Of course, in some fields there are hybrids, books with elements of both genres. If this is what you want to write most, look for publishers who produce that type of book, or, if you approach other publishers, prepare a persuasive case to put to them that this is a book they could publish.

Your choice of publisher (high/low status) and type of book (academic or textbook) may be shaped by your career goals or by your desire to supplement your income. It is possible to do both, but that probably means writing two books. In that case, your decision is which to progress first.

Once you have a statement of interest from a publisher, which brings no guarantee of a contract, you write a full-blown proposal, using their template. After you have done that, the commissioning editor will probably suggest changes, which you make, as far as is possible. This step may result in a subtle or considerable shift of focus for your book, since you are still developing your ideas, or there may be no more than revisions to do at this stage. Once the commissioning editor is happy with the revised proposal, it will be sent out to reviewers.

Reviews come back and are copied to you. You do further revisions, if the editor wants to take it forward at this stage. Or it may be dropped at this point. Then you wait while the commissioning editor persuades others in the publishing company, including those on the financial side, that they should publish your book. If that works, the commissioning editor will send you a contract.

Your contract will seem quite legal in style, which is appropriate, since it is, after all, a contract. What may interest you more is the information it contains about royalty percentages (10 per cent is probably acceptable), the number of free copies that you will receive when your book is published and, perhaps in a covering letter, details of the delivery schedule. This is where your final and interim deadlines are specified, and you must alert the publishers immediately to any changes in schedule you need. Any delay will shift their slot for the production of your book, but this is manageable if you give them plenty of notice. If there are any clauses in the contract that you do not accept, such as the one about the publishers having the right to publish your next book, check with the publishers, but it may be acceptable for you simply to delete the clause and initial it.

Then you write your book. You might already have submitted 'sample chapters', but only when you have the contract do you write the manuscript. Otherwise, you risk writing a book that is neither exactly what anyone wants nor sufficiently focused through discussion with a publisher.

There will doubtless be variations in this process, and there may be people with experience of different commissioning processes whom you can consult. The more you know about this whole process, the better. Ask those who have been through the process before.

The best approach is to follow the publisher's template for book proposals, but the following template will help you prepare. If your target publisher does not include all of the headings, you can strengthen your proposal by dealing with one or two of them under their headings. The final length of your proposal will be six or seven pages, single-spaced. Once you have filled it all in, ask several people whose judgement you trust and who know the area, and your potential publisher, if possible, to read your draft.

Template for book proposals

NAME OF PUBLISHING COMPANY

BOOK PROPOSAL

TO *Your contact at publisher*
FROM *Your name*
Your address and/or institution
phone
fax
email

CONTENTS *1. Pre-publication Review*
2. Outline of Contents (chapter headings and summaries)
3. Sample Material (chapters, introduction, publications)

DATE

1. **Pre-publication Review**

- **Name and qualifications of author**
- **Address and telephone**

  Home, work or both? phone
  fax
  email

- **Present appointment**
- **Career to date**

  Dates   Posts

- **Publications**

  In this area/in another area
  Comment on one or two, stating relevance to the proposed book, in terms of content, if not approach or style, for example. Show your awareness of the need to change content, style, approach for your proposed book.

  (Continued)

(Continued)

- **Provisional title of proposed work**
  See titles in publisher's current list for examples of titles they have approved.
  Make your working title descriptive and functional, rather than 'catchy'.
- **Subject of proposed book and academic level**
  Describe in terms that speak to experts and non-experts.
- **Purpose of book and way it is achieved**
  Purpose and/or aims or objectives: to ... [list of verbs]
  Method: 'This book will ... Each chapter will ...'
- **Why the book is needed**
  Rationale, context, recent developments, other publications

  'This book is needed because ... There is a growing literature on ... Over the past ten years ... A trend towards/away from ... A need for more information about/in support of ... There is no single text that addresses ... This book will ... My approach draws on years of experience/research/teaching'
- **Principal UK market for the book**
  Do a quick web search and specify markets, or use your current knowledge of the market to generalise more widely.
  'The readership for this book is ... The market for this book is ... This book will have relevance for several disciplines/courses/professions because ... in that ...'
- **Secondary UK markets**
  Consider all possibilities, even if only to rule some out, for example education/professional, undergraduate/postgraduate, 'Guardian readers', continuing professional development, updating, etc.
- **Market in the USA or Europe**
  Consider all possibilities, even if only to rule some out, for example education/professional, undergraduate/postgraduate, continuing professional development, updating, etc.
- **As the course textbook/required text**
  Specify courses, levels, numbers of students.
  'Courses on which this book will be a required text are ...'
- **As one of the course textbooks/recommended text**
  Specify courses, levels, numbers of students.
  'Courses on which this book will be a recommended text are ...'
- **As supplementary reading**
  Specify courses, levels, numbers of students.
  'Courses on which this book will be a recommended text are ...'

(Continued)

(Continued)

- **Professional staff who would use this book**
  Think about different professions.
- **Competitive titles available**
  Review each book separately, say what each does, according to its stated aims (often on the back of the book) and say how your book differs from that. Make a synthesising comment at the end of your review, saying what your book does that existing books do not. 'Existing books deal with ... do a good job of ... are excellent for ... For example, ... aims to ... covers a lot of ground ... focuses on ... is aimed at ... The best known title is ... What it does not do is ...'
- **Advantages of this book over others**
  'The proposed book will focus on ... in more detail ... will provide more ... will be aimed at ... provides a new ... complements existing books by ...'
- **How quickly the book will become out of date**
  About five years? 'It would probably need to be revised after ... years'
- **Approximate number of words**
  As agreed with [contact person at publisher with whom you have discussed this proposal, and say so here] ...
- **Illustrations**
  Approximate number of tables, graphs, photos that you will use.
  Type/style of graphical representations of explanations, models, analyses, etc.
- **Time to delivery of final manuscript**
  Years/months 'from approval of this proposal'.
- **Referees/people qualified to review this proposal**
  Full names, titles, addresses, phone, fax, email, etc.
  Check that they are willing and positive.
- **Further information for evaluation of this proposal**
  Sample material, experience of editing, conference organisation, etc.
- **Chapter headings**
  Attached in separate file.
  Signature(s) .... Date ....

2. Outline of Contents (chapter headings and summaries)

Provide the following

- *chapter titles*
- *authors (if appropriate)*

(Continued)

(Continued)

- *subheadings for all chapters*
- *one or two paragraphs on each chapter*
- *length of each chapter*

3. Sample Material (chapters, introduction, papers)

Full drafts of chapters, or copies of your papers (in print or in progress).
Not chapters of your thesis. Your aim should be to show (a) that you can write, (b) that your writing has been peer reviewed, positively, and (c) that you can complete a writing project.
One or two paragraphs introducing each chapter, its contents, rationale, and how it fits into your overall story line, theme or argument for the proposed book.

Once you have published your book, you have another communication role: promoting your book. For example, you can organise a book launch, inviting interested parties, supportive colleagues, friends, family, in what may be more of a social event than an academic ritual. You can run more than one launch, of more than one type. Your publisher may attend conferences where you present, and you can hold a launch there, drawing it to the attention of one of your peer groups.

There are many other types of promotional activity, each requiring you, potentially, to communicate your work in different ways to different groups (Baverstock, 2001). In the process, you may find that you develop other ideas for other books. Perhaps the best form of promotion, in the sense that it has the widest circulation and the largest audience, is the media.

Writing for the media

Writing for the media brings you into contact with the widest, largest audiences available. Newspapers, magazines, television and radio have much wider circulation figures than any academic journal is ever likely to achieve. More people will find out about your work in the media than in any form of academic communication.

Some academics appear to take up a position of superiority towards colleagues who are successful at communicating through the media. This raises the question of what your goal as a writer is: to satisfy these academics' standards, or to improve your academic profile, or to find ways to communicate your work to different audiences?

In addition, it is becoming more important to communicate your research to the wider community. It can add value to your research. It is one way of building your institution's or research group's profile. Your funders may value it.

As in any other form of writing, however, you have choices to make about content, structure and style: will your words be 'loosely packed or indigestibly squashed' (Hicks, 1999: 63)? There are a few key principles, of which the following may be useful for researchers who are just starting to write for the media:

- One specific example may be more valued than a comprehensive list.
- Finding a topical angle may attract an editor's attention more quickly.
- Decide on whether your material belongs in 'news' or 'features' and contact the right person for that section.

In some instances, however, you have to give your ideas over to a professional writer, perhaps during a phone conversation. Even when you are the sole author of an article, you may not have complete control over what is finally printed under your name.

Once the article is published in the newspaper or magazine, there may be some immediate responses, unlike in academic journals. For example, if you have worked hard to simplify your ideas for a wide audience, you may find that there are some academics who want to position your work as 'simplistic'. On one occasion, when a feature writer for the *Times Higher Education Supplement* and I discussed a possible article about my work, I suggested that the article could focus on the introduction to my book *How to Write a Thesis*, titled, deliberately, provocatively, 'How to Write 1000 Words an Hour'. I suggested some points to the feature writer in a phone conversation, and these were duly included in the article. One week after publication of the article, a letter was published in response:

> The advice given by Rowena Murray in her book *How to Write a Thesis* … is not as ridiculous as it first sounds.
>
> There is a misbelief that writing should await inspiration. In fact, the most productive and satisfying way to write is habitually, regardless of mood or inspiration. Writers who overvalue spontaneity tend to postpone writing, and if they write at all, they write in binges that can be associated with fatigue.
>
> Writers who are writing regularly in reasonable amounts benefit from greater productivity and creativity. (Griffiths, 2002: 13)

If you get this type of response, it pays not to be over-sensitive. Although 'Not as ridiculous as it first sounds' sounds negative, there are positives: (a) my book was featured in the *Times Higher* and (b) the author of the letter makes several positive points, endorsing approaches taken in my book.

The implications of this scenario for other writers are that while we need to disseminate our ideas in this medium, we also have to face up to people's reactions. Does this mean that we should write in less provocative, perhaps less topical, ways? Or should we continue to use that tactic to capture the journalist's attention? There are advantages to having our work featured in the mass media that we cannot get from other forms of publication, but there are often side-effects. It is not possible to control what a journalist writes, but it is possible to focus their thinking in your discussions with them and perhaps in notes you email to them.

You do have to be careful. The person who wrote the case study at the end of this chapter, who was doing a part-time PhD while in a full-time job, having worked in journalism for three years, alerts us to the danger of the question from the media, 'Would you say that …?' If you are asked, for example, 'Would you say that lecturers/ lawyers/teachers/engineers are dinosaurs?', then the safe answer is 'no'. If you do not actually say 'no', you may be quoted saying something more extreme than you would wish to be seen to be saying, particularly in print. In other words, as you are translating your words for a wider audience, be careful that someone does not push that process just a little too far.

This is not to say that you should be put off communicating about your work through the media. In fact, it could be argued that there should be much more communication about academic work in the media. Otherwise its social, academic or economic value – or 'value added' – may diminish, or be perceived as diminished. At worst, its value may not be perceived at all. Perhaps those who choose not to communicate through the media have been 'burned' in the past, because they did not like what a journalist did with their words, or because they felt their work was misrepresented in some way. Perhaps they were too precious about the journalist not using exactly what they were 'told to write'. Whatever the reason, it is a missed opportunity.

If you are offered formal training in this area, accept it. The example used in this section should indicate to you how much there is to be learned about communicating with and through the media. This chapter has provided basic hints and tips, but there is much more to it than can be covered here.

Presentations

This section covers key skills in presenting for academic and other contexts. Your most important consideration may be another shift of style and the words you use in presenting your work to different audiences. Even different academic audiences will have different expectations of your presentations. Your first task is therefore to think through the criteria they will use, either explicitly or implicitly. Standard questions, such as 'What will your presentation provide that might interest them?', can usefully be modulated to 'How will they judge the content of your presentation?'

It can be argued that if your content is good, then your presentations will be fine. People in academic settings can be heard saying this about both academic writing and presenting: if your research is indeed going well, you have no need to worry. Of course, there is some truth in this: you must have something to show for the time, effort and funding expended in your research (although that may not be the main message of your presentations). Your task is to persuade your audience that your work is progressing, that the progress is coherent and that you can communicate it coherently. In other words, even if your work is outstanding, your audience can still be critical. There is value in this, since genuine critique may give you the best indication of how to strengthen your work.

For researchers, therefore, particularly research students, a presentation is a particular type of task, often with a particular purpose: for work-in-progress presentations you have to report on work completed, but also on work that is still ongoing, questions that are still not answered, tangents you have avoided, even potential directions for the next step in your research that remain unclear or only half-formed.

- You have to show some measure of achievement, while demonstrating an understanding of the work still to be done and a sensible strategy for doing it.

- You must provide detail while still giving the overview to show the coherence of the whole project, showing how it all fits together.

- You must be honest in your appraisal of your work, without undermining it, showing an element of internal critique, while anticipating refutations.

- You have to strengthen the case for what you are doing, and have done, while demonstrating your understanding of alternative approaches, their strengths and their weaknesses in general and specifically in the context of your project.

- After your presentation, in discussion, you have to defend your work against critiques, without undermining the questioner, other researchers or yourself.

Research-in-progress, as a story line, is suited to a narrative or process structure. Do not worry that these structures are too simplistic for research; you can always represent what you are doing as a series of events or steps, in which each follows the previous one logically, moving towards an endpoint that connects with the starting point. This requires you, of course, to make that logic and the links between the steps quite explicit. In addition, you can highlight key words: 'Evidence of … increased/ reduced … benefits of … financial savings … value …'. You may qualify some of these statements with words such as 'Apparent … indications of … further research is needed to establish …'. Once you have this logical structure, you may still be asked probing questions. These will help you to develop your thinking, and probably your writing, further.

The purpose and form of your presentation are, therefore, likely to be very different from those of your thesis (see Table 9.1 for a comparison). Clearly, all of the items listed in Table 9.1 are options, though there is a shift towards more economy of style and, perhaps, less detail for presentations. You may find that you have to make up for this in the discussion after your presentation. It depends on your audience, but you can anticipate questions and prepare to provide more detail on the points you decide to make in your presentation.

You should state your presentation's (not your project's) aims and objectives. If you can formulate these in one short sentence, perhaps even in one verb, so much the better. The temptation is always to say more and to define and justify your aims. Try to separate those steps out from your opening sentences and, above all, pause after you

Table 9.1 Differences in purpose and form between a thesis and a presentation

Thesis	Presentation/Poster
Verbal	Visual
Persuasion	Stimulus for discussion
Long sentences	Short
Complex structures	Direct style
Building up to main point	Main point first
Define and explain	Show and illustrate
Presenting an argument	Giving key messages
Closure	Contingent/partial/interim closure

have said your one-sentence statement of presentation aims to let it sink in. If you run on to your next sentence, you are not really managing your audience's listening as well as you can. Even expert audiences, those who are already highly attuned to your subject or to related research, will appreciate this.

Explicitly say what you are going to do in your presentation and what you hope to achieve. Otherwise your audience has to work this out for themselves as you go along. What do you expect from them – to listen, to interact, to ask questions after you have finished talking?

Presentations: aim/purpose/objective?

- To inform (not a purpose in itself – to inform of what, to what extent/level)?
- To give feedback
- To show progress
- To ask questions
- To contextualise your work
- To make connections with others' work
- Looking back, taking stock
- Looking ahead, the next steps/possible directions

Whatever purpose you choose – and it should, usually, be related to what you were asked to do in your presentation and/or the prevailing culture in the environment in which you are presenting – it gives your presentation focus if you say so at the start. If you do not, you are asking the audience to work it out for themselves, which some will do, but others will not bother, and some will not be able to. Alternatively, if you plan to deviate from existing conventions, you should say that and say why.

One good way of clarifying your ideas and deciding which points need to be illustrated, as well as sequencing information, is storyboarding, a process used in many forms of media production, including film and television. It involves roughing out each of your slides on paper, identifying the content and the information to be discussed and putting a rough time on the duration that the slide will appear on the screen, as well as editing out unnecessary information. This forms a fairly detailed overview of your talk and provides a useful guide to work to.

Invest time in establishing a 'look and feel' for your presentation. Some people think this means using the same software templates for all of your slides. However, it is more effective to create a standard format for each presentation by making the following the same on all of your slides: background, titles, sub-headings, typeface, body text, branding, all chosen to suit the nature of your subject. You can take a format from the software provided, but it is better to tailor it to your presentation, just as you would your content. You may think this is all just so much superficial 'polishing' – it is, again, more important to make sure the content is right – but visual devices are additional ways for you to signal the coherence of your presentation. More importantly, you are using elements of what is, after all, a visual medium to make your writing, in a sense, visual.

Many people write slides as they would any other form of writing, but the visual medium works best if you adapt your style. In addition to words, you can use space and layout to make your points. Instead of sentences, link words and paragraphs, use lists, headings and fragments (incomplete sentences).

Because space is limited, use your most concise, and precise, style. Prune your words until they fit the space available. Use a more direct style on your slides and, perhaps, in your speech, than you would in your writing. Or you could use the direct style in your slides and a more formal or academic style in your speech. For your slides, the graphics experts (see references in Murray et al., 1997) tell us that good practice means restricting the words to the following limits:

- 65 characters per line

- 10–11 words per line

- 8 lines of text maximum. Less is better.

In order to see if your words fit these limits, view them in the appropriate software. You might find that you write more concisely if you enlarge your text, in bold, to type your first draft. You will soon see when you are over the recommended limit and you can prune the words as you go along.

To illustrate the process of producing direct, concise writing, here are three drafts of a written text from earlier in this section. Note how the style is gradually pruned from prose style, as for the printed page, to a more concise style, as for notes, then to an even more concise style for the slide.

Prose style for chapter

In sentences with links: 85 words

> Many people write slides as they would a report or a letter, but this medium works best if you adapt your style. The difference is that, for a visual medium like slides, writing has to be visual. Space and layout are used to enhance your points. In other words, instead of sentences, link words and paragraphs, you use lists, headings and fragments (incomplete sentences). Because space is limited, use your most concise, and precise, style. Prune your words until they fit the space you have.

Notes style for slides

In shorter sentences: 25 words

1. Adapt your style for this medium
2. Sentences & paragraphs > lists, headings & fragments
3. Prune to fit the limited space you have

Slides style

As a list, using parallelism: 14 words

- Change your style
- Use lists, headings and fragments
- Prune your points

Different styles can be used at different points in your presentation:

Opening phase: Questions

- What questions will you answer in your presentation?

- Can you write them as one-liners like this?

- Can you keep unanswered questions till the end, to prompt discussion/show the limits of your work?

Middle phase: Bullets

- Write short sentences

- Or fragments

- To relate or separate ideas

- Use indents to show hierarchy of points

- Prune your points: 10 words or less

End phase: Sentences

- Writing the conclusions as sentences has a different effect

- You can make a series of statements

- This can be more provocative, or just clearer or more precise

- These could be a series of 'should' statements: what should be done?

How will you make continuity explicit in your presentation?

Creating continuity

- Running header

- Sequence words, e.g. Problem … Solution, Questions … Answers

- Narrative words, e.g. Phase 1, Stage 2, Initial … Final

- If there is *no* link, a change of style/layout can show it visually

This example shows how you can – and probably should – translate the words you use into visual terms. There are many other principles of good practice, some of which are covered in the slides and poster websites referenced at the end of this chapter, including technical information, design features, use of colour, diagrams and fonts/typeface.

Case study: Making research accessible

Rowena Murray

I worked in journalism for several years and thought that I knew a fair bit about communicating for 'non-academic' audiences, in 'non-academic' media, like TV and newspapers, but when I did a short course on media training I realised that I had forgotten much of what I had learned as a journalist. You forget just how much you have to change your writing, the language you use, for a wider audience. Certain terms just will not work. 'Phenomenology', for example, will mean nothing to the general reader. In fact, some academics will not know what it means and many will have their own views on the rigour of this method, but here I realise that I am straying into academic territory again.

It is probably not the case that we 'forget' who we are writing for or talking to; it is just that it is so easy to slip back into academic language because this is the language we use all the time, and, some would say, it is the 'correct' language for talking about research. However, in my view, it is quite difficult to make the transition from the academic audience to the 'general reader'. It is obvious that we should make a 'style shift', but it is not at all obvious how to do it. Knowing more about it has not made it easier to do. It is hard work.

This was made clear to me during a media training course, when we were asked to write a short piece, pitching our research for the *Richard and Judy Show* (BBC). This made me realise that I had to think very differently about my academic work. We all found this task quite difficult. The tutor, who works in the media, gave us marks for our writing. One of the academics did quite badly. It is not that he writes badly, but that he failed to make the shift to the other audiences. Interestingly, no one seemed concerned that this was an inappropriate task – although that would have been an interesting debate. Instead, we all wrote our pieces and subjected them for review. This experience suggests that I still had a lot to learn about writing for the media, and that the best way to learn about it was to ask someone who regularly writes in that context.

In my case, since I was doing my PhD while in a full-time academic post, it also helped me support other PhD students to make their work more understandable to undergraduates. However, only yesterday I found myself talking about my research using the words 'Activity theory … phenomenographic' and names like Vygotsky. It is very easy to slip back into your own specialist language, or your own particular way of using a specialist term, and you can quickly lose an audience this way.

(Continued)

(Continued)

The starting point should always be what your audience already knows about your subject, but research students tend to focus on the technical issues of their problem, rather than the meaningful problem for real life. In our university, postgraduates have to do a poster display on their research, and this forces them to think about what they are doing in these terms.

When people respond to your presentation, you may realise that they have got the wrong end of the stick. For example, someone thought I was looking at the gendered aspect of discourse – people form their own associations of ideas. Therefore, as a speaker, you have to be clear about what your issue is. Of course, you can never be absolutely sure where people are coming from – they will always have their own ideas about what you are doing, and about what they think you should be doing, and you have to learn from that. I am writing here also as a member of staff, since I can see that students have this problem and I can recognise why it happens.

Perhaps the key challenge is not only talking about your own work in different ways, but also talking about others' work. You feel a pressure not to misrepresent them. This is particularly true in my area, where I am bringing different ideas together; I am always conscious that I am not going into enough depth.

Is this 'dumbing down'? Some people may choose to call it that, but that is unfortunate. It is a real problem if your subject – or the social sciences generally – are not accessible. For research students there is an additional problem: if you cannot express ideas in ways that people understand, you begin to wonder if there really is an idea there. There is a risk of losing the subtleties that jargon covers. Being able to say what a chapter of your thesis is about, in a sentence, does not need to be 'dumbing down'. It may, in fact, be the opposite. It takes a certain amount of thought to make it concise.

This was drawn to my attention when my supervisor said to me, early on in my PhD, 'You're in the swimming pool, but it's time you touched the sides'. It was time for me to establish what my focus was. That was my biggest problem at that stage. I found that the more presentations I gave about my work – to different audiences – the better I was at this, and the more focused my research and writing became.

Conclusion

If you are genuinely to communicate your research to different groups, you cannot get caught up in the debate about the relative status – in the academic world – of different forms of communication. Perhaps the last word is that you should no longer see it as an 'either-or' debate; in the current climate there are important reasons for aiming at both academic and non-academic communications.

Academic communication is not the only way to influence thinking, research, policy or practice; in fact, some would say it is not even the most effective way. In so-called non-academic communication you may have to relinquish control to the professional writers, but you may learn a fair amount about communicating in the process.

Further reading

Baverstock, A. (2001). *Marketing Your Book: An Author's Guide*. London:
A & C Black.

Harman, E. and Montagnes, I. (eds) (1976) *The Thesis and the Book*. Toronto: University of Toronto (reprinted, 2000).

Hicks, W., Adams, S. and Gilbert, H. (1999) *Writing for Journalists*. London:
Routledge.

Murray, R. (2000). *Writing for Publication* (video pack, with notes). Glasgow: University of Strathclyde. Contact to order: S.Mitchell@strath.ac.uk

Murray, R. (2002). *How to Write a Thesis*. Maidenhead: Open University Press/ McGraw-Hill.

Murray, R. (2005). *Writing for Academic Journals*. Maidenhead: Open University Press McGraw-Hill.

Murray, R., Thow, M. and Strachan, R. (1997). Visual Literacy: Designing and Presenting a Poster. *Physiotherapy*, 84(7), 319–27.

For more detail on creating visuals and verbals for posters and slide presentations, see:

• http://www.strath.ac.uk/Departments//CAPLE/poster

• http://www.strath.ac.uk/Departments//CAPLE/slides

• http://www.strath.ac.uk/Departments//CAPLE/writersgroup

See also:

Boden, R., Kenway, J., and Epstein, D. (2004). *The Academic's Support Kit*. London: Sage.

Schuck, P. (2002). Writing for different audiences. http//www.law.yale.edu/outside/html/Public_Affairs/275/yls-article.htm

Those Who Can ...? Teaching as a Postgraduate

10

David Mills with Lucy Atkinson

- Teaching undergraduates can be an excellent experience in preparation for an academic career and a very good way of getting a deeper and more rounded knowledge of the discipline. It is also an opportunity to earn a little extra money.

- However, there are also less rewarding aspects of postgraduate teaching and without adequate preparation and training, it can be very demanding.

- This chapter provides advice about the how and why of teaching undergraduate tutorials, including how to deal with student problems, assessment and feedback.

- It also outlines the sources of mentoring and support that should be available to new teachers.

Teaching students can be the most exhilarating and rewarding aspects of working in higher education. There is no better way of deepening one's understanding of a theoretical argument or critical debate than communicating it to others. Many academics began their teaching careers as postgraduates and remain deeply committed to linking their teaching and research. One's first experiences of facilitating a seminar or delivering a lecture can be deeply formative, the first step in an academic apprenticeship. Being a student yourself, you'll understand the pressures and issues students face, and so you can play a very influential role in their learning.

Yet teaching as a postgraduate is also demanding, time-consuming and often a low-status affair. As a research student, there are many competing demands on you. Teaching experience counts for less than research 'output' when it comes to applying for academic jobs. So you need to think carefully about why you are teaching, how best to prepare, the support you'll need, the academic and pastoral issues you might face, and how it might help you develop your future career. While institutions will have different expectations of their postgraduate teachers, the demands and rewards of teaching cross national and disciplinary boundaries. This chapter addresses each issue in turn. It ends by interviewing Lucy Atkinson, an Edinburgh postgraduate who has taught throughout her PhD.

Why teach?

As student–staff ratios continue to increase, universities increasingly rely on postgraduates to help with undergraduate teaching. Most lead weekly tutorial groups or seminars that accompany a lecture course. Although some postgraduates do give lectures, and even run graduate seminars, this chapter focuses on tutorial teaching.

There are lots of reasons to teach while doing postgraduate research. You may be doing it in order to pay your way through the PhD, or as a requirement of a university-funded studentship. You may be doing it to try out the academic life, to develop a valuable new skill, to make yourself more employable, or simply to help out your supervisor. Not everyone is offered the opportunity, however, and tutorial teaching may be given to those 'in the know' rather than being openly advertised.

Whatever your rationale for teaching, it is important to be clear about the drawbacks as well as the benefits. The actual weekly contact time with students is a fraction of your overall workload. As well as preparing for each tutorial or class (which may mean sitting in on the course lectures), you will probably hold office-hours, respond to student queries by email and have your share of marking. In a recent survey of UK postgraduate teachers in the social sciences (Whitecross and Mills, 2003) tutors took two hours on average to prepare for each seminar. Those with less experience took proportionately longer. The art of carving out time for your own research is a vital one.

Your tasks will be easier if explicit departmental or institutional support is offered to postgraduate teachers. Before you agree to teaching, find out how you'll be supported. At a very minimum, you need to be able to contact the course lecturers, do your photocopying, get advice and guidance, and have some office space. Many institutions do now provide postgraduate tutors with some generic basic training, although this can be of differing quality. Departmental handbooks or web-based resources for tutors are invaluable sources of disciplinary-specific reference and guidance, and save you having to ask repeated questions of the administrative staff. If they don't exist, encourage your institution to produce them. Do also find out if postgraduate teachers are included in departmental meetings or emails, so you feel part of the teaching team. These might seem small matters, but they'll stop you from feeling quite so marginal within your institution and will ensure that your opinions and feedback are heard. The last part of this chapter returns to some of these issues.

Tutorial teaching 101

As a postgraduate who teaches, you may have any of a number of titles – teaching assistant (TA), associate lecturer, visiting tutor, teaching fellow or graduate tutor. Despite the terminological diversity, the job is likely to be the same – leading (or facilitating) a number of tutorials each week. Tutorials have many roles. Ensuring that students have understood the lecture is only the first. They are places for developing broader intellectual and analytical skills in reading, presenting and communicating ideas, as well as working within a team, nurturing critical thinking and promoting independent learning. Tutorials have the further role of academic socialisation and identity formation, and in providing students with an invaluable peer support network. Many of these academic skills are just as important as the substantive course 'content'.

Handled well, tutorials and seminars can be very creative and provocative learning environments. They are also unpredictable, and depend heavily on the personalities and relationships within the group, and also on participants' expectations of the session. One tutorial group can effervesce, while the next can be mind-numbingly dull. That isn't necessarily your fault.

It may seem obvious, but familiarising yourself with the intended 'learning outcomes' of the course as a whole is vital. If one is not already arranged, try and schedule a meeting with the other tutors and the course convenor to talk through the course before it begins. What is the lecturer hoping that students will gain from doing the course? What ideas, theories, methods or skills are they aiming to convey? What questions does he or she seek to raise in the students' minds? These should be the spring-board for your own aims for your tutorial teaching. You may find it helpful to write these down and to return to them during the course.

The first session

In teaching, first impressions most definitely count. Your initial tutorial will set the tone for the rest of the semester, or even the year, so you want to ensure that it goes well. Even things like seating arrangements matter, so take time to prepare the room. Arranging chairs into a circle breaks the classroom monotony and makes discussion easier – neither students nor tutors should need to hide behind desks.

Your students will appreciate a hand-out listing the key information they'll need for the semester, including your plans for how the group is to be run, a list of everyone's names and your contact details, as well as a reminder of assessment deadlines, etc. It will also serve the double purpose of appearing organised and committed!

Find out as much as you can about your students, not least their names. What experiences and skills do they bring to the classroom? Do they know each other? If not, get them to introduce the person sitting next to them. Give them a couple of minutes to chat in order to inform their introduction. Ask them to talk about their expectations and aspirations for the course and their degree as a whole. The more you know about your students, the more you can tailor their learning accordingly. You'll have to take a regular record of attendance, so getting to know people's names quickly makes this task easier and demonstrates your interest in them as individuals.

What climate do you want to create in the tutorials? Your mood will be infectious, so be enthusiastic and make sessions enjoyable. You want to create a space for engaged and creative learning, where questioning and critical thinking can be fun. But you also want your students to work hard. You might like to establish some seminar house rules, such as no one person dominating discussions. At the very least, you could use the first session to explain how you'd like the tutorials to be structured and the preparation you expect them to do for each week.

Ideas for tutorials

There are lots of ways to facilitate tutorials or small-group teaching sessions. The tried-and-tested format is to have a student presentation followed by a discussion. Just because everyone else in your department relies on this approach does not mean that you have to. Indeed, this can be one of the most difficult formats to make work successfully at undergraduate level. Too much pressure is put on the student presenters, and often the task they are set is vague or unreasonably large. They have to summarise the readings, be confident about putting forward ideas, and then take responsibility for getting a dialogue going. What if they haven't done any preparation? Or worse still, they simply don't show up? And the format can mean everyone else gets away with doing little or no reading. All too often, this leads to the tutorial leader having to fill in the silence with an impromptu lecture, defeating the whole purpose of the tutorial.

There are stimulating alternatives. Why not set the students a collective task to complete as a group or within small break-out groups? As an example: ask them to come up with three questions about a set-text that they would like to explore further. You will find that dividing the group into twos or fours (or both, sequentially) can be rewarding, especially as a way of involving those who hesitate to contribute to whole-group discussions. A few of the many websites that offer university teachers advice or ideas are listed at the end of the chapter.

Some of the most successful tutorials need no elaborate structure or direction on your part. They are simply a thoughtful and constructive dialogue around issues raised in the readings or the lecture. Facilitating such conversations is rather less easy than it looks. You don't want to dominate, but you do want it to progress and cover the important issues, while recognising that the tangents it goes down are often revealing too. You need to learn the art of asking 'open' rather than 'closed' questions, questions that encourage reflection, narrative, description and trying out ideas rather than neat answers. Give your own opinions if appropriate, but always be wary of talking too much.

If you find it hard to keep the conversation lively, why not experiment with a group brain-storming session to get the tutorial going? Alternatively, ask the students to do poster presentations, organise debates, read and discuss a passage of writing or collec-tively fill in work-sheets. Other ideas that encourage active and engaged learning include role-plays or problem-based learning. The latter, sometimes shortened to PBL, covers a variety of structured learning techniques that ask groups of students to define their own research problem in relation to a topic, and to work as a team over the following week developing a presentation around the problem they have set them-selves (Owen and Mills, 2003).

Some people find that asking students to facilitate small-group work (with or without you) can be empowering. As you get more experience, you will develop the confidence to try new things. You might want to ask the students about approaches they think work well. Don't be too ambitious, however, and remember that there is often resistance, from both students and staff, to new ways of doing things. A seminar format where everyone is expected to participate might challenge a student *habitus* defined by passivity and the retort 'That's not the way Dr X does it'. It is sometimes easier to innovate with first-year students, who are less attached to departmental micro-traditions.

How to handle problems

Lots of things can, and sometimes will, go wrong in your tutorials. Some students will dominate. Others will silently brood, not contributing. There may be individual personality clashes, and sometimes the group is just too big. Having more than 12 to 15 students changes the classroom dynamic, forcing more reliance on small-group work. Lack of preparation by students is a perennial issue, as is dealing with a group with a mix of abilities (and motivations). Personal crises or family problems aren't necessarily left outside the classroom either. The skill is in being attentive to individual needs and factors while also accepting that a group will inevitably have its leaders and its followers.

There is a burgeoning range of books and websites (see end of chapter) that offer advice and teaching tips for dealing with such situations. There is no harm in returning to the ground rules, or seeking agreement with students on the appropriate amount of reading preparation for each class. Remember also to take into account other deadlines that the students might be facing. As they are budding social scientists, encourage your students to think about power-dynamics in the classroom and how they play out along the fault-lines of gender, language, ethnicity, nationality or cultural capital.

A perennial problem for students in the social sciences is engaging with social theory and its seemingly obscure languages and codes. Graff, in his entertaining *Clueless in Academe* (2003), offers some invaluable ways of dealing with this in the classroom and in your students' writing. He points out that academic and popular styles of argument and debate are less polar opposites than one might imagine, and that even the most 'difficult' theoretical expositions are leavened by more accessible moments of explanation and position-taking. He recommends students to 'talk the talk of the academic world' by doing their own criticisms of academic discourse (Graff, 2003: 246).

Remember that your adrenaline will flow, especially if it is your first teaching gig. Don't pretend to know all the answers. Your job is to help students ask the right questions, and to ask them in provocative and enlightening ways. Unless you are an unreconstructed positivist, there are unlikely to be definitive solutions! Rather than spend too long preparing for every eventuality, acknowledge your own limits. If you find a piece of theoretical writing hard to comprehend, you can guarantee that your students will too. Your willingness to admit this makes you human. Turn problems into solutions – organise a seminar discussion around a collective close reading and discussion of a passage of writing that is particularly difficult. And don't deny your own intellectual agency – you don't just have to regurgitate points made in the lecture. Why not occasionally challenge the lecturer's interpretation, or point to the strength of other perspectives on the topic?

Running the perfect tutorial

There is no such thing as a perfect tutorial. People learn in unpredictable ways, at different paces, and will take markedly dissimilar things from the weekly hour they spend in a room with you. One of the joys of an imagination honed by the social sciences is that tightly prescribed 'learning outcomes' are taken with a pinch of salt – pedagogy's unintended consequences are often the most rewarding. That said, as facilitator, you define the atmosphere, and the learning environment matters. Emphasise and model the importance of creating an atmosphere that is collaborative rather than competitive. One student-run seminar I once facilitated was powered by cups of tea and a biscuit tin, filled by a different person each week. And does the tutorial always have to be held in a classroom?

One thing that may not be covered in your training course is the pastoral dimension of the teacher–student relationship. You may find yourself asked for advice or support on personal matters, especially if your students feel that you are more approachable and less likely to divulge information than full-time members of staff. Academic and personal concerns are often very intertwined. If there can be no firm guidelines on how to respond and act on personal disclosures from students, a good rule is to try to restrict your competencies to academic matters, referring students where appropriate to university counselling services or to the appropriate member of staff.

Assessment

Conventional academic wisdom views assessment as a necessary chore. The daunting nature of the task is symbolised by looming piles of unmarked essays. From the point of view of students, this is precisely the aspect of the course that matters most. How is their performance to be judged, how often, and with what criteria? All too often assessment is an after-thought to course design. Ideally, the modes and criteria for assessment should be the first thing to consider in designing courses or thinking about teaching, as they will inevitably structure the way students approach their learning.

While you are unlikely to be involved in designing assessment, as a tutor you will invariably be marking written work. It is worth thinking through the rationale for assessment, especially if this has not been part of your training. What is being judged, and why? Ideally, you should be briefed by the lecturer who designed the assignment and given the opportunity to ask questions. Your department is likely to have explicit marking criteria that detail the quality of work expected to meet different grades, but these criteria will need to be tailored for different courses and different types of assessment. It may look straightforward, but in the social sciences, there is always a subjective quality to the judgement of work. It is good practice for new teachers to work alongside more experienced markers, and for work to be double-marked or moderated, but this is not always possible.

When marking, there is much to think about. Should one be encouraging, and so mark leniently at the start of the year? How should one deal with students with special needs (such as dyslexia) or second-language students? Whether you should mark down poor style and grammar should be covered by departmental/university policy. There is also your time and workload to consider. How long should one spend on each script? There may be departmental or university policies around these issues, but they are also topics to raise with your peers and the course convenor/lecturer.

As important as the written grades you assign are the types of feedback, both written and oral, that you provide to students. Formative (as opposed to summative) assessment is invaluable in helping students to learn. Do seek guidance on offering feedback, for it is a delicate art. You want to treat all students equally, not being too destructive, but also not overwhelming people with suggestions. Some marking gurus suggest that three written comments are enough. Another thought is to always start with something positive.

If you can meet students to hand back work, this offers further opportunities to discuss and contextualise your comments. Better still, why not encourage your students to think about their writing skills by asking them to give each other feedback on drafts of their own work before they submit an assignment. You may also want to run a tutorial specifically on essay writing, using one of the many hand-outs that proffer wisdom on writing, bibliographic referencing, and 'answering the question'. If your course is assessed by written exam, you will be asked to help them prepare for that. Increasingly, creative teachers are using a variety of other forms of assessment, such as reflective diaries, book reviews or group project work. Each develops different genres of writing and each requires a different approach to assessment.

Students get very worried about their written work. Expect to be asked repeatedly by your students about assignments and the best ways of preparing for them. The trick is to channel such anxieties in a productive way, so that they both feel reassured and can learn more about the demands being made of them.

As assessment procedures become more transparent, assertive students are more able to challenge and query marks, especially if their degree classification is seen to depend on continuous assessment. What would you do if confronted by an angry student who insists that their essay deserves 60 per cent and not 57 per cent? After staying calm, and not being intimidated, the best advice would be to refer all queries to an academic member of staff. Departments will (or ought to have!) clear procedures for dealing with student complaints and appeals.

You may also face the issue of plagiarism. Plagiarism is a portmanteau word that covers a gamut of issues, from a lack of familiarity with scholarly conventions to the blatant copying of someone else's work. Your department will have a policy on student plagiarism, and it will repay spending some time discussing it with students, so that they know what might not be acceptable, and that their work will be marked accordingly. Why not also talk with your students about ways of putting other people's ideas into one's own words, and the whole scholarly citation apparatus? If worried about a particular case, it would be as well to seek advice.

Feeling supported: training, mentoring and feedback

Universities across the globe are increasingly dependent on part-time and postgraduate teachers. If postgraduate teachers are trainees, then teaching responsibilities should be accompanied by effective and ongoing training. In our survey (Whitecross and Mills, 2003), most respondents believed that disciplinary-specific training courses, ideally delivered within departments themselves, would be of much greater value than generic courses. As one student said of his course, 'it seemed to lack hands-on advice and a sense of the reality of the classroom'. And such courses are not just for those at the start of their teaching career. They are a useful way to continue to reflect and learn from one's teaching experience. Find out about the quality of those offered in your institution.

In an ideal world, one full-time member of staff would take responsibility for the overall development and training of new postgraduate teachers. This has the additional benefit of ensuring that the support and development of graduate teachers by full-time staff is recognised and not simply another extra administrative burden. Yet the time and responsibilities such posts entail are still only rarely recognised by institutions and departments.

Some institutions do allocate departmental mentors for postgraduate teachers. This relationship can be invaluable, but it depends greatly on the commitment of the individual mentor. Mentors may not be aware of the issues facing teachers on a particular course. As one of our respondents commented, some 'have very little idea about our circumstances and are not interested either'.

If you have urgent concerns and queries, and the lecturer or course convenor is difficult to get hold of, cultivate your relationship with departmental administrators – they are a vital source of insider-knowledge. Alternatively, find out if you have an official representative who can raise issues at staff meetings. But remember that the informal support you get from other tutors will be the most valuable of all.

Feedback

Teachers need feedback, and need it on a regular basis. In the UK, most universities have adopted a version of course evaluation questionnaires – a disliked and humdrum affair, where the different aspects of a course and its teaching are ranked on a scale of 1 to 5. The exercise, usually carried out in a hurry at the last session of a course, is treated as a bureaucratic imposition. Often there is little opportunity for students to comment separately on the tutorials. You will gain far more from informal weekly snippets of feedback, such as when students arrive or depart. It might be worth planning a space for more structured feedback into your tutorials on a regular basis.

Equally important is getting feedback from departments. One way of doing so is to have a regular meeting with the course lecturer/convenor. Ideally, such sessions serve to iron out problems, help tutors reflect and assess their teaching performance, and act as a form of professional development for postgraduates. It also helps tutors situate their courses within the learning objectives for the degree as a whole. Such initiatives would also make postgraduate teachers feel a valued part of a teaching team. Another possibility is instituting peer-reviewing of teaching. Of those who responded to our UK survey, 75 per cent wanted more departmental involvement in reviewing and offering feedback to student teachers (Whitecross and Mills, 2003). Full-time staff can get involved without having to be reviewed themselves!

The bigger picture: teaching as a career?

When you apply for permanent academic lectureships, although teaching experience is valuable (see Chapter 11), you are likely to be judged primarily on your research productivity. Unfortunately, there are diminishing rewards for those who teach on temporary contracts for more than one or two years after completing their PhD (Husbands and Davies, 2000, Mills and Harris, 2004). Paradoxically, too much teaching experience can damage one's CV, unless you have been able to combine full-time teaching responsibilities with an active publication record.

The issuing of formal employment contracts to tutors has long been the practice in US universities. It is increasingly common in the UK and elsewhere. If this is not the case (and in our survey of UK anthropology departments, less than half the teaching assistants received written contracts; Whitecross and Mills, 2003), it is important to clarify just what you will be expected to do, your rates of pay, and the institutional and departmental support that is available. Will you get paid for office hours, for marking, and what about sick pay or travel costs? Informal working arrangements can seem appealing to departments, but also leave tutors vulnerable and unsupported. Under European Union employment legislation, fixed-term employees have the same rights as those on permanent contracts. On the other hand, an overly legalistic approach to part-time employees by institutions can institutionalise and reinforce the perpetual marginality that many postgraduate teachers already feel (Bryson, 2004).

There is a global trend towards the separation of research and teaching responsibilities within universities. In the UK, institutions are increasingly employing temporary lecturers on one-year (or even nine-month) rolling contracts as a way of meeting the problems of unpredictable student numbers and staffing needs (Association of University Teachers, 2004; Husbands, 1998), despite national agreements on minimising the use of casualised labour. Because no statistical data is collected on those working less than a quarter of the time, it is hard to know how many postgraduate teachers there are in the social sciences within the UK (Gibb, 2004). While there are growing efforts to raise the profile and professional aura of teaching (the UK's new Higher Education Academy being a case in point), part-time and temporary university teachers remain a low-status workforce, and teaching-related promotion criteria are less common than they might be. Joining a union may be a useful step, but in the UK conditions of work and pay tend to depend on local bargaining, and so conditions vary widely.

Universities in the USA have long relied on temporary 'adjunct' staff, and Sharff and Lessinger (1999) refer to adjunct faculty as 'free-way flyers' as they struggle to make a living by teaching in different institutions. There is a growing literature on Graduate Teacher activism, such as the Yale strikes of 1995 and 1996, and the conditions under which this flexible labour force live and work. In response, disciplinary and professional associations are beginning to address the exploitation of postgraduate teachers and part-time staff (Nelson, 1997, 2003). Lessons learnt in the USA are likely to be increasingly relevant elsewhere. If your department or institution has not already addressed the conditions under which its postgraduate teachers work, or the support and professional development it offers, now might be the time to raise it. Much of this comes down to confidence. As one postgraduate tutor put it, 'teaching assistants need to value themselves enough to change things'.

Case study: An interview with a postgraduate teacher

Lucy Atkinson has taught throughout her PhD in Anthropology at Edinburgh University, which is on the lives of refugee children from the Democratic Republic of Congo in camps in rural Zambia. She has taught on three courses: two in social anthropology and one on social and political theory. As well as running tutorials, she has also been senior tutor for the social anthropology courses, a paid administrative role.

What have been the most rewarding aspects of teaching as a postgraduate?
I really enjoy tutoring, even if I find it hard to put my finger on why! I like having a relationship with the students. I feel that I am a good tutor and this is confirmed in the feedback they give me, and it's always nice to do something you're good at! I love anthropology and so discussing it is always rewarding, especially if you are able to communicate that enthusiasm to others.

I find teaching has a highly positive impact on my own work. Taking tutorials is a good way of counterbalancing the ever-narrowing focus on your own research topic. It can often offer ways to make that topic richer. On several occasions I have found in student's work references that I had either forgotten, not considered or even was unaware of, but that turned out to be very relevant to my topic. A more indirect benefit is the chance to discuss broader theoretical issues with students.

I am also rewarded by the impact I can have on others' learning. It is very satisfying to show students, who might be having problems with theoretical ideas, the ways I came to get a better understanding of the issues. We are much closer in time and experience to the issues and learning that the students are facing, and this means that we can guide them in ways they can relate to. It is great when students engage with and become enthusiastic about the topic.

And the hardest part?
Being limited by the course curriculae and teaching conventions of the department. As tutors we are aware of the specific difficulties the students are having and potential

(Continued)

(Continued)

ways in which the course could be changed, but these are difficult to communicate and put into practice. The face-to-face aspect of most postgraduate teaching means that you are often in agreement with students on an issue but are unable to change the institutional traditions and ways of working. We are not considered members of staff by the department, but we are by our students.

It also takes up a lot of time, especially the first time you do a course. It can be incredibly frightening to think that you are the only point of contact that students have with the academic 'staff', and that you can influence up to 50 per cent of their grade. How much more do you really know than them? But once you get started this influence works in your favour.

What skills do you think you've gained, and how useful will they be for your future work?
I haven't yet decided whether to work in applied anthropology or in academia, so the usefulness of the skills I've gained will vary depending on where I end up. To be honest, this was not my motivation in deciding to tutor, so I don't think much about it. But I have learnt to prepare for all eventualities, to work with different group dynamics, and to get a balance between encouragement and correction. I've also learned that often you know more than you think!

How, if at all, have you balanced your teaching commitments with your own PhD research?
At times this has been very difficult. At least there are the holidays! The hardest thing is marking – this can take over completely. Despite my good intentions to always do some thesis-writing every day before doing the marking, invariably I end up unable to concentrate as I worry about getting the marking done in time. It is also amazing how much time is taken up with emails from tutees, as I try to reply even when it is a simple 'Sorry I was not in the tutorial'.

I find that it is better to have all my tutorials on one day and to do the preparation either the night before, or on the same morning. This is easy enough if the preparation is simple but at times, when more is needed, I try to do it immediately after the tutorials. At least that way the rest of the week is relatively free. This works for me but I know others who prefer to have tutorials at the same time on several days as this helps to structure their day.

(Continued)

(Continued)

Can you tell me a bit about what the role of 'senior tutor' involves?
As senior tutor I was responsible for 'recruitment' of postgraduate teachers this year. We try to give all the PhD students the option of teaching as a way to supplement their income. But this means trying to arrange meetings and organising the timetable in the same week that they are arriving and signing up for their own courses. What makes it rather crazy is that there is no way of knowing who will turn up or how to contact them. It probably means that some people sign up for tutoring and then regret it and others don't know about it until it is too late and everything is organised. The distribution of teaching responsibilities can be a bit of a lottery.

Have you been involved in campaigning within your institution to improve the conditions of postgraduate teachers? How successful has this been?
I am lucky that our teaching conditions are not specific to my department but to an interdisciplinary school of which we are a part. This means that if improvement is needed there are always people with whom to share the burden of campaigning. We do have contracts and the conditions and rates of pay are specified. We also get handbooks that are quite useful, but these are no longer specific to the department or the discipline. The one thing I intend to do while working as senior tutor is to create a folder of disciplinary-specific teaching resources for our tutors.

Conclusion

For as long as undergraduate teaching has a relatively low priority in 'research-led' institutions, permanent academic members of staff will tend to undervalue postgraduate teachers. Undergraduate students will always view them differently. You are the member of 'staff' with whom they have the most contact and you can have a powerful impact on their learning experiences. Betwixt and between, your status as an intermediary is one reason teaching as a postgraduate is both challenging and rewarding. Do seek out a variety of teaching opportunities, but be mindful of the possibilities and limits they offer for your academic career. Meantime, enjoy every moment.

Further reading

Online web resources for postgraduate teachers in the social sciences

Sociology, Anthropology, Politics (C-SAP): www.c-sap.bham.ac.uk

As well as a range of case studies, C-SAP is developing a page of resources for those teaching for the first time.

Higher Education Academy: www.heacademy.ac.uk

The UK Higher Education Academy has useful resources for part-time teachers, providing advice, case studies, support materials and bibliographies.

Forster, F., Hounsell, D. and Thompson, S. (eds) (1995). *Tutoring and Demonstrating: A Handbook*. Published by the Centre for Teaching, Learning and Assessment at the University of Edinburgh in association with the Universities' and Colleges' Staff Development Agency. Available online at: http://www.tla.ed.ac.uk/services/tutdems/handbook.htm

While this publication is now several years old, the online version offers practical and sensible generic advice for new lecturers and tutors on small-group work, assessment and feedback.

The Handbook for Economics Lecturers: http://www.economics.ltsn.ac.uk/handbook

Many have found this online handbook for economics lecturers useful.

Hess, J. (2003). Using the Internet for contingent faculty organizing. *Jump Cut* 46. http://www.ejumpcut.org/archive/jc46.2003/links.html

This is a useful set of links to organisations mobilising and supporting part-time and graduate student teachers within US higher education. For those in the UK wishing to join a union, both the Association of University Teachers (AUT) and the National Association of Teachers in Further and Higher Education NATFHE offer very much reduced membership rates for postgraduate teachers. See www.aut.org.uk and www.natfhe.org.uk

NATFHE/NPC/NUS Employment Charter (2003). (for postgraduate student academic and academic-related staff): www.npc.org.uk/essentials/publications

This charter, published on the UK National Postgraduate Committee (NPC) web-site, lists the basic principles to be accorded to postgraduates who are employed to teach. The NPC site (www.npc.org.uk) has a number of other resources, and represents the interests of postgraduates in the UK.

Holland, S. (n.d.). *Part-time Teaching: A Good Practice Guide*. English Subject Centre. Report No. 9. Available at: www.english.heacademy.ac.uk

Though written for teachers of English, this report has some useful advice.

What Next?
Career paths

11

Jeanette Holt

- There is a wide range of career opportunities available to social scientists, not only in universities, but also in social research outside academia and in many jobs where a social science background is useful or essential.

- This chapter describes the career options available to social science postgraduates.

- It advises how to present your talents and experience most effectively to potential employers.

- This chapter also recommends sources of further information and suggests how to locate vacancies.

Having enrolled on your Masters or doctorate in social science, you will no doubt be interested to find out what careers are available to you. The other chapters in this book are concerned with helping you to manage your course and learn some of the requisite skills you will need for your chosen career. The purpose of this chapter is to help you to identify the various career directions that you could take.

A recent survey (Teacher Training Agency, 2004) of 1,044 graduates aged 21–35 found that one in four are bored at work and wished to change career. Half of those questioned said that they had fallen into jobs rather than chosen them carefully. This chapter is designed to help you to avoid this and to assist you to make an informed decision about your future career.

It is divided into three sections: the first is a broad description of various career options, the second is about considering your transferable skills and how you can market these to a potential employer and the third is about sources of vacancies and job-hunting strategies.

The entry requirements given throughout are only for work in the UK. If you live elsewhere and are intending to work in your home country, you will need to check the requirements using either the Key Graduate Careers websites listed in at the end of the chapter, your own particular university careers service or the relevant professional association.

Career options for postgraduate social scientists

Careers in academia

Researchers

Researchers may work within academic departments or specialised research centres at universities, for example the Centre for Housing Research and Urban Studies at Glasgow University, the Social Policy Research Unit at the University of York and the Social Policy Research Centre, University of New South Wales in Australia. Research centres employ some permanent researchers with grades linked to academic lecturers and some short-term contract staff. Alternatively, many university teaching departments recruit researchers but usually on short-term contracts. There are fewer lecturing posts but they tend to have a better career structure and a far higher proportion of permanent posts.

Entry requirements: Research posts generally require a postgraduate qualification in a relevant subject, either a Masters containing research methods modules or a doctorate. Although research posts are open to Masters and PhD graduates, some university departments prefer the latter.

Lecturers

Higher education (university) lecturers teach subjects to undergraduate and post-graduate students using a variety of methods, including group lectures, seminars, tutorials and laboratory work. Lecturers' teaching skills are now subject to assessment. Lecturers must pursue their own areas of specialist research and there is considerable pressure to get published as they are required to contribute to the department's research profile. There are also many administrative duties and the work can involve pastoral responsibilities with students. Other activities include attending conferences and establishing links with outside organisations such as employers and public organisations. Bidding for research grants and attracting funding is another aspect of the job.

Entry requirements: Lecturing posts generally require someone who has a PhD or is working towards one. Evidence of the ability to produce original research is essential and having been published will give a distinct advantage. Teaching experience, preferably with undergraduates, would also help your case. Many research students take up part-time teaching, which helps when applying for lecturing posts (see Chapter 10). In addition, evidence of excellent analytical and communication skills is most important.

If you are considering an academic career it is worth asking yourself the question 'Why?' Few academics have chosen this career path because of the salaries involved. Starting salaries are comparable with some graduate jobs (e.g. teaching, market research, social research and personnel), but fall far short of salaries in law, accountancy, business and finance and consultancy. Good reasons for wanting to pursue an academic career include having an enthusiasm for your subject and wanting to pass this on, determination to make progress in your field and having an ability to plan your own work. Other good reasons include being able to work independently as well as part of a team and being prepared to work long hours but enjoying some flexibility and autonomy within this.

Employers: universities and colleges of higher education and specialised postgraduate institutions such as law and business schools.

Careers in academia are very competitive and it is worth noting that only about 40 per cent of social science PhDs end up in academia. You may therefore wish to consider using your skills and knowledge in a different environment. So what are the other options?

Other careers in research

Social researchers outside academia

Social researchers design, formulate, conduct and manage social research projects. They interpret results and disseminate findings. Research can be on a wide range of social issues, such as ethnicity and gender, ageing, crime, media, housing, transport, health care, education, environment, unemployment, economic trends and forecasts, and population structure and migration. There is a trend towards policy research, especially working for the government, where analysis is required for policy development, review and evaluation. Work activities include using a brief received from a client to decide upon the most appropriate and creative method to design a research project using either quantitative or qualitative methods, carrying out or coordinating fieldwork to gather information, analysing results and preparing a report on findings, disseminating results both orally and in writing, and providing research-based advice, sometimes with an action plan.

Entry requirements: Some employers will accept graduates with just a first degree in a relevant subject, which includes social research methods and statistics. Most employers prefer a taught Masters degree in social research or a research degree (PhD). Generally the Masters is preferred because in the past it has provided a better skill-set than the PhD. The Economic and Social Research Council (the UK's leading research funding agency addressing economic and social concerns) is now insisting that PhD students funded by them receive training in research methods and this should enhance their employment prospects in general.

Other skills and personal qualities required include: communication skills – the ability to relate well to different types of people, give clear presentations and write reports; numerical skills – confidence in using statistical techniques and computer software; organisational skills – the ability to prioritise, give attention to detail and work to deadlines; and analytical skills – the ability to analyse complex problems and suggest creative solutions. In addition, previous work experience in research, including market research interviewing, in administration or in social support roles is helpful.

Employers:

- Central government. Government research officers are employed in various government departments, including Health, Education, Statistics, Justice, Employment and Parliamentary Services. Researchers are also employed by some government agencies. Central government websites contain more information. There is a new government social research website with more details at www.gsr.gov.uk

- Local government. Research opportunities exist in policy units and departments such as social services, housing and education.

- Market research organisations. Many of these regularly conduct social research and some have specialist social research divisions and take on graduate trainees, for example NOP, British Market Research Bureau (BMRB) and MORI. More experienced social researchers are also employed by agencies. The Market Research Society (www.mrs.org.uk) is a good place to find out more about companies.

- Independent research organisations, charities and pressure groups. There are many independent non-profit-making research organisations, for example the National Centre for Social Research in London and the International Institute for Sustainable Development in Canada. A significant number of social researchers are employed in this sector. 'Think tanks' such as the Australia Institute (TAI) and the Adam Smith Institute also come under this category. Think tanks produce policy papers on topical issues, often with recommendations influenced by their political perspectives. Many charities employ their own permanent researchers to evaluate their policies, for example, the National Society for the Prevention of Cruelty to Children (NSPCC), New Zealand Drug Foundation, the Academy for Educational Development (AED) in Washington and pressure groups such as Amnesty International. They may also recruit researchers on a short-term basis to carry out a single study or evaluation.

- National Health Service. The NHS employs researchers in specialist fields, such as health policy and evaluation.

- Trade unions. Vacancies for researchers are scarce because many trade union research departments are quite small. In smaller unions researchers usually perform other roles, such as press officer. The Trades Union Congress (TUC) employs a number of research staff in its economics department but applicants tend to have a higher degree plus relevant work experience.

- Media. The BBC recruits researchers to do broadcasting audience research and programme research. This often means working on short-term contracts.

- Consultancies. Some social researchers are employed by management or business consultancies, for example Cordis Bright and MEL Research, which offer consultancy support to the health and social care sector.

More information and a newsletter is available on the Social Research Association (SRA) website: www.the-sra.org.uk

Political researchers

Research officers are employed by major political parties in order to advise policy makers and campaign staff and provide up-to-date information. This information is used to develop new policies, which support the party's aims. The work of Parliamentary research assistants includes scanning newspapers and specialist publications, liaising with pressure groups, drafting letters and speeches and assisting with routine constituency work.

Entry requirements: Entry is possible with a first degree in a relevant subject or a Masters degree that provides knowledge of policy issues. Work experience is essential and academic or social research would be particularly relevant. Evidence of commitment to a party and knowledge of the political system will be looked for. Other requirements include numerical skills, communication skills and confidence in dealing with influential people.

Employers: All the parties represented at Westminster and the European Parliament employ researchers although the major parties employ more. Competition for jobs is stiff with often more than 100 applicants per post. Parliamentary research assistants are employed by members of the House of Commons or European Parliament. Researchers may also be employed to give support to the party's representatives on local authorities. For more information, look at 'Working for an MP' on www.W4mp.org

Market research executives

Market research executives conduct and control research into what people think, want, buy and do. Their findings are used to influence product, service and policy development and the way services and products are marketed. Market researchers usually focus on either quantitative or qualitative research methods.

Typical work activities include talking with clients to develop a brief, devising and writing questions to gain data, and deciding the size and nature of the sample group. Other activities include deciding how to collect the information, calculating the cost of the project and training a team of interviewers to conduct the research, using statistics and software to interpret the data and producing a written report of the findings.

Entry requirements: This is a career that is open to graduates of all disciplines, but psychology, business studies, languages, sociology, maths and statistics, politics and economics are particularly useful. A postgraduate qualification is not needed but can be useful, as many employers will look for quantitative research skills. There are several postgraduate courses recognised by the Market Research Society (MRS). To be successful you will need to have a strong interest in research, the ability to cope under pressure, good communication skills, especially in giving presentations and writing reports, excellent numerical, analytical and IT skills, and organisational and problem-solving abilities. Previous experience of interviewing people is also useful.

Employers: Market research agencies vary in size from 500-plus staff to two or three people. Their role is to answer questions asked by other organisations commissioning research. A list can be found in the *Research Buyers Guide*, produced by the Market Research Society, which is also available online at www.rbg.org.uk. Large businesses and manufacturers also employ market researchers to coordinate research and sometimes their role overlaps with marketing.

Professional practitioners

Rather than research, you may be interested in a career in other professional roles where your transferable skills would be used. Most of these professions include research activities as part of the job description.

Economists

Economists provide analysis and specialist advice concerning economic aspects of policy in order to solve practical problems such as investment demand and resource planning. They may be involved in advising the government, financial institutions, industrial companies, trade associations and international organisations. Economists carry out research, collect and analyse data and monitor trends. They may be involved in forecasting future demands (e.g. skills in the labour market) and may specialise in industry, finance or development, analysing factors affecting economic performance and helping to formulate strategy.

Entry requirements: Competition for jobs is intense, so a first or 2.1 in economics (or, less often, in another discipline) is required and a postgraduate course is desirable. You will need to have good research skills, good communication skills, time management and organisational skills plus the ability to handle complex numerical and statistical data.

Employers: The largest employer is the Government Economic Service, part of the Civil Service. Other employers include regional development agencies, local authorities, universities, research institutes, management consultancies, banks, securities companies, specialist consultancies, insurance firms and other commercial organisations. You can find more information about this and related careers on the Prospects website (the UK's official careers website) at www.prospects.ac.uk, and from the Government Economic Service at www.ges.gov.uk and the Society of Business Economists at www.sbe.co.uk

Psychologists

If your academic background is in psychology or you are willing to take a conversion course, you may be interested in the following careers.

Clinical psychologists are responsible for using psychology to assess and treat patients in health-care settings and conduct research into mental and physical illness. Only about one in three applicants for the Doctorate in Clinical Psychology are successful and previous work experience as an assistant psychologist/research assistant or similar is a requirement for the course. However, in the UK there is a shortage of clinical psychologists so, once trained, the prospects are good.

Counselling psychologists use psychological techniques and theories to help clients with a range of problems and life issues (e.g. depression, anxiety, bereavement and eating disorders).

Educational psychologists apply psychology to the learning, behavioural, social and emotional difficulties of children and youngsters and advise parents, teachers and other professionals. The training route for educational psychology is currently in transition, so you will need to check the British Psychological Society (BPS) website (www.bps.org.uk) for the latest information.

Health psychologists are responsible for applying psychological theories to find ways of improving the standard of health and healthcare of the population. This is often more of a research role.

Occupational psychologists apply psychology to people at work and the organisations they work for. They may be involved in giving advice about staff selection and assessment, training, work design and organisational change.

Forensic psychologists work mainly for the prison and probation service. They make assessments of offenders and give treatment on a one-to-one and group basis.

Neuropsychologists – neuropsychology is a post-qualifying specialisation and one of the most quickly advancing areas of research. It involves meeting the needs of people with neurological disorders. The work is usually conducted by qualified clinical psychologists but other trained psychologists can also specialise in this area.

Entry requirements (for all the above psychology careers): You will need a degree accredited by the British Psychological Society (BPS) for the Graduate Basis for Registration or an accredited psychology conversion course. You will also need the appropriate postgraduate specialist qualification and, in some cases, work experience.

More information about routes into these careers and how to become chartered is available on the BPS website (www.bps.org.uk) and the Prospects website (www. prospects.ac.uk. select 'Explore Types of Jobs').

Employers: Depending on your specialist area you could work for the health service, an independent research organisation, central government, local government, the prison or probation service, industry or commerce, a charity, a consultancy or a further/higher education institution.

There are also non-accredited areas of psychology. These are careers that do not currently have a division within the BPS. For more information, contact the following websites:

Ergonomist/human factors specialist – refer to the Ergonomics Society www.ergonomics. org.uk

Environmental psychologist – refer to the Prospects website: www.prospects.ac.uk

Sports psychologist – contact the British Association of Sport and Exercise Science (BASES): www.bases.org.uk. The BPS has set up a committee to look into the accreditation of sports psychology courses.

Psychotherapist – although some psychologists are psychotherapists, the BPS does not accredit training courses for people who are not already chartered psychologists. More information is available from the British Association of Counsellors and Psychotherapists (BACP): www.bacp.co.uk

Social supportive roles

Social workers

Social workers give support to individuals, families and groups who are in need of help within the community. This may include helping people with specific needs, such as mental health problems, children at risk, people with disabilities, elderly people, the homeless and the disaffected. The work involves conducting interviews and writing assessments with recommendations for action. Accurate records and reports need to be kept as these may be used in court cases. Social workers offer information and advice to their clients. They also liaise with many different agencies and are members of multidisciplinary teams.

Entry requirements: Social work is open to graduates of any discipline although a social science degree could increase your chances. Some relevant work experience/voluntary work is required plus a professional postgraduate two-year diploma/MA course in social work or the two-year 'accelerated' degree, unless you already have a three-year degree in social work. In Scotland there is also a fast-track graduate scheme. Personal qualities such as the ability to keep calm in a crisis, be a good listener and observer and be able to think on your feet and make good decisions under stressful circumstances are extremely important.

Employers: More information is available from www.socialworkcareers.co.uk

Probation officers

The work involves carrying out risk assessments of offenders and providing supervision programmes designed to help to reduce the risk of re-offending. Probation officers present pre-sentence reports to the courts and draw up supervision plans for offenders. They liaise with police and prison colleagues, and housing and social services departments. Their responsibilities include rehabilitation of offenders and some work with victims.

Entry requirements: The training involves studying for a two-year Diploma in Probation Studies, delivered by nine regional consortia working with higher education institutions. Work experience or voluntary work with people who have difficulties is essential plus excellent communication skills, both written and verbal, and an understanding of different cultural and ethnic backgrounds. You would also need to be very perceptive about people, assertive (to cope with difficult behaviour) and creative (in order to come up with ideas to help offenders change their patterns of behaviour). Training for probation work is different in Scotland and Northern Ireland where the qualification is still the Diploma in Social Work.

Employers: More information is available from the Home Office website at www. probation.homeoffice.gov.uk

There are a number of other careers where a background in social sciences provides useful transferable skills and is relevant. However, most of the careers listed below involve doing some further training, either full-time or part-time, while in employment:

- Community worker

- Housing manager/adviser

- Information scientist/librarian

- Health promotion/education officer

- Public sector administrator/manager

- Charity administrator/fundraiser

- Clinical audit

- Teacher – primary/secondary/further education

- Careers adviser/personal adviser

- (Associate) Mental health practitioner

- Quality assurance adviser

- Personnel/HR manager

- Counsellor

- Speech and language therapist

- Occupational therapist

- Operational researcher

- Management consultant

- Recruitment consultant

- Civil Service fast streamer

- Prison governor

- Journalist

- Advertising executive

- PR officer

- Public affairs consultant

- Media analyst

More information on these careers and others is available on the Prospects website and in your university careers service library. In addition, approximately two-thirds of graduate jobs are open to graduates of any discipline. You may feel you need some help with self-assessment in order to find out which of these careers would match your skills, interests, values and personality. If so, you can look at the following websites:

- Prospects website – 'What job would suit me?': www.prospects.ac.uk

- Kiwi Careers – 'Pathfinder': www.kiwicareers.co.nz

- Keirsey Temperament Sorter: www.keirsey.com

- UKGRAD: www.grad.ac.uk

- My Future: www.myfuture.edu.au

- Career Development Manual, University of Waterloo: www.cdm.uwaterloo.ca

University careers services also have tools such as:

- MBTI – a personality type indicator

- Prospects Planner – a computer-aided careers guidance system

- A careers guidance interview

- Careers management skills programmes

Case study: A graduate with an MSc in Social Research reflects on his own career path

John started his career by achieving a 2.1 BSc Social Administration from Loughborough University. His final-year project was concerned with evaluating community services for people with learning disabilities. On completion of this he was offered the opportunity to stay for a further two years to study a MPhil in the same subject. Following this, he stayed at the university to work as a research assistant and studied part-time to achieve a PhD. However, although he only stayed 15 months as a research assistant, it took him five years' part-time study to complete the PhD.

(Continued)

(Continued)

By the end of his research post, John felt that research was not of sufficient immediate relevance for him and that he wanted to make more of a difference to other people's lives. He therefore found a job for two years as a social work assistant working on a community project with people with learning difficulties. In effect doing the work of a social worker, he decided to qualify by studying the Masters in Social Work course at Trent University.

John then became a qualified social worker and worked as a generic social worker with Nottingham County Council Children's Services. He stayed in this post for four and a half years, involved in child protection activities.

His next move was to a specialist post in adolescent mental therapy as a member of a multidisciplinary child and family therapy team. Doing his own research helped him to keep his knowledge up to date and provided the basis for presentations.

John then secured a senior social worker's post with Surrey Social Services Family Centre. Four years later a manager's post, 'Assistant Team Manager', became vacant in a neighbouring centre. As a manager, John was involved in reviewing and evaluating what could be provided with the staffing resources available and was again trying to assess what had worked and why and how to be more effective.

At this point, John was at a crossroads in his career. He could either take the route of therapist/manager or opt for a career in research and evaluation. He decided to study for a part-time MSc in Social Research at the University of Surrey.

John found that the Masters course enabled him to switch career ladders without losing too much in terms of salary. It also gave him just the right skills-set to help him to change career direction. The course confirmed for him that his greatest interest was in evaluation and research. Having been a practitioner, John could reflect on the impact that research could make, provided that it was applied to real-life situations. He felt that his experience in therapeutic social supportive roles had helped him in his research work because the quality of his research often depended on the relationships he had built up with people.

On completion of his Masters course, John secured a job as Senior Evaluation Officer for the NSPCC, which had been advertised in a national newspaper. He is responsible for evaluating the policies and services offered by the NSPCC to abused children. John still conducts interviews himself with practitioners using qualitative methods and is a project manager monitoring the work of two other evaluation

(Continued)

(Continued)

officers. His job has a development function so he is responsible for piloting new approaches and training other staff in evaluation methods. He evaluates various NSPCC campaigns by meeting groups of young people and asking them about how effective the campaigns are for them. He also uses many other skills, such as managing time, negotiating with clients and communication.

His career path shows that he has not been afraid to try a new route. His example also shows that it is now quite common to have more than one career and to re-train at some point in life.

Marketing yourself to an employer

Key skills

The first step is to be aware of your key skills and how these match with what employers are looking for. Sometimes postgraduates make the mistake of thinking employers are only interested in their academic ability. However, they are also interested in other transferable skills. Table 11.1 is a list of key skills that are popular with employers. For each one they would be seeking evidence from you – not just from your academic experience, but also from other areas of your life.

When applying for a job it is worth making a list of the competencies or key skills that the employer has highlighted in the 'person spec' or 'job description' and then listing examples of your own evidence for possessing these skills. You will need to incorporate these skills with your evidence for them in your CV or application form.

There is a very useful skills audit that you can use on the UKGRAD website (www. grad.ac.uk). The Windmills Programme also has a useful 'Skills Check' (www. windmills programme.com).

Constructing a targeted CV

A CV is essentially a marketing document, through which you are trying to impress a potential employer and demonstrate why you are the ideal person for the job. This

Table 11.1 Key Skills

Key skill	Examples of evidence
Communication	Written – thesis, published papers Oral – teaching and presentations
Team work	Employment when you have been part of a team, team assignments and projects
Time management	Examples of when you have had to prioritise work and establish a schedule in order to meet a deadline
Organisational	Examples of events you have organised (perhaps extra curriculum activities) and meetings you have arranged
Problem-solving	Examples of obstacles you have needed to overcome at work or in your studies
Analytical skills	What methods have you used (e.g. quantitative/qualitative) and with what degree of success?
Computing/IT	What specialist software, databases and statistical packages can you use?
Research	What methods can you use and what has been the outcome?
Independent working	When have you needed to be a self-starter? What initiatives have you taken?

means that your CV needs to be targeted to the needs of the employer as outlined in the 'person spec' or 'job description'.

There are no hard rules for constructing a CV. The format can range from the traditional 'chronological CV' to a 'skills-based CV', but it needs to be relevant to the job and interesting to read. The 'Prospects' website 'Applications and Interviews' section shows different CV formats.

Although there are no rules, there are some basic principles.

How long should it be?

Put yourself in the employer's shoes and consider that on average he/she is so busy that only about 30 seconds will be spent looking at your CV. Therefore try to keep your CV down to two pages of A4 with a third page for publications/conferences if needed. The exception to this is for academic posts where the university will want to know more details about your research, your degree content, project work and any publications. In this case a longer CV is acceptable, with an appendix including publications, papers given at conferences, etc. There are some useful examples of different types of CV for PhD students applying for academic and other research type posts on the UKGRAD website (www.grad.ac.uk).

What should I include?

Be ruthless and try to give only relevant information. Think about the most important facts about you and give supporting evidence to make it more convincing. Don't forget to include leadership roles within university societies and positions of responsibility held outside academia.

How should I present it?

You can experiment but always aim for a logical order with relevant information under appropriate headings. Start with your most recent education and employment, then the rest in reverse chronological order. You do not need to write 'CV' at the top, just put your name in bold as a heading. You can embolden key words and headings and use bullet points with action verbs such as 'negotiated' and 'initiated' to break up the text. Use good quality paper, white or neutral coloured and produced by a printer, not photocopied. Do not fold or staple your CV. Sending your CV by email is fine but you may wish to check that it has been received. Always ask someone to proof read your CV to make sure there are no spelling or grammatical errors.

How do I demonstrate my key skills?

If you are constructing a skills-based CV, you will probably list your key skills on the first page with headings and appropriate evidence. Your 'employment' section will then be shorter and will include the name of the employer you worked for, the title of the job that you did, the dates you worked there and your main responsibilities.

If you write a chronological CV, you may wish to have a separate section with the heading 'Key skills' where you identify your most appropriate skills for the post and give evidence for them. Alternatively, you may wish to mention your skills under the relevant job in the 'Employment' section and then mop up any extras such as 'languages, IT, leadership' in a shorter 'Additional skills' section. Figure 11.1 is an example of a chronological CV.

LINDSAY PARKER

Cathedral Court
University of Poppleton
Poppleton PP2 5XH

Tel: 01999 63218
Mobile: 07796 703885
Email: l.parker21@poppleton.ac.uk

Date of Birth: 19 May 1982

Career Objective: To apply my research skills and knowledge of housing as a social researcher specialising in housing policy.

EDUCATION

2004–2005 University of Surrey, Guildford
MSc in Social Research Methods
Subjects include: Research Design, Data Analysis, Field Methods, Discourse and Documentary Analysis, SPSS, Qualitative & Quantitative Techniques
Dissertation: Statistical analysis of longitudinal data on graduate employment using SPSS

2000–2003 University of Sussex, Brighton
BA (Hons) European History (2:1)
Subjects included: Modern French Thought, Life History Research, History of Political Thought, French and German
Final year project: An investigation into class and political conflict

1993–2000 Ridge School, Farnham
A Levels (2000) – History (B), Economics (B), French (C), German AS (C)
GCSEs (1998) – 9, including Maths (B) and English Language (B)

EMPLOYMENT

2003–2004 **Clerical Officer, Bristol City Council Housing Department**

Responsibilities included:

- Providing secretarial support for committees
- Arranging and servicing meetings
- Researching and preparing reports
- Answering public enquiries on all aspects of social housing

Vacation Work
1998–2000 Retail Sales: W.H. Smith
Tele-Sales: Direct Marketing Ltd.

KEY SKILLS

Teamwork Worked successfully in team of four on group research project (our project achieved commendation from panel of social researchers)
Computing Regular user of SPSS, PowerPoint, Word, and Excel
Languages Speak conversational French and German – currently undertaking structured course with certification
Communication Experienced in delivery of oral and written reports to academic and commercial audiences
Analytical Competent with a range of parametric statistics

AWARDS AND PRIZES
University Departmental Prize for Best Final Year Project (2003)
School   Awarded the Duke of Edinburgh's Gold Award (2000)

POSITIONS OF RESPONSIBILITY AND INTERESTS
Union   Secretary of Rag Committee. Actively involved in organising events which raised £20,000 in support of the National Children's Home
Sports   Regular 2nd XI player for University of Surrey Football Team Organised departmental five-a-side soccer tournament
Writing   Regular contributor to *Bare Facts*, the student newspaper
Voluntary   Worked with homeless people in London one day a week for a year (2001)

REFEREES
Academic   *Previous employer*

Figure 11.1   An example curriculum vitae

Do I need to send a covering letter?

Yes, always include a covering letter and use it to demonstrate your writing skills and to draw attention to the highlights on your CV. Although it need not be very long (one page of A4 is plenty), it needs to be carefully thought out and should convey enthusiasm and your key selling points for the job. Figure 11.2 is an example of a covering letter for a Masters student who is applying on 'spec' to a housing association for a research position.

Further information

Different countries tend to favour different styles of CV, so for other countries refer to Thompson (2000) and www.eurograduate.com

Your address
The date

Dr C. Goodman
Principal Research Officer
Roseberry Housing Association
Queen Anne's Gate
London SW1Y 2AG

Dear Dr Goodman,

I am currently on the MSc in Social Research Methods at the University of Surrey and am available for employment from September 2005.

(Continued)

I am writing in response to your entry in the *Directory of Social Research Organisations in the UK*, which mentions that you specialise in research into housing policy. I wish to enquire whether you may currently or in the near future have any openings for a Research Assistant. As you will see from my enclosed CV, I can offer a considerable amount of relevant experience, including:

- Recent experience of a year's employment in a local authority housing department undertaking administrative support for the Housing Committee;
- A degree and MSc which have included several courses and a dissertation related to social research and housing policy in Europe and the UK;
- Evidence of my teamworking and interpersonal skills, through my achievements and responsibilities in extra-curricular areas, e.g. my position as Secretary of the Rag Committee and my voluntary work with homeless people. ...
- Experience of using computers, e.g. SPSS to analyse and interpret statistics as well as a range of packages, including Microsoft Word, Excel and PowerPoint.

I am very keen to apply my skills and experience in an organisation such as yours because .... If you would like any further information I would, of course, be very happy to supply it.

Thank you for considering my application and I do look forward to hearing from you.

Yours sincerely

Figure 11.2   An example covering letter

Case study: A Job-hunting strategy

Emily graduated from a Masters in Social Research in 2002. Here she describes her own job-hunting strategy.

Emily works as a research consultant with a small private company. The latter provides consultancy support, policy and financial analyses to the health and social care sector. Emily works on project and programme evaluations for Sure Start Partnerships. Sure Start aims to improve the social well-being of young children and their parents by various programmes, such as teaching parenting skills. Emily evaluates six programmes, which involves doing background research, contacting clients, doing surveys of parents, designing questionnaires, training interviewers, analysing, findings and writing reports.

Emily has a degree in Social Policy and International Studies. She studied part-time for the Masters in Social Research while still working as a commercial database assistant. Following her Masters she worked as a research fellow on a temporary contract in a university.

(Continued)

(Continued)

When the project was coming to an end Emily decided to make an appointment with her university careers adviser in order to get help with her CV and ideas of where to look for jobs. As a result of this she found several suitable jobs advertised in Wednesday's *Guardian,* including her current post. She also emailed her CV 'on spec' to MORI, MVA Research and BMRB. In response, she was called for an interview with MORI and offered a job by them. In all she applied for six jobs and was offered two. In her experience there are plenty of jobs and lots of new private agencies. During a three-week period she found 8–10 jobs advertised. She advises students to be realistic about money because starting salaries are not that great.

In terms of qualifications and skills, Emily feels that the Masters course really gave her the skill-set she needed in her current job. She also feels that having a friendly manner is important because she needs to make people feel that they can trust her. She needs to be able to relate to all sorts and finds that good eye contact helps. It is also important to be good at multi-tasking. As deadlines are often given to her by people who do not give her the data in time, she needs to be diplomatic but also able to confront people.

Emily advises current students to start looking at job adverts to see what is out there. When you are ready, she suggests replying to job adverts but also applying 'on spec'. She has noticed that qualitative skills are very much in demand, just as much as quantitative skills. Her recommendation is to use your university careers service and ask for advice on your CV. In addition, practise doing psychometric tests, especially verbal and numerical reasoning, and practise your interview technique.

Finding job advertisements

For some sources of vacancies, mostly in the UK but also including some graduate sites for other countries, see the 'Sources of vacancy information' section at the end of this chapter. If you are interested in working in another country, then the Prospects website has a very useful section on 'working abroad' with a country-by-country index. In addition, you may wish to look for useful links by using the Eurograduate website (www.eurograduate.com), the overseas jobs website (www.overseasjobs.com) and the World Careers Network (www.wcn.co.uk). If you are an international student looking to work in the UK, you will find more information on www.workingintheuk.gov.uk. You will also be able to find out more information from your university careers service.

Speculative applications

Many postgraduates still find work by targeting specific employers who are of interest and sending off a letter plus CV on 'spec' to them. If you are intending to use this approach, send your CV and covering letter to a named contact, point out your key selling points and tell them why you are interested in this type of work and this employer. You can mention in your covering letter that you will contact them by phone in about two weeks to check that they received your CV. There is a list of publications containing suggestions of possible employers to contact in the Further Reading section at the end of this chapter.

Timing of applications

Some major employers have a recruitment cycle with set closing dates. Others recruit when they need people. You will need to be aware of employers' training schemes where there is a set closing date each year. Listed below are some examples of those where you would need to apply before the closing date in order to start in the September of the following year.

- Clinical psychology training – applications need to be submitted by 1 December.

- Social work training courses – applications need to be submitted by 15 December.

- Government economist – applications need to be made in the early autumn.

- Probation officer – adverts for trainee probation officers usually appear during the spring.

- Graduate Training Schemes with employers have varied closing dates but some large employers close their applications as early as 31 December. Financial companies and public sector management schemes tend to recruit early.

You can check closing dates on the occupational profiles on the Prospects website or at your university careers service. University careers services often arrange employer presentations and careers fairs. Many other employers recruit on a rolling basis all year round.

The importance of networking

Not all job vacancies appear as advertisements. It is estimated that about three-quarters of available jobs are filled by word of mouth or by internal candidates. Hence, many postgraduates still find jobs by using their own personal contacts. You may wish to think about your current contacts, such as supervisors and lecturers, contacts made through a placement or work experience, commercial/industrial partners in your research, and family and friends.

Other sources for networking include attending conferences and workshops, joining professional associations and meeting employers at Careers Fairs, using your university careers service, contacting your university alumni association and participating in voluntary work or temporary paid work.

Conclusion

This chapter has provided some ideas of careers that are suitable for postgraduate social scientists. The chapter has illustrated the importance of marketing yourself to an employer as being a well-rounded individual with formal qualifications particularly in research, but also possessing other key personal skills. It has also been designed to help you to consider some job-seeking strategies. Deciding on a career is a journey and there are people, such as your careers adviser and lecturers, who will be pleased to help you along the way.

Further reading

Ali, L. and Graham, B. (2000). *Moving On in Your Career: A Guide for Academic Researchers and Postgraduates*. London: Routledge Falmer.

Careers Staff at Flinders University and Australian National University (2004). *A Degree of Certainty: Career Options for Postgraduate Research Students. Carlton, Victoria, Australia: Graduate Careers Council of Australia Ltd.*

Goldsmith, John A., Komlos, J. and Gold, P.S. (2001). *The Chicago Guide to Your Academic Career*. Chicago: University of Chicago Press.

Sources of lists of possible employers whom you could contact regarding speculative applications:

Bulmer, M., Sykes, W. and Moorhouse, J. (1998). *Directory of Social Research Organisations (UK)*. London and New York: Mansell.

The Social Research Association Members' Directory – produced every two years plus the newsletter has a 'contacts' section.

Current Research in Britain: *Social Sciences* – published annually by Cartermill International, this provides information about higher education/independent research projects.

Research Buyers Guide – produced by the Market Research Society (published annually and available online at www.rbg.org.uk), this lists organisations offering market research services.

The Association of Qualitative Research Directory – published annually and available online at www.aqr.org.uk, it lists practitioners.

The Voluntary Agencies Directory (2004) – produced by National Council for Voluntary Organisations (NCVCO).

Sources of vacancy information

Key Graduate Careers websites (vacancies, careers information, directories of employers and useful links):

Prospects, UK: www.prospects.ac.uk

Gradlink, Australia: www.gradlink.edu.au

Kiwi Careers, New Zealand: www.kiwicareers.govt.nz

Workopolis, Canada: www.workopoliscampus.com

CACEE (Canadian Association of Career Educators and Employers): www.cacee.com

Campus work link: www.campusworklink.com

Graduate Careers Ireland: www.gradireland.com

Hobsons, International: www.hobsons.com

Monster, covers New Zealand, UK, Canada, Australia, USA: www.monster.com

Graduate Opportunities, Australia and New Zealand: www.graduateopportunities.com

JobWeb US careers advice and vacancies: www.jobweb.com

Your university careers service vacancy bulletin: Your careers service's web pages

Academic posts

Academics 360 (international links to faculty positions by discipline):
www.academics360.com

Academic jobs website, UK: www.jobs.ac.uk

The Times Higher Education Supplement (Fridays): www.thesis.co.uk

The Guardian Educational Supplement (Tuesdays): www.guardianunlimited.co.uk

Association of Commonwealth Universities: www.acu.ac.uk/adverts

University websites PhD jobs: www.phdjobs.com

Find a postdoctoral research post: www.findapostdoc.com

Researchers in general

PhD Jobs: www.phdjobs.com

Social Sciences Research Grapevine: www.sosig.ac.uk

The Social Research Association Newsletter: www.the-sra.org.uk

The Australian Sociological Association: www.tasa.org.au

Academy of Social Sciences in Australia: www.assa.edu.au

The Market Research Society: www.mrs.org.uk

Prospects Today and Prospects Directory: www.prospects.ac.uk

University of London Virtual Careers Website links for postgraduate researchers:
www.careers.lon.ac.uk/

The Association of Qualitative Research: www.aqr.org.uk

The Guardian (Wednesday): www.guardianunlimited.co.uk

The Times Educational Supplement: www.tes.co.uk

Civil Service: www.careers.civil-service.gov.uk; www.gsr.gov.uk

Australian Government Online Directory: www.gold.gov.au

National Health Service: www.jobs.nhs.uk

Doctorjob: www.doctorjob.com

Hobsons website and Directory: www.hobsons.com

Public sector database: www.jobsgopublic.com

Charities: www.jobsincharities.co.uk

Psychologists and social support

BPS Appointments Memorandum (vacancies for assistant and qualified psychologists): www.appmemo.co.uk

The Australian Psychological Society: www.psychology.org.au

Australian Association of Social Workers: www.aasw.asn.au

The Guardian (Tuesday and Wednesday): www.guardianunlimited.co.uk

Health Service Journal, EMAP weekly: www.hsj.co.uk

National Health Service: www.jobs.nhs.uk

Local government jobs: www.lgjobs.com

Community Care Magazine: www.communitycare.co.uk

Probation Service: www.probation.homeoffice.gov.uk

Prison Service: www.hmprisonservice.gov.uk

Human Resources/Personnel: www.peoplemanagement.co.uk

Economists

The Economist (weekly): www.economist. com

The Financial Times (daily): www.ft.com

Government Economic Service: www.ges.gov.uk

Hobsons Finance Casebook: www.hobsons.com

Target City and Finance: www.doctorjob.co.uk

Prospects Directory: www.prospects.ac.uk

Hobsons Directory: www.hobsons.com

The Economic Society of Australia: www.ecosoc.org.au

Specialist recruitment agencies

Recruitment and Employment Federation: www.rec.uk.com

Glossary

Abstract A summary, often about 100 words in length, of the main conclusions, findings, and methods of a published research article.

Advisory group (steering group) A group of interested people and/or experts (possibly including representatives of sponsors, q.v.) who meet regularly but infrequently to offer guidance and advice to a principal investigator (q.v.). A steering group has some power to enforce its decisions, while an advisory group may only proffer advice.

Beneficence The principle of beneficence states that one should do good to others, when one can do that with minimal risk or expense to oneself.

Bioethics The study of the ethical and moral implications of biomedical advances, such as in genetic engineering and new health treatments.

Community of practice A community of practice is a group of people who share similar objectives. In pursuit of these, they work with the same tools, deploy similar skills and express themselves in a common language. Through such common activity, they may come to hold similar beliefs.

Computer-mediated communication Communication between people through computer interfaces. Examples of computer-mediated communication (CMC) include email, instant messaging, and video conferencing over the internet.

Copyright A set of rights over intellectual property which control its reproduction and distribution for a limited time.

Database right A right that prevents unauthorised copying of the contents of a database.

Empirical research Research that analyses data collected from the social world through instruments such as surveys or interviews.

Executive summary A short summary of a research project, intended for decision-makers, that emphasises the implications and recommendations of the research, rather than its theory and methods.

Fair use An exception to the rule that copyright materials may not be reproduced without the permission of the copyright holder: brief quotation for non-commercial, especially research and educational uses, is permitted under the fair use doctrine provided that the source is properly acknowledged.

Focus group A focus group is a form of qualitative research in which a group of people are asked for their attitudes or opinions about a topic. Questions are asked in an interactive group setting where participants are free to talk with other group members. An online focus group is one in which the members communicate using computer-mediated communication (q.v.), such as a chat room or bulletin board on the internet.

Funding organisation   An organisation that funds social research. Examples include research councils (q.v.), national and local government, charitable foundations, and business.

Gantt chart   A diagram with time as the horizontal axis in which each task in a project is represented by a bar covering the period during which the task is expected to last. A Gantt chart can be used to calculate how long a project should take and to identify the critical tasks which, if delayed, will delay the whole project.

Informed consent   The idea that patients embarking on medical treatment and, by extension, respondents to surveys and other types of social research, should have the right to be informed about the objectives, risks and consequences of the experience that they are about to encounter and then, having understood this information, must give their consent before the medical treatment takes place or they participate in the research.

Intellectual property   Ideas and concepts, including inventions and discoveries, computer programs, databases, and formulae that have some market value and which are legally owned by someone or some organisation.

Learning outcome   The knowledge and skills that students are intended to acquire as a result of following a course of study.

Literature review   A summary description of the scholarly literature relevant to a research topic, preferably organized in a structured way.

Magnitude of risk   The weight of the consequences that may occur if a risky event comes to pass.

Meta analysis   A statistical method of combining the results of a collection of analyses, each reported in a separate research study. Analysing the results of a number of studies can yield more accurate estimates than any one alone.

Milestone   Milestones are points in a project at which decisions are needed; for example concerning which of several methods will be adopted as the basis for the next phase of the project.

Moral right   An author of a work has the moral rights to be identified as its author and to prevent publication of a modified version of the work.

Multidisciplinary and interdisciplinary research   Research that draws on the traditions of more than one discipline. Multidisciplinary research uses ideas from more than one discipline side by side, while interdisciplinary research attempts to combine or meld the ideas of different disciplines.

Nonmaleficience   The principle of nonmaleficience states that one should do no harm to others. In practice, this means that researchers should take all reasonable steps to ensure that no harm occurs to subjects by virtue of their participation in the study.

Participant observation   Participant observation involves the researcher living in a social setting, participating to some degree in the culture and activities of a group, while observing the social life around him or her. It may also involve interviewing group members.

Patent   A right for a limited time to prohibit the use of an invention by manufacturing, using or selling products or processes, granted by governments in exchange for the open publication of the details of the invention.

PICO formula   Population, Intervention, Control, Comparison or Context, Outcomes. An acronym that indicates the main ingredients of a systematic review (q.v.).

Prevalence of risk   The likelihood that some event with undesirable consequences will come to pass.

Primary research   Research that collects and analyses data from primary sources, that is, directly from the social world, such as by surveys, observation and documents.

Principal investigator   A principal investigator is the person chiefly responsible for the conduct of a research project. He or she may be assisted by co-investigators.

Protocol   The plan of an investigation or research study, and so also a description of the stages and methods used in a research study.

Registered rights   Rights conferred on intellectual property (q.v.) when the property is registered at an intellectual property office. For example, rights to a trade mark (q.v.) only become enforceable once the mark has been registered.

Research assistant, Research fellow, Researcher   Someone who works on, and has a salary paid from a research project. The terminology varies between employers, but generally a research assistant is more junior than a research fellow. The term, 'researcher', although not as common, has the merit of being gender and status neutral.

Research contract   A contract between a research organisation and a sponsor (q.v.) in which the organisation undertakes to carry out a project in return for an agreed payment. Research contracts are almost invariably agreements between organisations, although it is the Principal investigator (q.v.) who is responsible for performing the research.

Research council   An independent government agency established to fund a nation's research, usually using public money. Those wishing to conduct research may apply to a research council for money to support their work, covering staff salaries, the cost of surveys, travel expenses, etc.

Sample   Those from a population who are actually observed or studied in a research project. The aim is to select a sample from the population (e.g. using a random process, or by choosing representative individuals) in such a way that it is possible to make inferences (statistically, or in other ways) about the population from evidence drawn just from the sample.

Secondary research   Research that analyses already existing data, which has been initially collected for another purpose, either for another research project or for some administrative reason.

Sponsor   An organisation giving support to a research project by providing money, access to data, access to respondents, or in other ways. Sponsors usually expect some return for their support, such as a copy of the research findings, and may request rights over the research, for example, to suppress or delay inconvenient results.

Supervisor/supervisory team   The person or people who are responsible for guiding research conducted as part of doctoral study, and for mentoring a PhD student.

Systematic review   A literature review that has been created using systematic methods, including methods for locating all relevant scholarly articles and for evaluating the research described in those articles.

Trade mark   A distinctive sign used by a business to identify itself and its products to consumers. A trade mark may be a name, a symbol, a phrase, a logo, or an image. A trade mark needs to be registered (q.v.) in order that its owner can prevent its unauthorised use by others.

Unregistered rights   Rights that arise immediately that intellectual property (q.v.) is created. For example, as soon as a book is written, its author possesses copyright (q.v.), without the need to carry out any registration procedure.

Voluntary consent   A participant gives voluntary consent when he or she freely consents to take part in a study. Consent may not be entirely voluntary when the participant stands in a subordinate position to the researcher (as a result of differences in status, power or education, for instance) or where the participant is coerced through threats or bribes to take part. *See also* informed consent.

Web log (weblog, blog)   A form of diary published on the world wide web. Bloggers usually add an entry to their blogs every few days, describing their activities and/or commenting on world events.

References

Adenekan, S. (2005). Academics Give Lessons on Blogs. *BBC News Online,* http://news.bbc.co.uk/1/hi/education/4194669.stm (23.01.05).

Adler, P.A. and Adler, P. (2002). The Reluctant Respondent. In J.F. Gubrium and J.A. Holstein (eds), *Handbook of Interview Research: Context and Method* (pp. 515–535). Thousand Oaks, CA: Sage.

Alexander, V. (2001). Analysing Visual Materials. In N. Gilbert (ed.), *Researching Social Life* (pp. 343–357). London: Sage.

Ali, L. and Graham, B. (2000). *Moving on in Your Career: A Guide for Academic Researchers and Postgraduates.* London: Routledge Falmer.

Annas, George J. and Grodin, Michael A. (1992). *The Nazi Doctors and the Nuremberg Code.* New York: Oxford University Press.

Arksey, H. and Knight, P. (1999). *Interviewing for Social Scientists: An Introductory Resource with Examples.* London: Sage.

Association of University Teachers (2004). *The Unequal Academy: UK Academic Staff 1995–96 to 2002–3.* London: Association of University Teachers, http://www.aut.org.uk/index.cfm?articleid=917

Atkinson, R. (2002). *Does Gentrification Help or Harm Urban Neighbourhoods? An Assessment of the Evidence-base in the Context of the New Urban Agenda.* Centre for Neighbourhood Research Paper No. 5. Glasgow and Bristol Universities, http://www.neighbourhoodcentre.org.uk/research/research.html

Barter, C. and Renold, E. (2003). Dilemmas of Control: Methodological Implications and Reflections of Foregrounding Children's Perspectives on Violence. In R. M. Lee and E.A. Stanko (eds), *Researching Violence: Essays on Methodology and Measurement* (pp. 88–106). London: Routledge.

Baverstock, A. (2001). *Marketing Your Book: An Author's Guide.* London: A and C Black.

Baym, N. (2000). *Tune In, Log On: Soaps, Fandom and Online Community.* London: Sage.

Beauchamp, T.L. and Childress, J.F. (2001). *Principles of Biomedical Ethics* (5th edn). New York: Oxford University Press.

Becker, Howard (1986). *Writing for Social Scientists: How to Start and Finish Your Thesis, Book or Article.* London: University of Chicago Press.

Becker, Howard (1998). Visual Sociology, Documentary Photography, and Photojournalism: It's (Almost) All a Matter of Context. In J. Prosser (ed.), *Image-based Research: A Sourcebook for Qualitative Researchers* (pp. 84–96). London: Falmer Press.

Becker, Howard (2004). *Writing for Social Scientists.* Chicago: University of Chicago Press.

Bell, J. (1993). *Doing Your Research Project: A Guide for First-time Researchers in Education and Social Science* (2nd edn). Buckingham: Open University Press.

Belo, R. (2004). Blogs take on the mainstream, http://news.bbc.co.uk/2/hi/technology/4086337.stm (23.01.05).

Berger, J. (1972). *Ways of Seeing.* London: Penguin.

Berry, R. (1994). *The Research Project: How to Write it.* London: Routledge.

Best, S.J. and Krueger, B.S. (2004). *Internet Data Collection.* London: Sage.

Boaz, A., Ashby, D. and Young, K. (2002). *Systematic Reviews: What Have They Got to Offer Evidence-based Policy and Practice?* Working Paper 2. ESRC UK Centre for Evidence-based Policy and Practice, Queen Mary, University of London, http://www.evidencenetwork.org

Boaz, A. and Pawson, R. (forthcoming). The Perilous Road from Evidence to Policy: Five Journeys Compared. *Journal of Social Policy.*

Boshier, R. (1990). Socio-Psychological Factors in Electronic Networking. *International Journal of Lifelong Education*, 9(1), 49–64.

Bowling, B. (2004). Why I Think Academics Should Take Part in Public Inquiries. *The Higher,* 13 February 2004.

Braunack-Mayer, A. and Hersh, D. (2001). An Ethical Voice in the Silence of Aphasia: Judging Understanding and Consent in People with Aphasia. *Journal of Clinical Ethics,* 12(4), 388–396.

Brink, P.J. and Wood, M.J. (1994). *Basic Steps in Planning Nursing Research: From Question to Proposal* (4th edn). Boston, MA: Jones & Bartlett Publishers.

British Educational Research Association (2004). *Ethical Guidelines for Educational Research.* London: BERA, http://www.bera.ac.uk/publications/pdfs/ETHICA1.PDF

Brown, J.S. and Duguid, P. (1991). Organizational Learning and Communities of Practice: Toward a Unified View of Working, Learning, and Innovation. *Organization Science*, 2(1), 40–57.

Bryson, C. (2004). *Strategic Approaches to Managing and Developing Part-time Teachers.* York: Learning and Teaching Support Network, www.heacademy.ac.uk

Bulmer, M., Sykes, W. and Moorhouse, J. (1998). *Directory of Social Research Organisations (UK).* London and New York: Mansell.

Burgess, J. (2004). *Creativity/Machine: Creativity, Culture and Technology.* http://hypertext.rmit.edu.au/~burgess/

Campbell, R., Pound, P., Pope, C., Britten, N., Pill, R., Morgan, M., et al. (2003). Evaluating Meta-ethnography: A Synthesis of Qualitative Research on Lay Experiences of Diabetes and Diabetes Care. *Social Science and Medicine*, 56(4), 671–684.

Careers Staff at Flinders University and ANU (2004). *A Degree of Certainty: Career Options for Postgraduate Research Students.* Carlton, Victoria: Graduate Careers Council of Australia.

Chaplin, E. (1994). *Sociology and Visual Representation.* London: Routledge.

Cleveland Inquiry. (1988). *Report of the Inquiry into Child Abuse in Cleveland 1987.* CM 412. London: HMSO.

Christie, A. and Gare. S. (2004). *Blackstone's Statutes on Intellectual Property* (7th edn) Oxford: Oxford University Press. With companion website for new developments at http://www.oup.com/uk/booksites/content/0199273057/

Cohen, Kris (2005). Photos Leave Home: Research Notes from a 1-year ESRC Study about Personal Photography and the Web (Oct 2004–Oct 2005). Retrieved from http://www.photosleavehome.blogspot.com (26.01.05).

Cook, Trevor (2002). *A User's Guide to Patents.* London: Butterworths.

Coomber, R. (1997). Using the Internet for Survey Research. *Sociological Research Online*, 2(2), http://www.socresonline.org.uk/socresonline/2/2/2.html

Cooper, H. (1998). *Synthesizing Research: A Guide for Literature Reviews.* London: Sage.

Correll, S. (1995). An Ethnography of an Electronic Bar: The Lesbian Café. *Journal of Contemporary Ethnography*, 24(3), 270–298.

Cuba, L. and Cocking, J. (1994). *How to Write about Social Sciences.* London: Harper Collins.

D'Andrade, R. (1995). Moral Models in Anthropology. *Current Anthropology*, 36(3), 399–408.

Davies, H.T.O., Nutley, S. and Smith, P. (2000). *What Works? Evidence-based Policy and Practice in Public Services.* Bristol: The Policy Press.

Davis, Jennifer (2003). *Intellectual Property Law* (2nd edn). London: LexisNexis UK.

de Koning, K. and Martin, M. (1996). *Participatory Research in Health: Issues and Explanations.* London: Zed Books.

Denscombe, M. (1998). *The Good Research Guide for Small-scale Social Research Projects*. Milton Keynes: Open University Press.

Denzin, N. (1999). Cybertalk and the Method of Instances. In S. Jones (ed.), *Doing Internet Research: Critical Issues and Methods for Examining the Net* (pp. 107–126). London: Sage.

Department of Health (2001). *Research Governance Framework for Health and Social Care*. London: Department of Health.

Dicks, B. and Mason, B. (1998). Hypermedia and Ethnography: Reflections on the Construction of a Research Approach. *Sociological Research Online*, 3(3), http://www.socresonline.org.uk/3/3/3.html

Ditton, J. (1977). *Part-time Crime: An Ethnography of Fiddling and Pilferage*. London: Macmillan.

Dreher, M. (1994). Qualitative Research Methods from the Reviewer's Perspective. In J.M. Morse (ed.), *Critical Issues in Qualitative Research Methods* (pp. 281–297). Thousand Oaks, CA: Sage.

Dubois, D., Holloway, B., Valentine, J. and Cooper, H. (2002). Effectiveness of Mentoring Programs for Youth: A Meta-analytic Review. *American Journal of Community Psychology*, 30(2), 157–197.

Economic and Social Research Council (2005) *Postgraduate Training Guidelines*. Swindon: ESRC, http://www.esrcsocietytoday.ac.uk/ESRCInfoCentre/Images/Postgraduate_Training_Guidelines_2005_tcm6-9062.pdf

Economic and Social Research Council (2005) *Research Funding Guide*. Swindon: ESRC, http://www.esrcsocietytoday.ac.uk/ESRCInfoCentre/Images/res_funding_guide_tcm6-9734.pdf

Economic and Social Research Council (n.d.) *Pressing Home Your Findings: Media Guidelines for ESRC Researchers*. Swindon: ESRC.

Economic and Social Research Council (n.d.) *Key conditions for ESRC Studentships*. Swindon: ESRC, http://www.esrcsocietytoday.ac.uk/ESRCInfoCentre/Images/sect2_tcm6-5494.pdf

Egan, M., Petticrew, M., Ogilvie, D. and Hamilton, V. (2003). New Roads and Human Health: A Systematic Review. *American Journal of Public Health*, 93(9), 1463–1471.

Egger, M., Davey-Smith, G. and Altman, B.G. (2001). *Systematic Reviews in Health Care: Meta-analysis in Context*. London: BMJ Books.

El Dorado Task Force (2002). *Final Report*. Arlington, VA: American Anthropological Association, http://www.aaanet.org/edtf/final/preface.htm

Ess, C. and AoIR Ethics Working Committee (2002). *Ethical Decision-making and Internet Research: Recommendations from the AoIR Ethics Working Committee*. www.aoir.org/reports/ethics.pdf

Ezzy, D. (2002). *Qualitative Analysis: Practice and Innovation*. Sydney: Allen and Unwin.

Faden, R.R. and Beauchamp, T.L. (1986). *A History and Theory of Informed Consent*. New York: Oxford University Press.

Fielding, N. (1982). Observational Research on the National Front. In M. Bulmer (ed.), *Social Research Ethics: An Examination of the Merits of Covert Participant Observation* (pp. 80–104) London: Macmillan.

Fielding, N. (1988). *Joining Forces*. London: Routledge.

Fielding, N. (1993). Ethnography. In N. Gilbert (ed.), *Researching Social Life*. (pp. 154–171) London: Sage.

Fielding, N. (1999). Research and Practice in Policing. *Police Practice and Research*, 1(1), 1–29.

Fielding, N. and Conroy, S. (1990). *Investigating Child Sexual Abuse*. London: Police Foundation/Policy Studies Institute.

Fielding, N. and Conroy, S. (1992). Interviewing Child Victims: Police and Social Work Investigations of Child Sexual Abuse, *Sociology*, 26: 103–124.

Fink, A. (1998). *Conducting Research Literature Reviews: From Paper to the Internet*. Thousand Oaks, CA: Sage.

Forbat, L. and Henderson, J. (2003). 'Stuck in the Middle with You': The Ethics and Process of Qualitative Research with Two People in an Intimate Relationship. *Qualitative Health Research*, 13(10), 1453–1462.

Forster, F., Hounsell, D. and Thompson, S. (eds) (1995). *Tutoring and Demonstrating: A Handbook.* Edinburgh: Center for Teaching, Learning and Assessment, http://www.tla.ed.ac.uk/services/tutdems/handbook.htm

Gaiser, T. (1997). Conducting Online Focus Groups: A Methodological Discussion. *Social Science Computer Review*, 15(2), 135–144.

Gibb, R. (2004). Seminar Culture(s), Rites of Passage and the Unmentionable in Contemporary British Social Anthropology. In D. Mills and M. Harris (eds), *Teaching Rites and Wrongs: Universities and the Making of Anthropologists.* Birmingham: C-SAP.

Gitlin, L.N. and Lyons, K.J. (1996). *Successful Grant Writing.* New York: Springer.

Gledhill, J. (1999). *Moral Ambiguities and Competing Claims to Justice: Exploring the Dilemmas of Activist Scholarship and Intervention in Complex Situations.* http://les.man.ac.uk/sa/jg/Moral%20Ambiguities.pdf

Goldsmith, J.A., Komlos, J. and Gold, P.S. (2001). *The Chicago Guide to Your Academic Career.* Chicago and London: University of Chicago Press.

Grady, K. and Wallston, B. (1988). *Research in Healthcare Settings.* London: Sage.

Graff, G. (2003). *Clueless in Academe: How Schooling Obscures the Life of the Mind.* New Haven, CT: Yale University Press.

Graves III, W. and Shields, M.A. (1991). Rethinking Moral Responsibility in Fieldwork: The Situated Negotiation of Research Ethics in Anthropology and Sociology. In C. Fluehr-Lobban (ed.), *Ethics and the Profession of Anthropology: Dialogue for a New Era* (pp. 132–151). Philadelphia: University of Pennsylvania Press.

Grayson, L., Boaz, A. and Long, A. (2004). Organising Social Care Knowledge: In Search of a 'Fit for Purpose' Classification. *Journal of Integrated Care*, 12(1), 42–48.

Grayson, L. and Gomersall, A. (2003). *A Difficult Business: Finding the Evidence for Social Science Reviews.* Working Paper 19. London: ESRC UK Centre for Evidence-based Policy and Practice, Queen Mary, University of London, http://www.evidencenetwork.org

Gregg, M. (2004). McGregg: Quasi-academic Thoughts of a Brisbane Research Fella. Retrieved from http://hypertext.rmit.edu.au/~gregg (26.01.05).

Griffiths, M. (2002). *The Times Higher Education Supplement*, 6.8.02: 8 (Letter).

Hagaman, D. (1996). *How I Learned Not to be a Photojournalist.* Lexington: University of Kentucky Press.

Hall, J.C. (2003). *Mentoring and Young People: A Literature Review.* Research Report 114, Glasgow: Scottish Centre for Research in Education (SCRE), http://www.scre.ac.uk/cat/1860030742.html

Hammersley, M. and Atkinson, P. (1994). *Ethnography: Principles in Practice.* London: Tavistock.

Harman, E. and Montagnes, I. (eds) (1976). *The Thesis and the Book.* Toronto: University of Toronto (reprinted 2000).

Harper, D. (1998). An Argument for Visual Sociology. In J. Prosser (ed.), *Image-based Research: A Sourcebook for Qualitative Researchers* (pp. 24–41). London: Falmer Press.

Hearnshaw, L.S. (1979). *Cyril Burt: Psychologist.* London: Hodder and Stoughton.

Hess, J. (2003). Using the Internet for contingent faculty organizing. *Jump Cut* 46. http://www.ejump-cut. org/archive/jc46.2003/links.html.

Hewson, C., Yule, P., Laurent, D. and Vogel, C. (2003). *Internet Research Methods: A Practical Guide for the Social and Behavioural Sciences.* London: Sage.

Hicks, W., Adams, S. and Gilbert, H. (1999). *Writing for Journalists.* London: Routledge.

Hine, C. (2000). *Virtual Ethnography.* London: Sage.

Hodkinson, P. (1993). Net.Goth. Online Communications and (Sub)cultural Boundaries. In D. Muggleton and R. Weinzierl (eds), *The Post-subcultural Reader.* Oxford: Berg.

Holland, S. (2004). *Part-time Teaching: A Good Practice Guide.* English Subject Centre Report No 9. York: The Higher Education Academy, http://www.english.heacademy.ac.uk

Homan, R. (2001). The Principle of Assumed Consent: The Ethics of Gatekeeping. *Journal of Philosophy of Education*, 35(3), 229–343.

Hornblum, A.M. (1998). *Acres of Skin: Human Experimentation at Holmesburg Prison*. New York: Routledge.

Husbands, C.T. (1998). Assessing the Extent of Use of Part-time Teachers in British Higher Education: Problems and Issues in Enumerating a Flexible Labour Force. *Higher Education Quarterly*, 52(3), 257–282.

Husbands, C.T. and Davies, A. (2000). The Teaching Roles, Institutional Locations and Terms and Conditions of Employment of Part-time Teachers in United Kingdom Higher Education. *Journal of Further and Higher Education*, 24(3), 337–362.

International Committee of Medical Journal Editors. (2001). *Uniform Requirements for Manuscripts Submitted to Biomedical Journals: Writing and Editing for Biomedical Publication*. Philadelphia, PA. http://www.icmje.org

Israel, M. (2000). The Commercialisation of University-based Criminological Research in Australia. *Australian and New Zealand Journal of Criminology*, 33(1), 1–20.

Israel, M. (2004a). *Ethics and the Governance of Criminological Research in Australia*. Sydney: New South Wales Bureau of Crime Statistics and Research. http://www.lawlink.nsw.gov.au/bocsar1.nsf/files/R55.pdf/$file/R55.pdf

Israel, M. (2004b). Strictly Confidential? Integrity and the Disclosure of Criminological and Socio-Legal Research. *British Journal of Criminology*, 44(5), 715–740.

Israel, M. and Hay, I. (2006, in press). *Research Ethics for Social Scientists*. London: Sage.

Jacob, R., Alexander, D. and Lane, L. (2004). *A Guidebook to Intellectual Property* (5th edn). London: Sweet and Maxwell.

Johnson, William A. (2004). *The Sociology Student Writer's Manual* (4th edn). Upper Saddle River, NJ: Pearson Education.

Jones, H. and Benson, C. (2002). *Publishing Law* (2nd edn). London: Routledge.

Jones, S. (1999). *Doing Internet Research: Critical Issues and Methods for Examining the Net*. London: Sage.

Jungnickel, K. (2003a). 73urbanjourneys.com. Retrieved from http://www.73urbanjourneys.com (26.01.05).

Jungnickel, K. (2003b). No. 73 Bus Blog. Retrieved from http://www.73bus.typepad.com/73stories/

Kagan, A. and Kimelman, M. (1995). Informal Consent in Aphasia Research: Myth or Reality? *Clinical Aphasiology*, 23, 65–75.

Kellehear, A. (1989). Ethics and Social Research. In J. Perry (ed.), *Doing Fieldwork: Eight Personal Accounts of Social Research* (pp. 61–72). Waurn Ponds, Vic.: Deakin University Press.

Kelly, M. (1998). Writing a Research Proposal. In C. Seale (ed.), *Researching Society and Culture* (pp. 111–122). London: Sage.

Kendall, L. (2002). *Hanging Out in the Virtual Pub: Masculinities and Relationships Online*. London and Berkeley, CA: University of California Press.

Kidder, L. (1981). Qualitative Research and Quasi-Experimental Frameworks. In M.B. Brewer and B.E. Collins (eds), *Scientific Inquiry and the Social Sciences*. San Francisco: Jossey-Bass.

Kovats-Bernat, J.C. (2002). Negotiating Dangerous Fields: Pragmatic Strategies for Fieldwork Amid Violence and Terror. *American Anthropologist*, 104(1), 208–222.

Kuper, A. (1995). Comment. *Current Anthropology*, 36(3), 424–426.

Lewis, G., Brown, N., Holland, S. and Webster, A. (2003). *A Review of Ethics and Social Science Research for the Strategic Forum for the Social Sciences: Summary of the Review*. York: Science and Technology Studies Unit.

Lewis, J. (2002). Research and Development in Social Care: Governance and Good Practice. *Research Policy and Planning*, 20(1), 3–10.

Lock, D. (2003). *Project Management*. Aldershot: Gower.

Locke, L.F., Spirduso, W.W. and Silverman, S.J. (1983). *Proposals that Work* (3rd edn). Newbury Park, CA: Sage.

Lowman, J. and Palys, T. (2001). Limited Confidentiality, Academic Freedom, and Matters of Conscience: Where does CPA Stand? *Canadian Journal of Criminology*, 43(4), 497–508.

Mackintosh, N.J. (ed.) (1995). *Cyril Burt: Fraud of Framed?* Oxford: Oxford University Press.

Mann, F. and Stewart, F. (2000). *Internet Research and Qualitative Research: A Handbook for Researching Online*. London: Sage.

Maylor, H. (2002). *Project Management* (3rd edn). London: Prentice Hall.

Maxwell, J.A. (1996). *Qualitative Research Design: An Interactive Approach*. Thousand Oaks, CA: Sage.

McGrath, C. (n.d.). *Influencing the UK Policymaking Process*. Swindon: Economic and Social Research Council.

Miles, M.B. and Huberman, A.M. (1994). *Qualitative Data Analysis* (2nd edn). Thousand Oaks, CA: Sage.

Milgram, S. (1977). Ethical Issues in the Study of Obedience. In S. Milgram (ed.), *The Individual in a Social World* (pp. 188–199). Reading, MA: Addison-Wesley.

Miller, D. and Slater, D. (2000). *The Internet: An Ethnographic Approach*. Oxford: Berg.

Mills, D. and Harris, M. (2004). *Teaching Rites and Wrongs: Universities and the Making of Anthropologists*. Birmingham: C-SAP.

Murray, R. (2000). *Writing for Publication* (video pack, with notes). Glasgow: University of Strathclyde. Contact to order: S.Mitchell@strath.ac.uk

Murray, R. (2002). *How to Write a Thesis*. Maidenhead: Open University Press/McGraw-Hill.

Murray, R. (2005). *Writing for Academic Journals*. Maidenhead: Open University Press/McGraw-Hill.

Murray, R., Thow, M. and Strachan, R. (1997). Visual Literacy: Designing and Presenting a Poster. *Physiotherapy*, 84(7), 319–327.

Nardi, P. (2003). *Doing Survey Research: A Guide to Quantitative Methods*. London: Allyn & Bacon.

National Health and Medical Research Council (2004). *Report of the 2002–2003 Human Research Ethics Committee (HREC) Annual Report Process*. Canberra: NHMRC, http://www.nhmrc.gov.au/ publications/_files/hrecarp.pdf

Nelson, C. (ed.) (1997). *Will Teach for Food: Academic Labour in Crisis*. Minneapolis: University of Minneapolis Press.

Nelson, C. (2003). Moving River Barges: Academic Activism and Academic Organizations. In B. Johnson, P. Kavanagh and K. Mattson (eds), *Steal this University: The Rise of the Corporate University and the Academic Labour Movement*. New York: Routledge.

Neumann, W.L. (1994). *Social Research Methods: Qualitative and Quantitative Approaches* (2nd edn). Boston: Allyn & Bacon.

NHS Centre for Reviews and Dissemination (2000). *Fluoridation of Drinking Water: A Systematic Review of its Efficacy and Safety*. CRD Report No. 18. York: NHS Centre for Reviews and Dissemination, http://www.york.ac.uk/inst/crd/fluorid.htm

NHS Centre for Reviews and Dissemination (2001). *Undertaking Systematic Reviews of Research on Effectiveness: CRD's Guidance for Those Carrying Out or Commissioning Reviews*. CRD Report No. 4: 2nd edn. York: NHS Centre for Reviews and Dissemination, http://www.york.ac.uk/inst/crd/ report4.htm

Nicholl, J. (2000). The Ethics of Research Ethics Committees. *British Medical Journal*, 320, 1217.

Noblit, G.W. and Hare, R.D. (eds) (1988). *Meta-ethnography: Synthesizing Qualitative Studies*. Newbury Park, CA: Sage.

Norman, S. and Chartered Institute of Library and Information Professionals (Great Britain) (2004). *Practical Copyright for Information Professionals: The CILIP Handbook*. London: Facet.

Norris, C. (1993). Some Ethical Considerations on Field-Work with the Police. In D. Hobbs and T. May (eds), *Interpreting the Field: Accounts of Ethnography* (pp. 123–143). Oxford: Clarendon Press.

Oakes, J.M. (2002). Risks and Wrongs in Social Science Research: An Evaluator's Guide to the IRB. *Evaluation Research*, 26(5), 443–479.

O'Connor, M. and Woodford, F. (1978). *Writing Scientific Papers in English*. Tunbridge Wells: Pitman.

Oliver, P. (2004). *Writing Your Thesis*. London: Sage.

Oringderff, J. (2004). My Way: Piloting an Online Focus Group. *International Journal of Qualitative Methods*, 3(3), Article 5.

Owens, P. and Mills, D. (2003). *Problem Based Learning: A Handbook for Staff and Students*. Includes video and guidance notes. Available from www.c-sap.bham.ac.uk/resources/publications/default. htm

Padfield, T. (2004). *Copyright for Archivists and Users of Archives* (2nd edn). London: Facet.

Patton, M. (2002). *Qualitative Research and Evaluation Methods* (3rd edn). London: Sage.

Pawson, R. (2002). Evidence-based Policy: In Search of a Method. *Evaluation*, 8(2), 157–181.

Pawson, R. (2004). *Assessing the Quality of Evidence in Evidence-based Policy: Why, How and When?* Working Paper No. 1. ESRC Research Methods Programme. Swindon: Economic and Social Research Council, http://www.ccsr.ac.uk/methods/publications/

Peck, J. and Coyle, M. (1999). *The Student's Guide to Writing*. Basingstoke: Macmillan.

Petticrew, M. (2001). Systematic Reviews from Astronomy to Zoology: Myths and Misconceptions. *British Medical Journal*, 322(7278), 98–101, http://www.bmj.com/cgi/content/full/322/7278/98

Pink, S. (2001). *Doing Visual Ethnography*. London: Sage.

Pole, C. and Lampard, R. (2002). *Practical Social Investigation: Qualitative and Quantitative Methods in Social Research*. Harlow, Essex: Prentice-Hall.

Punch, K.F. (1998). *Introduction to Social Research: Quantitative and Qualitative Approaches*. London: Sage.

Punch, K.F. (2000). *Developing Effective Research Proposals*. London: Sage.

Reid, E. (1996). Informed Consent in the Study of On-Line Communities: A Reflection on the Effects of Computer Mediated Research. *The Information Society*, 12, 169–174.

RESPECT (2004). *Code of Practice for Socio-Economic Research*. Brighton: RESPECT project. http://www.respectproject.org/code/respect_code.pdf

Rezabek, R. (2000). Online Focus Groups: Electronic discussions for research. *Forum Qualitative Sozialforschung/Forum: Qualitative Social Research* [On-line Journal], 1(1). http://www.qualitative-research.net/fqs-texte/1-00/1-00rezabek-e.htm

Rhind, D. (2003). *Great Expectations*. London: Academy of Learned Societies in the Social Sciences.

Sapienza, A. (2004). *Managing Scientists: Leadership Strategies in Scientific Research* (2nd edn). New York: Wiley-Liss.

Scheper-Hughes, N. (1995). Propositions for a Militant Anthropology. *Current Anthropology*, 36(3), 409–420.

Sharff, J. and Lessinger, J. (1999). Sweatshopping Academe: Capitalism and the Part-time Academic in US Universities. In L.G. Basch, L.W. Saunders, J.W. Sharff and J. Peacock (eds), *Transforming Academia: Challenges and Opportunities for an Engaged Anthropology* (pp. 43–63). Arlington, VA: American Anthropological Association.

Social Sciences and Humanities Research Ethics Special Working Committee (2004). *Giving Voice to the Spectrum*. Ottawa: Interagency Advisory Panel on Research Ethics, http://www.pre.ethics.gc.ca/english/workgroups/sshwc/SSHWCVoiceReportJune2004.pdf

Teacher Training Agency (2004). *Survey of Graduates in Full-time Employment*. Conducted by PCP Data Ltd. London: Teacher Training Agency http//www.tta.gov.uk/php/read.php?articleid=2129& sectionid=283

Thomas, J. (1996). Introduction: A Debate about the Ethics of Fair Practices for Collecting Social Science Data in Cyberspace. *The Information Society*, 12, 107–117.

Thompson, M. (2000). *The Global Resume and CV Guide*. New York: Wiley.

Tinker, A. (2004). National Survey of University Research Ethics Committees: Their Role, Remit and Conduct. *Association of Research Ethics Committees Newsletter*, 14, 9–11.

Tinker, A. and Coomber, V. (2004). *University Research Ethics Committees: Their Role, Remit and Conduct*. London: King's College London.

Tisdall, E.K.M. (2003). The Rising Tide of Female Violence? Researching Girls' Own Understandings and Experiences of Violent Behaviour. In R.M. Lee and E.A. Stanko (eds), *Researching Violence: Essays on Methodology and Measurement* (pp. 137–152). London: Routledge.

van den Hoonaard, W.C. (ed.) (2002). *Walking the Tightrope: Ethical Issues for Qualitative Researchers*. Toronto: University of Toronto Press.

Wakeford, N. (1998). Urban Culture for Virtual Bodies: On Lesbian 'Identity' and 'Community' in San Francisco Bay Area Cyberspace. In R. Ainley (ed.), *New Frontiers of Space, Bodies and Gender* (pp. 176–190). London: Routledge.

Walker, J. and Taylor, T. (1999). *The Columbia Guide to Online Style*. New York: Columbia University Press.

Wallis, R. (1977). The Moral Career of a Research Project. In C. Bell and H. Newby (eds), *Doing Sociological Research* (pp. 149–167). London: George Allen and Unwin.

Webster, A., Lewis, G. and Brown, N. (2004). *Developing a Framework for Social Science Research Ethics: Project Update*. York: Science and Technology Studies Unit, http://www.york.ac.uk/res/ref/docs/update250604.pdf

Wesch, M. (2003). Nekalimin.net: A Developing Digital Ethnography of a Papua New Guinea People in the Midst of 'Development'. Retrieved from http://www.people.virginia.edu/%7Emlw5k/ (26.01.05).

Whitecross, R. and Mills, D. (2003). *Professional Apprenticeship or Contract-Labour? A Survey Report on the Use of Teaching Assistants within UK Anthropology Departments*. Birmingham: C-SAP, www.c-sap.bham.ac.uk/resources/publications/default.htm

Wilson, C. (2002). *Intellectual Property Law in a Nutshell*. London: Sweet and Maxwell.

Wright Mills, C. (1959). *The Sociological Imagination*. New York: Oxford University Press.

Ziman, J. (1991). Academic Science as a System of Markets. *Higher Education Quarterly*, 45, 41–61.

Zimbardo, P.G., Maslach, C. and Haney, C. (1999). Reflections on the Stanford Prison Experiment: Genesis, Transformations, Consequences. In T. Blass (ed.), *Obedience to Authority: Current Perspectives on the Milgram Paradigm* (pp. 193–237). Mahwah, NJ: Lawrence Erlbaum Associates.

Index